CAPITAL STRUCTURE OF CORPORATE SECTOR

By
DR. JAGANNATH PANDA
Professor
P.G. Department of Commerce,
Berhampur University
Berhampur
&
DR. ASHOK KUMAR PANIGRAHI
Reader
Department of Management,
RITEE Business School, Raipur

DISCOVERY PUBLISHING HOUSE PVT. LTD.
NEW DELHI-110 002

Published by:
Tilak Wasan
DISCOVERY PUBLISHING HOUSE PVT. LTD.
4383/4A, Ansari Road, Darya Ganj
New Delhi-110 002 (India)
Phone : +91-11-23279245, 43596064-65
Fax : +91-11-23253475
E-mail : parul.wasan@gmail.com
discoverypublishinghouse@gmail.com
web : www.discoverypublishinggroup.com

***First Edition:* 2012**

ISBN: 978-81-8356-999-6

Capital Structure of Corporate Sector

Printed at:
Shree Balaji Art Press
Delhi

Preface

How do firms choose their capital structures? In his answer to this question, Prof. Stewart C. Myers, then President of American Finance Association in 1984 said that 'we don't know'. Despite decades of intensive research, and hundreds of papers after Modigliani and Millers' seminal work, surprisingly there is lack of consensus even today among the finance experts on this basic issue of corporate finance. In practice, it is observed that finance managers use different combinations of debt and equity. Academicians and practitioners alike have found it difficult to find out how a firm decides its capital structure in the perfect capital markets of the west as well as in the imperfect capital markets, as in India. This has led to an upsurge in research on company finance, particularly aimed at understanding how companies finance their activities and why they finance their activities in these specific ways.

The present book is aimed at to find out the trend and pattern of financing by the Indian companies in the private sector. The sheer size and diversity of the Indian capital market are, on their own, more than sufficient reasons for investigating Indian company financing in depth. In addition, the liberalization of the market offers a unique laboratory for evaluating the development of companies as liberalization proceeds.

In this book, we have tried to find out the ways in which different companies at different times and in different institutional environments have financed their operations; and to identify possible implications of these financing patterns. We have analyzed the financing pattern of 300 Indian private sector companies, comprising of 20 different sectors for the period 1999-2000 to 2007-2008, duly grouping them on the basis of their region, size, age, and nature etc.

The central issue of our investigation was to examine empirically the existence of inter-firm and inter-industry differences in the capital structure of Indian firms and to identify the possible sources of such variation in capital structure. We have tried to find out the factors that determine the financing pattern of capital structure of Indian companies, particularly in the private sector. Going beyond this, we have also examined the impact of liberalization and changes noticed due to liberalization, on the capital structure of Indian companies.

We hope the research scholars, faculty members and working executives will find this book more useful and rewarding.

We are thankful to Discovery Publishing House for their support in getting this book published.

Dr. Jagannath Panda

Dr. Ashok Kumar Panigrahi

Contents

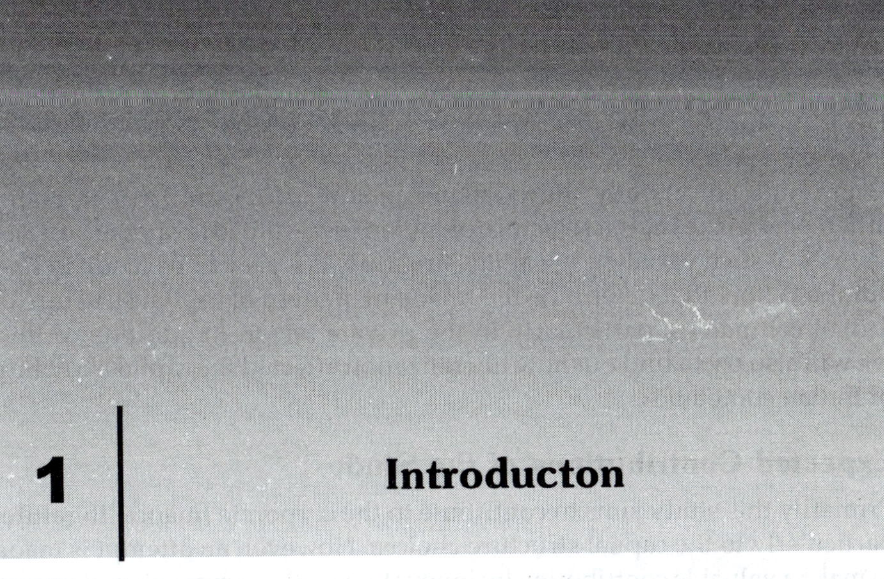

1 Introducton

The Background and Motivation of the Study

In the last two decades, there has been an upsurge in research on company finance, particularly aimed at understanding how companies finance their activities and why they finance their activities in these specific ways. In practice, it is observed that finance managers use different combinations of debt and equity. A practical question therefore is: What motivates them to do so? More fundamental questions to be answered are: (1) Does use of debt create a value? (2) If so, do firms gravitate towards an optimum mix of debt and equity?

In theory, it is argued that the financing decision is irrelevant under perfect capital markets. When, within the framework of perfect capital markets, taxes and bankruptcy costs are assumed, the financial economists argue that an optimum capital structure, which maximizes the market value of the firm (or minimizes cost of capital), can exist. But, in case of an imperfect market, the views differ greatly and, as a result, till date, no universally accepted model has been developed on this crucial issue. Firms in developing countries like India, are found following different financing policies—some aggressive and some conservative. Hence, it needs to be investigated that how Indian finance managers decides the financing mix, whether all finance managers follow the same principle and if so, than why? And, for that purpose one need to know whether the ratio of financing mix in the capital structure of all the Indian companies is same or not. It can be found out only by examining the existence of variations in the capital structures of different companies of different sectors. The proposed research is intended to examine the trend and pattern of financing the capital structure of Indian companies. The central issue we will address is to examine empirically the existence of inter-firm and inter-industry differences in the capital structure of Indian firms and identify the possible sources of such variation in capital structure. Efforts will be made to find out the factors that determine the financing pattern of capital structure of Indian companies, particularly in the private sector. In addition to this, we will also try to find out how liberalization affected the capital structure of Indian companies.

Expected Contributions of the Study

Primarily this study aims to contribute to the corporate finance literature, particularly to the capital structure choices. However, an attempt is made to make a valuable contribution by innovating on the rich existing literature in three major ways. First, in order to provide a more comprehensive view on the subject, both theoretical and empirical approaches are undertaken. All the chapters are devoted to a review of existing theoretical and empirical literature on the capital structure decision controversy, with emphasis on current thinking.

The second way by which this study attempts to innovate on existing academic work is by concentrating on emerging, as opposed to developed, markets. Our literature review shows that most of the theoretical and empirical studies that deal with financing decisions are US-based. However, many emerging markets are, as implied by the name, in the middle of a process of change, growth and liberalization, which provide an interesting testing ground for western-based corporate theory. This study which is entirely based on Indian firms is likely to provide an insight to the capital structure decision of Indian companies.

The third way by which innovation is sought in this study is by synthesizing corporate financing theory with the phases of liberalization that took place in India in 1990's. Chapter—4 investigates the impact of liberalization on the capital structure decisions. Effort is made to compare and contrast the capital structure decisions of Indian firms before and after liberalization.

Structure and Scope of the Study

This study which is specifically conducted for the purpose of our Doctoral Theses is divided into nine chapters. The 'Introduction' chapter deals with the background and motivation of the study where the objectives and purpose of the study is stated along with the research area and the problems in the field of research and the expected contribution of the study, which is devoted to report how the research is innovative, novel or extends existing approaches to a problem.

Before turning to the analysis of how Indian firms were taking financing decisions in pre and post liberalized era, Chapter —2 'Concept of Capital Structure' takes stock of current thinking and evidence on the basics of capital structure. It starts with the meaning of capital structure, the importance of capital structure, the relationship between cost of capital and capital structure and how cost of capital affects the capital structure decisions. Here various theories on capital structure are presented to substantiate the relation between the cost of capital and capital structure. The other things discussed in this chapter include components of capital structure, optimal capital structure, determinants of capital structure, essential features of sound capital mix, capital gearing and changes in capital structure etc.

In Chapter—3 titled as 'Sources of Corporate Finance', the various sources of financing capital structure are discussed in detail and the major sources of finances for Indian Companies are also discussed. Effort is also made to find out the best source of finance, after knowing the relative advantages and disadvantages of each source. In choosing the best source of finance, it is essential to know the merits and demerits of all the sources. Both debt and equity financing offer a number of advantages and disadvantages. Unfortunately, there is no magic proportion of debt that a company can take on. The debt-equity relationship varies according to industries involved, a company's line of business and its stage of development. However, because investors are better off putting their money into companies with strong balance sheets, common sense tells us that these companies should have, generally speaking, lower debt and higher equity levels. Along with debt and equity financing, we have tried to give a brief overview of other sources of corporate financing also.

Chapter—4 turns attention to the liberalization of Indian economy and its impact on capital structure of Indian Corporate. The chapter started with the research findings of capital structure of Indian corporate before liberalization. Then we started analyzing the impact of liberalization on capital structure of Indian Corporate. We tried to show how with the waves of liberalization, privatization and globalization, the corporate world has started wooing equity capital in a big way. The arrival of a matrix of new financial instruments such as commercial papers, asset securitization, factoring and forfeiting services, and the market related interest rate structure and their stringent conditions for lending, force modern enterprises to court equity finance. We tried to find out the changes observed in the capital structure of Indian companies in post-liberalization period and the reasons for that.

While reviewing the literatures on this topic in Chapter—5, we found a handful of noteworthy contributions published by a number of experts.

All these studies have helped to understand the dynamics of this crucial issue better but have not been able to come to a definite conclusion as to how firms determine their optimal capital structure. So, the present study was planned to make another attempt to resolve this contentious issue. It may be pointed out that the study has not included the effect of factors like agency and bankruptcy costs, as they are difficult to measure in the Indian scenario.

Chapter—6 titled as 'Methodology and Tools for Analysis' is fully devoted to the aspects like nature of the data, source of data, selection and classification of sample, methodology designed for the study, period of study, tools and techniques adopted, hypotheses of the study and the objectives of the study etc. In this chapter it is clearly stated as to how we will proceed in this study in a step by step manner.

For our study purpose, only secondary data is used which is sourced from the website *www.moneycontrol.com.* The information relating to nature of industry, size, age, state and region, company background, value of total assets and annual financial statements of sample companies for the period 1999-2000 to 2007-2008 have been obtained from the same. Keeping in view the scope of the study, it was decided to select companies on the basis of purposive sampling rather than taking the whole thing. Our sample consists of 300 firms from a heterogeneous set of 20 different sectors. For our study purpose we have taken the data of top 15 companies of each sector selected on the basis of their total assets value as on 31st March 2008. The study excludes financial and securities sector companies, as their financial characteristics and use of leverage are substantially different from other companies.

For the purpose of analysis, we have classified the total sample companies according to their age, size, region and the industry or sector. Two important techniques of analysis, i.e., ratio analysis and funds flow statement analysis have been selected to study the capital structure as these two methods are widely used for the study.

In Chapter—7 titled as 'Empirical Analysis of Total Sample Companies', we did an extensive analysis of the capital structure of the sample companies in total. The different sources from where the corporate sector has raised the funds and the ways and means by which the so raised funds have been utilized have been analyzed in detail. The analysis of the study is based on the historical funds flow statements of each company. For the total sample, the aggregate of (300 companies) individual sources of funds and their investment in acquiring different assets has also been made.

The measurement of company financial structure has been subject to considerable debate, in which there are two interlinked strands. The first question concerns the source of data: whether to use the aggregate company sector statistics that form the basis of the national accounts, or individual company accounts data from company reports. The second question is conceptual: whether to use balance sheets (stocks of assets and liabilities) or flows of funds (sources and uses, or cash flows) to measure financing. Within this second question, there are further issues: particularly whether to use market values or book values in calculating balance sheet data; and whether and how to use gross or net sources and uses if flows of funds are the chosen basis of measurement. In deciding these questions, the central issue is to determine the purposes for which the data are to be used. This point has not always been addressed in the literature on this debate, and this has resulted in some confusion in deciding which methods are the most appropriate. Here we would like to make it clear that, for our study purpose we have taken the balance sheets of the sample companies from the website *www.moneycontrol.com* and prepared funds flow statements of each individual company so as to find out the various sources from which they have raised funds and the purpose of utilization of the raised funds. This chapter highlights the structure of corporate finance in India.

In Chapter—8 which is designed for the variable wise analysis of the data, we have proposed to conduct the analysis of the capital structure of sample companies after grouping them into different variables. In attempting to study differences in funds flow and capital mix across firms, a variable-wise analysis of funds flow and capital structure of the sample companies has been undertaken. Accordingly, the sample companies were classified on the basis of region, industry or sector, size-group and age-group. The main purpose was to understand the financing trend of sample companies and to conduct an analysis of investment patterns of sample companies by using suitable statistical tools. The result so found will be related to the hypothesis set earlier.

In last chapter i.e. in conclusion we have tried to throw some lights towards the aim and utility of the study, detailed summary of each chapter and contribution of the study, scope for further extension of the study and promising research ideas.

Limitations of the Study

We would like to make it clear that, mainly there are four main limitations of this thesis. First, the thesis relies on empirical procedures as in the corporate finance literature rather than construction of theoretical proofs on capital structure of firms in emerging markets. Thus the first main limitation of this thesis is that theoretical modelling of these issues as contained in the financial economics literature is not addressed here.

Second, it was purposely intended to produce stand-alone empirical papers in Chapters 2, 3, 4 and 5. To maintain their stand-alone status, it was found necessary to include brief reference to the relevant background literature, thereby inevitably leading to some limited amount of duplication between each of the stand-alone chapters and the literature survey in Chapter 5. However, we maintain that the repetition has been kept to the strictest minimum.

Third, the results obtained in our study are from a sample size of 300 firms taken selectively from 20 different sectors. Our presumption of 300 firms as the representative of India Inc is one of the biggest limitation of our study because the findings of these 300 firms will be taken as the findings of Indian corporate. Total dependence on secondary data could be also one of the limitations of our study.

At last, the empirical findings and conclusions contained in this thesis may be used by financial managers to inform policy decisions. However, it is not the intention of this thesis to generate policy-oriented findings for operation purposes. Thus the fourth main limitation of this work is that focus is not directed at the practical applicability of the findings.

2 Concept of Capital Structure

Introduction

Capital structure refers to the mix of long-term sources of funds, such as debentures, long-term debt, preference share capital and equity share capital including reserves and surpluses (i.e. retained earnings). Some companies do not plan their capital structure, and it develops as a result of the financial decisions taken by the financial manager without any formal planning. These companies may prosper in the short-run, but ultimately they may face-considerable difficulties in raising funds to finance their activities. With unplanned capital structure, these companies may also fail to economies the use of their funds. Consequently, it is being increasingly realized that a company should plan its capital structure to maximize the use of the funds and to be able to adapt more easily to the changing conditions.

Theoretically, the financial manager should plan an optimum capital structure for his company. The optimum capital structure is obtained when the market value per share is maximum. There is significant variation among industries and, among individual companies within an industry in terms of capital structure. Since a number of factors influence the capital structure decision of a company, the judgment of the person making the, capital structure decision plays a crucial part. Two similar companies can have different capital structures if the decision makers differ in their judgment of the significance of various factors. A totally theoretical model perhaps cannot adequately handle all those factors, which affect the capital structure decision. These factors are highly psychological, complex and qualitative and do not always follow accepted theory, since capital markets are not perfect and the decision has to be taken under in perfect knowledge and risk.

The board of directors or the chief financial officer (CFO) of a company should develop an appropriate capital structure, which is most advantageous to the company. This can be done only when all those factors, which are relevant to the company's capital structure decision, are properly analyzed and balanced. The capital structure should be planned generally keeping in view the interests of the equity shareholders and the financial requirements of a company. The equity shareholders, being the owners of the company and the providers of risk capital (equity) would be concerned about the ways of financing a company's operations. However, the interests of other groups, such as employee, customers, creditors, society and government, should also be given reasonable consideration. While developing an appropriate capital structure for its company, the financial manager should inter alia aim at maximizing the long-term market price per share. Theoretically, there may be a precise point or range within which the market value per share is maximum. In practice, for most companies within an industry there may be a range of an appropriate capital structure within which there would not be great differences in the market value per share. One-way to get an idea of this range is to observe the capital structure patterns of company's vis-à-vis their market prices of shares. It may be found empirically that there are not significant differences in the share values within a given range. The management of a company may fix its capital structure near the top of this range in order to make maximum use of favourable leverage, subject to other requirements such as flexibility, solvency, control and norms set by the financial institutions, the Security Exchange Board of India (SEBI) and stock exchanges.

Meaning of Capital Structure

Capital structure refers to the way a *corporation* finances itself through some combination of *equity, debt,* or *hybrid securities.* A firm's capital structure is then the composition or 'structure' of its liabilities. For example, a firm that sells ₹ 20 crores in equity and ₹ 80 crores in debts is said to be 20 per cent equity financed and 80 per cent debt financed. The firm's ratio of debt to total financing, 80 per cent in this example is referred to as the firm's *leverage.* It is a mix of a company's long-term debt, specific short-term debt, common equity and preferred equity. The capital structure is how a firm finances its overall operations and growth by using different sources of funds. Debt comes in the form of bond issues or long-term notes payable, while equity is classified as common stock, preferred stock or retained earnings. Short-term debt such as working capital requirements is also considered to be part of the capital structure. A company's proportion of short and long-term debt is considered when analyzing capital structure. When people refer to capital structure they are most likely referring to a firm's debt-to-equity ratio, which provides insight into how risky a company is. Usually a company more heavily financed by debt poses greater risk, as this firm is relatively highly levered. Thus, Capital structure refers to a mixture of a variety of long-term sources of funds and equity shares including reserves and surpluses of an enterprise. It hardly takes in its structure; the entire complex quantitative factors as well as qualitative attributes affecting investment decisions.

Importance of Effective Capital Structure

Capital structure is the combination of debt and equity that funds an organization's strategic plan. The 'right' capital structure supports strategic-financial goals, while optimizing flexibility and minimizing cost. Capital structure management can be approached by answering the question, what is the appropriate amount, mix, structure, and cost of debt and equity to support the organization's strategic-financial goals? The proper and strategic management of capital structure ensures access to the capital needed to fund future growth and enhance financial performance. The key benefits of effective capital structure management are increased capital access, added flexibility, and lower overall cost of capital. "Organized properly in an organization of any size, a capital structure can be easily adjusted to meet changes in interest rates and the changing shape of interest rate yield curves," notes Kenneth Kaufman, managing partner of Kaufman Hall. "Capital structures by themselves can lower the overall cost of capital and can maximize the return of assets versus the cost of liabilities. Clearly, the creatively managed capital structure has become a competitive advantage. Perhaps most important, over a 10 to 20-year planning horizon, the quality of an organization's capital structure can cost or save the organization millions of dollars."[1]

Cost of Capital and Capital Structure

The cost of capital is the company's cost of using funds provided by creditors and shareholders. A company's cost of capital is the cost of its long-term sources of funds: debt, preferred equity, and common equity. And the cost of each source reflects the risk of the assets the company invests in. A company that invests in assets having little risk in producing income will be able to bear lower costs of capital than a company that invests in assets having a higher risk of producing income. For example, a discount retail store has much less risk than an oil drilling company. Moreover, the cost of each source of funds reflects the hierarchy of the risk associated with its seniority over the other sources. For a given company, the cost of funds raised through debt is less than the cost of funds from preferred stock that, a senior claim over assets and income relative to preferred shareholders, who have seniority to common shareholders.[2]

Theories of Capital Structure

There are different theories of capital structure. David Durand propounded the net income approach of capital structure in 1952 (Durand 1952). This approach states that firm can increase its value or lower the cost of capital by using the debt capital. Net operating income approach is converse to this approach. This approach contends that the value of a firm and cost of the capital are independent to capital structure. Thus, the firm cannot increase its value by judicial mixture of debt and equity capital. These are two extreme approaches to capital structure. Solomon developed the intermediate approach to the capital structure in 1963. This traditional theory of capital structure pleads that value of the firm goes increase to a certain level of debt capital and after then it tends to remain constant with a moderate use of debt capital, and finally value of the firm decreases (Solomon 1963). Thus, this theory holds the concept of optimal capital structure.

The modern theory of capital structure began with the celebrated paper of Modigliani and Miller published in 1958. In this paper, they supported the net operating income approach and rejected the traditional theory of capital structure. They contend in their first proposition that the market value of any firm is independent to its capital structure and is given by capitalizing its expected return at the rate appropriate to the risk class. This was theoretically very sound but was based on the assumptions of perfect capital market and no tax world, which were not valid in reality. So, this was corrected in 1963. In correction, they incorporated the effect of tax on value and cost of the capital of the firm and contend that, in the presence of corporate tax, the value of the firm varies with the variation of the use of the debt due to tax benefit on interest bill.

Capital structure theories are concerned with explaining how the mix of debt and equity in the firm's capital structure influences its market value. Since the seminal paper by Modigliani and Miller (1958) and their proposition that the value of the firm is independent of its debt-equity mix, the two basic theories that have dominated the capital structure debates are the 'trade off theory' and the 'pecking order theory'. The trade off theory proposes that the optimal level of debt is where the marginal benefit of this source of finance is equal to its marginal cost. There is variation, however, among researchers on the view of what constitute the benefits and costs of debt. One benefit of debt, from the point of view of existing shareholders, is that bondholders have no voting rights. This makes external debt more attractive relative to external equity particularly in the case of small or tightly controlled firms, whose owners are reluctant to give up control. Some contend that, control considerations may be particularly relevant for the capital structure decisions of firms in emerging markets, due to the long tradition of family ownership.

Apart from control considerations another benefit of debt is the tax deductibility of interest payments at the corporate tax level. Specifically, Modigliani and Miller (1963) note that because interest payments are deducted in arriving at the profit figure on which tax is charged, these payments actually reduce the corporate tax liability. The corporate tax benefit of debt, however, may be offset, at least to some extent or in some cases, by the tax disadvantage of interest payments at the personal level. Indeed, Miller (1977) shows that capital structure may still be irrelevant when the benefit of the interest tax shield is fully offset by the disadvantage of interest income at the personal level. This may be the case when the effective personal tax rate on equity income, from both dividends and capital gains, is sufficiently lower than that on interest income. Further, as suggested by DeAngelo and Masulis (1980) the value of the corporate tax deductibility of interest also depends on the corporate tax level, whether the firm has generated taxable profits, and the availability of non-debt tax shields. Thus given non-debt tax shields such as capital allowances, tax credits, pension contributions, or tax losses carried forward, the trade off theory typically sets the corporate tax benefit of debt against costs that are associated with debt, such as financial distress.

Financial distress costs include the costs associated with bankruptcy, such as legal and administration fees and the costs incurred in liquidating assets. Liquidation costs are high if the value of the asset in liquidation is substantially less than its value in current use. This partly depends on the type of assets held. For example, the secondary market for specialized machinery is likely to be thin therefore liquidation costs for such assets are likely to be high. Likewise, intangible assets such as brand names, trademarks, or human capital have no value on liquidation hence liquidation costs for such assets will also be high. Brealey and Myers (2000) note that even before the firm is declared bankrupt, it may incur distress costs that are associated with being in a position of financial difficulties. These costs may be associated with lost reputation or manpower migration, which are likely to occur when it becomes known that the firm is financially distressed. In short, financial distress should be an important disadvantage of using debt and its costs should be weighed against the corporate tax advantage of debt. But corporate tax and financial distress are not the only benefit and cost of debt. Agency theory as articulated by Jensen and Meckling (1976) has further implications for the trade off theory of capital structure.

Jensen and Meckling developed the capital structure theory based on the agency costs in 1976. Firm incurs two types of agency costs—cost associated with the outside equity holders and cost associated with the presence of debt in capital structure (Jensen and Meckling 1976). Total agency cost first decreases and after certain level of outside equity capital in capital structure, it increases. The total agency cost becomes minimal at certain level of outside equity capital. Thus, this theory pleads the concept of optimal capital structure.

There are at least four agency-related benefits of using debt in the capital structure mix. First, conflicts of interests between managers and outside shareholders may be controlled by debt. Specifically, higher levels of debt in the capital structure of firms imply that managers hold a larger fraction of the firm's equity, which reduces agency problems by aligning the interests of managers with that of outside shareholders. Second, Jensen (1986) argues that higher level of debt implies a commitment to pay out more cash, which may otherwise be wasted by managers. Third, managers' tendency to over invest, in order to advance their self-interests, can be controlled through monitoring by lenders and by debt covenants. Forth, Harris and Raviv (1990) propose that debt in the capital structure generate information valuable in controlling agency behaviour. Particularly it is noted that for self-interest reasons, managers are always reluctant to liquidate the firm or to provide information that could lead to liquidation. This is the case even when liquidation is the best course of action from investors' point of view. However, debt is a disciplining device because default on debt obligations triggers an investigation of the firm. Such investigation, although costly in terms of legal fees and disruption to normal operations, generates information to investors and lead to the implementation of major changes and more efficient operating policies.

To summarize, agency theory predicts that debt should reduce conflicts between managers and outside owners because it increases the fraction of management's ownership, and because interest is a commitment to pay out cash. Further, debt is valuable because debt covenants restrict managers' freedom, and because default on debt triggers information and changes in policies. Bearing these agency-related benefits of debt, there are also agency-related costs to debt, which are due to conflicts of interests more expensive, more constraining and less available as a future source of finance. However, just as financial distress costs partly depend on the type of assets held, so is the between equity and debt holders of levered firms. One such conflict is over risk levels, and is commonly referred to as the problem of risk shifting or asset substitution. Accordingly, debt in the capital structure induces moral hazard problems by encouraging owners to engage in investments riskier than those anticipated by debt holders. By increasing the variance of cash flows, wealth is expropriated from debt holders because the level of interest required by them has been fixed before the shift in risk. This way if the risky projects are successful the extra gains accrue to shareholders while if the risky projects are unsuccessful the costs are shared among all security holders. Risk shifting behaviour has adverse effects on debt in the capital structure as it leads to debt becoming ability of equity holders to expropriate debt holders' wealth through risk-shifting actions also depends on the firm's asset structure. For instance, when growth prospects constitute a substantial part of the firm's assets, providing it with many alternative investments, this increases the opportunity for risk-shifting actions by equity holders. Similarly, Viswanath and Frierman (1995) argue that the potential for risk-shifting behaviour is directly related to assets' fungibility, or the ease with which the variance of cash flows to be generated from a particular asset may be altered. The similarity between intangibility and fungibility is noted. Thus Viswanath and Frierman (1995) remark that intangible assets such as the skills of lawyers of a law firm are fungible because it is difficult to monitor the type of cases in which these lawyers engage. In contrast a tangible fixed asset such as land is non-fungible. This is because it is relatively easy to monitor the way in which land is used, thus limiting the ease with which the variance of cash flows from the use of this asset may be altered.

From the above discussion it emerges that agency-related costs, that are associated with risk shifting behaviour by equity holders may be higher for firms with many intangible or fungible assets. However, risk shifting or asset substitution is not the only agency cost of debt. Another such cost is the cost associated with under investment. This problem applies particularly to firms in financial distress, when owners may be unwilling to invest even in good projects. Instead equity holders may prefer to receive higher dividends rather than the firm generating cash flows that may be sufficient to pay only those higher up on the payment list. Thus, under investment like asset substitution is an agency cost of debt that may reduce the benefits from the value of debt, in controlling the agency cost of equity. However, whether or not the agency costs and benefits of debt are considered, and whatever other non-agency related factors are assumed to constitute the benefits and costs of debt, central to the trade off theory is the idea of an optimal capital structure. This can be contrasted with the pecking order theory, where the central idea is that firms follow a preference order with respect to the various sources of finance.

The pecking order theory is due to Myers (1984) and is based on two realistic assumptions. The first assumption is the presence of asymmetric information between managers and outside investors. The second assumption is that mangers, acting in the interest of existing security holders, tend to issue securities when these are over valued. The first assumption implies that due to information problems outsiders do not know the true value of the firm but that they should use managers' actions as signals to this value. The second assumption implies that new issues should be interpreted as bad news and should therefore be met with price reductions. The combination of price reductions and issue expenses increases the cost of external funds relative to internal funds, and leads to preference by firms for the latter. It also implies that when internal funds are insufficient to meet the financing needs of the firm, external debt is preferred to external equity because it is less risky and less exposed to mis-pricing.

Thus there is a principle difference between the trade off and pecking order theories. This difference relates to the question of whether firms follow a target capital mix or whether capital structure is determined by the most preferred source that is available to the firm when the need for funds arises. However, while the distinction between these two theories may be clear-cut, the practical implications of pecking order, agency costs, trade off, and control considerations are difficult to disentangle. To distinguish between these theories as possible explanation for the capital structure decision, investigators typically study the relationships between leverage and other firm's characteristics. However, often the direction of correlation between leverage and a particular firm characteristic is consistent with more than one theory. This is a serious limitation to the investigation at hand as distinguishing between these theories, is precisely the aim here.

Components of Capital Structure

Capital structure is a business finance term that describes the proportion of a company's capital, or operating money, that is obtained through debt and equity. Debt includes loans and other types of credit that must be repaid in the future, usually with interest. Equity involves selling a partial interest in the company to investors, usually in the form of stock. In contrast to debt financing, equity financing does not involve a direct obligation to repay the funds. Instead, equity investors become part-owners and partners in the business and thus are able to exercise some degree of control over how it is run. A company's capitalization describes the composition of a company's permanent or long-term capital, which consists of a combination of debt and equity. A healthy proportion of equity capital, as opposed to debt capital, in a company's capital structure is an indication of financial fitness.[3]

The equity part of the debt-equity relationship is the easiest to define. In a company's capital structure, equity consists of a company's common and preferred stock plus retained earnings, which are summed up in the shareholders' equity account on a balance sheet. This invested capital and debt, generally of the long-term variety, comprises a company's capitalization, i.e. a permanent type of funding to support a company's growth and related assets. A discussion of debt is less straightforward. Investment literature often equates a company's debt with its *liabilities*. Investors should understand that there is a difference between operational and debt liabilities—it is the latter that forms the debt component of a company's capitalization—but that's not the end of the debt story.

Among financial analysts and investment research services, there is no universal agreement as to what constitutes a debt liability. For many analysts, the debt component in a company's capitalization is simply a balance sheet's long-term debt. This definition is too simplistic. Investors should stick to a stricter interpretation of debt where the debt component of a company's capitalization should consist of the following: short-term borrowings (notes payable), the current portion of long-term debt, long-term debt, two-thirds (rule of thumb) of the principal amount of operating leases and redeemable preferred stock. Using a comprehensive total debt figure is a prudent analytical tool for stock investors.

Unfortunately, there is no magic proportion of debt that a company can take on. The debt-equity relationship varies according to industries involved, a company's line of business and its stage of development. However, because investors are better off putting their money into companies with strong balance sheets, common sense tells us that these companies should have, generally speaking, lower debt and higher equity levels.

A company considered too highly leveraged (too much debt versus equity) may find its freedom of action restricted by its creditors and/or may have its profitability hurt as a result of paying high interest costs. Of course, the worst-case scenario would be having trouble meeting operating and debt liabilities during periods of adverse economic conditions. Lastly, a company in a highly competitive business, if hobbled by high debt, may find its competitors taking advantage of its problems to grab more market share.[4]

Theoretically, the financial manager should plan an optimum capital structure for his company. The optimum capital structure is obtained when the market value per share is maximum. There is significant variation among industries and, among individual companies within an industry in terms of capital structure. Since a number of factors influence the capital structure decision of a company, the judgment of the person making the, capital structure decision plays a crucial part. Two similar companies can have different capital structures if the decision makers differ in their judgment of the significance of various factors. A totally theoretical model perhaps cannot adequately handle all those factors, which affect the capital structure decision. These factors are highly psychological, complex and qualitative and do not always follow accepted theory, since capital markets are not perfect and the decision has to be taken under in perfect knowledge and risk.

Optimal Capital Structure

In finance, the most debatable topic is capital structure. The main issue of debate revolves around the optimal capital structure. There are two schools of thought in this regard. One school pleads for optimal capital structure and other does against it. Former school argues that judicious mixture of debt and equity capital can minimize the overall cost of capital and maximize the value of the firm. Hence, this school considers capital structure decision as relevant. Latter school of thought led by Modigliani and Miller contends that financing decision does not affect the value of the firm. Since value of the firm depends on the underlying profitability and risk of investment (Van Horne 2002). An appropriate capital structure is a critical decision for any business organization. The decision is important not only because of the need to maximize returns to various organizational constituencies, but also because of the impact such a decision has on an organization's ability to deal with its competitive environment. The prevailing argument, originally developed by Modigliani and Miller (1958) is that an optimal capital structure exists which balances the risk of bankruptcy with the tax savings of debt. Once established, this capital structure should provide greater returns to stockholders than they would receive from an all-equity firm.[5]

Despite its theoretical appeal, researchers in financial management have not found the optimal capital structure. The best that academics and practitioners have been able to achieve are prescriptions that satisfy short-term goals. For example, in a recent Harvard Business Review article, readers were left with the impression that the use of leverage was one way to improve the performance of an organization. While this can be true in some circumstances, it fails to consider either the complexities of the competitive environment, or the long-term survival needs of the organization.

We argue that the use of leverage either to discipline managers or to achieve economic gain is the 'easy way out', and, in many instances, can lead to the demise of the organization. The fact that an optimal capital structure has not been found is an indication of some flaw in the logic. We believe that the original question was framed incorrectly. Rather than: What is an optimal mix of debt and equity that will maximize shareholder wealth; it should have been: Under what circumstances should leverage be used to maximize shareholder wealth? Why? Because debt and equity have profound long-term implications for corporate governance that far exceed the exigencies of the moment.[6]

Determinants of Capital Structure

Capital structure of a firm is determined by various internal and external factors. The macro variables of the economy of a country like tax policy of government, inflation rate, capital market condition, are the major external factors that affect the capital structure of a firm. The characteristics of an individual firm, which are termed here as micro factors (internal), also affect the capital structure of enterprises. This section presents how the micro-factors affect the capital structure of a firm with reference to the relevant capital structure theories stated earlier.

Size of a Firm

The bankruptcy cost theory explains the positive relation between the capital structure and size of a firm. The large firms are more diversified, have easy access to the capital market, receive higher credit ratings for debt issues, and pay lower interest rate on debt capital. Further, larger firms are less prone to bankruptcy and this implies the less probability of bankruptcy and lower bankruptcy costs. The bankruptcy cost theory suggests the lower bankruptcy costs, the higher debt level. The empirical studies carried out during the 1970s, as suggested by this theory, also show the positive relation between the size of firms and capital structure. But results of some empirical studies do not corroborate with this theoretical relation.

Growth Rate

The agency cost theory and pecking order theory explain the contradictory relation between the growth rate and capital structure. Agency cost theory suggests that equity controlled firms have a tendency to invest sub-optimally to expropriate wealth from the enterprises' bondholders. The agency cost is likely to be higher for enterprises in growing industries which have more flexibility in their choice of future investment. Hence, growth rate is negatively related with long-term debt level. Pecking order theory, contrary to the agency cost theory, shows the positive relation between the growth rate and debt level of enterprises. This is based on the reasoning that a higher growth rate implies a higher demand for funds, and, ceteris paribus, a greater reliance on external financing through the preferred source of debt. For, pecking order theory contends that management prefers internal to external financing and debt to equity if it issues securities .Thus, the pecking order theory suggests the higher proportion of debt in capital structure of the growing enterprises than that of the stagnant ones.

Business Risk

Both agency and bankruptcy cost theories suggest the negative relation between the capital structure and business risk. The bankruptcy cost theory contends that the less stable earnings of the enterprises, the greater is the chance of business failure and the greater will be the weight of bankruptcy costs on enterprise financing decisions. Similarly, as the probability of bankruptcy increases, the agency problems related to debt become more aggravating. Thus, this theory suggests that as business risk increases, the debt level in capital structure of the enterprises should decrease. Studies carried out in western countries during 1980s show the contradictory evidence in this regard. The studies carried out in India and Nepal also show the contradictory evidence on the relation between the risk and debt level.

Profitability

The static trade-off hypothesis pleads for the low level of debt capital of risky firms. The higher profitability of firms implies higher debt capacity and less risky to the debt holders. So, as per this theory, capital structure and profitability are positively associated. But pecking order theory suggests that this relation is negative. Since, as stated earlier, firm prefers internal financing and follows the sticky dividend policy. If the internal funds are not enough to finance financial requirements of the firm, it prefers debt financing to equity financing. Thus, the higher profitability of the enterprise implies the internal financing of investment and less reliance on debt financing. Most of the empirical studies support the pecking order theory.

Dividend Payout

The bankruptcy costs theory pleads for adverse relation between the dividend payout ratio and debt level in capital structure. The low dividend payout ratio means increase in the equity base for debt capital and low probability of going into liquidation. As a result of low probability of bankruptcy, the bankruptcy cost is low. According to the bankruptcy cost theory, the low bankruptcy cost implies the high level of debt in the capital structure. But the pecking order theory shows the positive relation between debt level and dividend payout ratio. According to this theory, management prefers the internal financing to external one. Instead of distributing the high dividend, and meeting the financial need from debt capital, management retains the earnings. Hence, the lower dividend payout ratio means the lower level of debt in capital structure.

Debt Service Capacity

The higher debt level in capital structure increases the probability of bankruptcy and bankruptcy costs of the enterprises. Probability of bankruptcy refers to the chances of cash flows to be less than the amount required for servicing the debt. The debt service ratio measured by the ratio of operating income to total interest charges indicates the firms' ability to meet its interest payment out of its annual operating earnings. Therefore, the higher debt service ratio shows the higher debt capacity of the enterprises. Hence, the debt capacity theory suggests the positive relation between the debt service capacity and capital structure of the enterprises. But contrary to this theoretical relation, empirical studies show the negative relation.

Operating Leverage

The use of fixed cost in production process also affects the capital structure. The high operating leverage-use of higher proportion of fixed cost in the total costs over a period of time-can magnify the variability in future earnings. Both the bankruptcy cost theory and agency cost theory suggest the negative relation between operating leverage and debt level in capital structure. The bankruptcy cost theory contends the higher operating leverage, the greater the chance of business failure and the greater will be the weight of bankruptcy costs on enterprise financing decisions. Similarly, as the probability of bankruptcy increases, the agency problems related to debt become more aggravating. Thus, these theories suggest that as operating leverage increases, the debt level in capital structure of the enterprises should decrease.

Essential Features of a Sound Capital Mix

A sound or an appropriate capital structure should have the following essential features:

- Maximum possible use of leverage;

- A flexible capital structure;
- Avoidance of undue financial risk with the increase of debt;
- Use of debt within the capacity of the firm.

While we still cannot give an exact recipe, we can now present an approach for finding the best debt/equity mix. Long-term shareholder value results mostly from bottom-line growth. Therefore, the right mix must maximize the growth in long-term profits.

This mix is likely to be different for each individual situation. At one extreme may be start-ups. Because these may lose money in their initial years, and because they have neither cash flow nor much collateral to support debt, start-ups mostly need equity to enable growth. At the other extreme are leveraged buy-outs, where a team of investors takes over an existing company. If that company is profitable already, generates cash and has a healthy asset base, a buy-out can be financed mostly by debt.

The optimal mix of debt and equity has to be tailored for each situation. This requires some sophistication in financial modeling. The trick is to prepare financial projections under different scenarios and with different assumptions. The goal is to find the debt/equity mix that provides the highest expected long-term shareholder value.[7]

Investments into companies usually require both debt and equity. The optimal ratio needs to be carefully determined for each individual situation. It is unlikely that this ratio will consist of 100 per cent equity. If the long-term prospects are so poor that a company can never make sufficient profits to benefit from leverage then the opportunity is probably not worth pursuing. Conversely, relying on 100 per cent debt financing often places a heavy cash drain on companies and leads to sub-optimal growth.

Debt and equity financing should not be seen as substitutes for each other. Instead, they are very different in nature and complement each other. Debt needs to be repaid in cash. Equity needs to be rewarded with long-term profits. Depending on individual circumstances and opportunities the trick for each investment is to find the best mix of both. [8]

Capital Gearing

'Gearing' means the ration of different types of securities to total capitalization. The term, when applied to the capital of a company, means the ratio of equity share capital to the total capital and is known as 'capital gear ratio' or 'capital gearing'. J. Batty defines the term 'capital gearing' as "the relation of ordinary shares (equity shares) to preference share capital and loan capital is described as the capital gearing."

Thus the term 'capital gearing' is used to indicate the relative proportion of fixed cost bearing securities such as preference shares and debentures to the ordinary share capital in the capital structure. Interest of equity share holders is represented by the amount of share capital plus retained earrings and undistributed profits.

Capital gearing is the most crucial factor, which must be taken into account while preparing the financial plan of a company. The term 'gearing' means the ratio between the various types of securities to total capitalization. Capital gearing is the process that determines the proportion in the various accounts of securities, which are being issued.

Capital Gearing or structure means the decision about the ratio, which different types of securities will bear, to total capitalization. Capital gearing or structure is the fixation of the appropriate ratio between two or more types of securities and the ratio that each type of security will bear to the total capitalization.

Capital Gearing can be defined as, "The mixture of debt and equity in a firm's capital structure, which influences variations in shareholders profits in response to sales and EBIT variations." A company is stated to be highly geared when the proportion of the equity capital to the total capital is small or when the proportion of preference shares and debentures bearing fixed rate on dividend. On the other hand, the company is said to be low geared if it has a larger proportion of funds raised through the issue of equity shares without bearing any fixed rate of dividend.

In simple words, a company that has raises funds mostly by equity share is low geared while a company which has secured substantial proportion of its long term funds by the issue of preference shares, bonds, and debentures is highly geared.[9]

A large proportion of firms will consider some level of capital gearing as very few firms raise all of their financial requirements via equity shareholders. This assumes that managements are actively pursuing a shareholder wealth maximization objective and presumably using gearing to achieve that objective. Capital gearing does not account for extremely high levels by many firms as the common belief is the value of the firm is not maximized when excessive gearing levels are implemented. However, all firms will consider similar factors in determining what capital gearing ratio will best maximize shareholders 'returns. A summary of the main determinants of capital gearing which will influence a firm's decision on attaining the appropriate gearing ratio are:

1. ***The rate of tax:*** Depending on a companies taxable profit level, this will determine whether or not they would be in a position to

gain from debt financing. Debt financing will occur when there is tax advantages for paying of loan interest compared to paying of dividend interest.

2. ***Tax capacity:*** for a tax deductible expense to have value there is a requirement to have taxable income against which to set it. Consequently, companies with low earnings will tend to find having high gearing less effective.
3. ***Fluctuating sales:*** If a company has fluctuating sales, then it stands to reason that fluctuations in the returns paid to ordinary shareholders will also occur in direct relation to sales. This increases the risk to the shareholder in relation to their returns and subsequently could increase the risk of bankruptcy and overall lower the appeal for shares.
4. ***High operating gearing:*** Any company that has a high operating gearing can add risk to the shareholder returns and have a similar bankruptcy risk associated with fluctuating sales. A combination of fluctuating sales and high operating gearing will pose high risk to shareholders in general.
5. ***Nature of the firm's assets:*** Firms that have assets whose value is significantly greater as a 'going concern' than on a bankruptcy sale basis, will generally avoid high capital gearing due to the difference in value.
6. ***Costs of raising capital:*** Loan finance tends to be cheap to raise although most equity finance will come from retaining profits. An issue of shares can be relatively expensive and inevitably will be a factor in a firm's decision on capital gearing.
7. ***Capital servicing costs:*** One factor that cannot be overlooked when deciding on capital gearing will be the prevailing rates of interest that will be secured against any gearing decision.

Changes in Capital Structure

In this fast changing world of business, no scheme of capitalization or capital structure can be said as permanent. However, may be initially planned, the pattern of capital structure can never fully anticipate the future changes in the economy. So it becomes necessary to make changes in the capital structure to suit the changing needs of the company. Changes in capital structure may be sought as a means of easing tension and giving the corporation a better opportunity to pursue its purpose.[10] Adjust is also required in the capital structure to facilitate expansion, growth, revision, re-capitalization and re-organization. The changes may be in the form of re-capitalization or re-adjustment of capital structure.

There are many reasons which necessitate a change in capital structure. First of all, if the financial structure of a company has become heavy with fixed cost bearing securities, it results a great strain on the financial position. Here, the company wants to adjust its capital structure by redeeming preference shares and debentures out of the proceeds of new issue of equity shares. Secondly, when a company has a variety of securities, it may need to consolidate such securities to simplify the financial plan as and when the market conditions are favorable. Thirdly, a company may resort to split up its shares to make these more attractive to investors. This becomes important when the face value is very high. Fourthly, when companies want to make their short-term loans into long-term securities. Fifthly, changes in capital structure may take place due to capitalization of retained earnings by issue of bonus shares. A company may prefer to issue bonus shares out of its accumulated reserves to maintain a balance between preference - equity and equity-debentures. Sixthly, a change in the capital structure is resulted when equity shares, preference shares or new debentures are offered to clear the default in paying interest on debentures or repayment of debentures on their maturity. This also happens when dividends to its preference shareholders and their redemption have not been met due to shortage of necessary funds, resulting in a change in the capitalization. Seventhly, readjustment of capital structure is required in case of merger and expansion of companies in order to equate their shares. Lastly, a change in capitalization is necessitated to meet the legal requirements which may change from time to time.

Conclusion and Promising Research Ideas

In terms of promising research ideas, the question of whether the asset structure variable represents tangibility, or is a proxy for the availability of non-debt tax shield, clearly calls for further investigations. Similarly, more research is required to determine the role and importance of the contentious variables including the non-debt tax shield, debtors, profitability, and risk. Other extensions to this study could allow for interaction terms, industry classifications, or the addition of explanatory variables such as dividends or ownership structure. Furthermore, additional research could also help to distinguish the impact of group affiliation on the capital structure decision. Indeed, it could be argued that business groups' theories have been neglected by researches particularly given their dominant role in many business environments.

REFERENCES

1. http://findarticles.com/p/articles/mi_m3257/is_8_59/ai_n14920105
2. http://peregrin.jmu.edu/~drakepp/principles/module7/coc.pdf
3. http://www.enotes.com/small-business-encyclopedia/capital-structure
4. http://www.investopedia.com/articles/basics/06/capitalstructure.asp
5. http://www.westga.edu/~bquest/2002/rethinking.htm
6. http://www.westga.edu/~bquest/2002/rethinking.htm
7. http://www.dynamic-equity.com/vcmag03.htm
8. http://www.dynamic-equity.com/vcmag03.htm
9. http://quickfinancecheck.org/capital-gearing
10. Sharma R.K., Gupta S.K., Management Accounting, Principles and Practice, Kalyani Publishers, New Delhi, 1996, p. 16.20.

3 Sources of Corporate Finance

Introduction

Financing policy by firms requires managers to identify ways of funding new investment. The managers may exercise three main choices: use retained earnings, borrow through debt instruments, or issue new shares. Hence, the standard capital structure of a firm includes retained earnings, debt and equity; these three components of capital structure reflect firm ownership structure in the sense that the first and third components reflect ownership by shareholders while the second component represents ownership by debt holders. This is the pattern found in developing and developed countries alike. Thus, financing policy, capital structure and firm ownership are all strongly linked in explaining how economic agents form and modify their asset-acquisition behaviour through firms and capital markets, and thereby influence their incomes and returns to asset holdings, whether in the form of direct remuneration, capital gains or dividends.

Sources of Financing Capital Structure

The primary responsibility of financing a business venture is that of the owners of the business. However, loans and credits also meet the financial requirements of business firms. In sole proprietorship business, the individual proprietor generally, invests her/his own savings to start with. She/he may reinvest a part of the profits earned in course of time. She/he may also borrow money on her/his personal security or the security of assets. Similarly, the capital of a partnership firm consists partly of funds contributed by the partners and partly of borrowed funds. If necessary they may also decide to reinvest their own shares of profit. The company form of organization enables the promoters to raise necessary funds from the public, who may contribute capital and become shareholders of the company. In course of its business, the company can raise loans directly from banks and financial institutions or by issue of debentures to the public. Besides, profits earned may also be reinvested instead of being distributed as dividend to the shareholders. Thus, for any business enterprise, there are two sources of finance, that is, funds contributed by owners, and funds available from loans and credits. In other words, the financial resources of a business may be provided by owner's fund which is otherwise known as internal sources of finance and borrowed funds which is known as external sources of finance. The sources of finance can also be categorized as long-term and short-term sources depending the period of financing. The following are the most popular sources of business finance:

- Equity Shares
- Preference shares
- Retained earnings
- Debentures/Bonds of different types
- Loans from financial institutions and corporations
- Loans from commercial banks
- Public Deposits
- Lease Financing/Hire Purchase Financing
- Venture capital funding
- Asset securitization
- International Financing
- Trade credit
- Advances received from customers
- Various short-term provisions

Internal Sources of Finance

The major internal sources of finances for a company are given below:

PERSONAL SAVINGS

Quite simply, personal savings are amounts of money that a business person, partner or shareholder has at their disposal to do with as they wish. If that person uses their savings to invest in their own or another business, then the source of finance comes under the heading of personal savings.

RETAINED EARNINGS

A company generally does not distribute all its earnings amongst the shareholders as dividends. A portion of the net earnings may be retained in the business for use in the future. This is known as retained earnings. It is a source of internal financing or self financing or 'ploughing back of profits'.[1]

The profit available for ploughing back in an organization depends on many factors like net profits, dividend policy and age of the organization.

For any company, the amount of earnings retained within the business has a direct impact on the amount of dividends. Profit re-invested as retained earnings is profit that could have been paid as a dividend. The major reasons for using retained earnings to finance new investments, rather than to pay higher dividends and then raise new equity for the new investments, are as follows:

(*a*) The management of many companies believes that retained earnings are funds which do not cost anything, although this is not true. However, it is true that the use of retained earnings as a source of funds does not lead to a payment of cash;

(*b*) The dividend policy of the company is in practice determined by the directors. From their standpoint, retained earnings are an attractive source of finance because investment projects can be undertaken without involving either the shareholders or any outsiders;

(*c*) The use of retained earnings as opposed to new shares or debentures avoids issue costs;

(*d*) The use of retained earnings avoids the possibility of a change in control resulting from an issue of new shares.[2]

Another factor that may be of importance is the financial and taxation position of the company's shareholders. If, for example, because of taxation considerations, they would rather make a capital profit (which will only be taxed when shares are sold) than receive current income, and then finance through retained earnings would be preferred to other methods.

A company must restrict its self-financing through retained profits because shareholders should be paid a reasonable dividend, in line with realistic expectations, even if the directors would rather keep the funds for re-investing. At the same time, a company that is looking for extra funds will not be expected by investors (such as banks) to pay generous dividends, nor over-generous salaries to owner-directors.

WORKING CAPITAL

This is the short-term capital or finance that a business keeps. Working capital is the money used to pay for the everyday trading activities carried out by the business—stationery needs, staff salaries and wages, rent, energy bills, payments for supplies and so on. Working capital is defined as:

Working capital = current assets – current liabilities

Where, *current assets* are short term sources of finance such as stocks, debtors and the amount of cash and cash equivalents the business has at any point of time. Cash is cash in hand and deposits payable on demand (e.g. current accounts). Cash equivalents are short term and highly liquid investments which are easily and immediately convertible into cash. *Current liabilities* are short term requirements for cash including trade creditors, expense creditors, tax owing, dividends owing and the amount of money the business owes to other people/groups/businesses at any one time that needs to be repaid within the next month or so.

SALE OF ASSETS

Business balance sheets usually have several fixed assets on them. A fixed asset is anything that is not used up in the production of the good or service concerned—land, buildings, fixtures and fittings, machinery, vehicles and so on. At times, one or more of these fixed assets may be surplus to requirements and can be sold.

Alternatively, a business may desperately need to find some cash so it decides to stop offering certain products or services and because of that can sell some of its fixed assets. Hence, by selling fixed assets, business can use them as a source of finance. Selling its fixed assets, therefore, has an effect on the potential capacity of the business—the amount it can produce.[3]

External Sources of Finance

A business can raise funds from various sources. Each of the sources has unique characteristics, which must be properly understood so that the best available source of raising funds can be identified. There is not a single best source of funds for all organizations. Depending on the situation, purpose, cost and associated risk, a choice may be made about the source to be used. For example, if a business wants to raise funds for meeting fixed capital requirements, long term funds may be required which can be raised in the form of owned funds or borrowed funds. Similarly, if the purpose is to meet the day-to-day requirements of business, the short term sources may be tapped. A brief description of various sources, along with their advantages and limitations is given below:

Issue of Shares

The capital obtained by issue of shares is known as share capital. The capital of a company is divided into small units called shares. Each share has its nominal value. For example, a company can issue 1,00,000 shares of ₹ 10 each for a total value of ₹ 10,00,000. The person holding the share is known as shareholder. There are two types of shares normally issued by a company. These are equity shares and preference shares. The money raised by issue of equity shares is called equity share capital, while the money raised by issue of preference shares is called preference share capital.

EQUITY SHARES

There are different sources of long term finance which can be used to generate the finance for the business for long period of time. One of the most commonly used is Equity Shares; the issuing of equity shares is the most important source for raising the long term capital by the company. These shares are the best source because they are only paid back on winding up of company. Equity shareholders are the real owners of the company. Equity shareholders get dividend when the company is earning profits. A company can now issue different classes and kinds of shares to raise its owned capital. The kind of shares will be issued according to the needs of the company and preferences of the investors. There are two types of shares one is right shares. A public company may increase its subscribed capital by issue of right shares. Right shares are offered to the shareholders in proportion to their present holding often at a price which is less than the currently quoted price on the stock exchange.[4]

Equity shares are shares which do not enjoy any preferential right in the matter of payment of dividend or repayment of capital. The equity shareholder gets dividend only after the payment of dividends to the preference shares. There is no fixed rate of dividend for equity shareholders. The rate of dividend depends upon the surplus profits. In case of winding up of a company, the equity share capital is refunded only after refunding the preference share capital. Equity shareholders have the right to take part in the management of the company. However, equity shares also carry more risk.

Merits

The important merits of raising funds through issuing equity shares are given as below:

(*i*) Equity shares are suitable for investors who are willing to assume risk for higher returns;

(*ii*) Payment of dividend to the equity shareholders is not compulsory. Therefore, there is no burden on the company in this respect;

(*iii*) Equity capital serves as permanent capital as it is to be repaid only at the time of liquidation of a company. As it stands last in the list of claims, it provides a cushion for creditors, in the event of winding up of a company;

(*iv*) Equity capital provides credit worthiness to the company and confidence to prospective loan providers;

(*v*) Funds can be raised through equity issue without creating any charge on the assets of the company. The assets of a company are, therefore, free to be mortgaged for the purpose of borrowings, if the need be;

(*vi*) Democratic control over management of the company is assured due to voting rights of equity shareholders.

Limitations

The major limitations of raising funds through issue of equity shares are as follows:

(*i*) Investors who want steady income may not prefer equity shares as equity shares get fluctuating returns;

(*ii*) The cost of equity shares is generally more as compared to the cost of raising funds through other sources;

(*iii*) Issue of additional equity shares dilutes the voting power, and earnings of existing equity shareholders;

(*iv*) More formalities and procedural delays are involved while raising funds through issue of equity share.

PREFERENCE SHARES[5]

The capital raised by issue of preference shares is called preference share capital. The preference shareholders enjoy a preferential position over equity shareholders in two ways:

(*i*) Receiving a fixed rate of dividend, out of the net profits of the company, before any dividend is declared for equity shareholders; and

(*ii*) Receiving their capital after the claims of the company's creditors have been settled, at the time of liquidation.

In other words, as compared to the equity shareholders, the preference shareholders have a preferential claim over dividend and repayment of capital. Preference shares resemble debentures as they bear fixed rate of return. Also as the dividend is payable only at the discretion of the directors and only out of profit after tax, to that extent, these resemble equity shares. Thus, preference shares have some characteristics of both equity shares and debentures. Preference shareholders generally do not enjoy any voting rights.

Preference shares have a fixed percentage dividend before any dividend is paid to the ordinary shareholders. As with ordinary shares a preference dividend can only be paid if sufficient distributable profits are available, although with 'cumulative' preference shares the right to an unpaid dividend is carried forward to later years. The arrears of dividend on cumulative preference shares must be paid before any dividend is paid to the ordinary shareholders. A company can issue following types of preference shares:

Types of Preference Shares

1. *Cumulative and Non-Cumulative:* The preference shares which enjoy the right to accumulate unpaid dividends in the future years, in case the same is not paid during a year are known as cumulative preference shares. On the other hand, on non-cumulative shares, dividend is not accumulated if it is not paid in a particular year.

2. *Participating and Non-Participating:* Preference shares which have a right to participate in the further surplus of a company shares which after dividend at a certain rate has been paid on equity shares are called participating preference shares. The non-participating preferences are such which do not enjoy such rights of participation in the profits of the company.

3. *Convertible and Non-Convertible:* Preference shares that can be converted into equity shares within a specified period of time are known as convertible preference shares. On the other hand, non-convertible shares are such that cannot be converted into equity shares.

Merits

The merits of preference shares are given as follows:

(*i*) Preference shares provide reasonably steady income in the form of fixed rate of return and safety of investment;

(*ii*) Preference shares are useful for those investors who want fixed rate of return with comparatively low risk;

(*iii*) It does not affect the control of equity shareholders over the management as preference shareholders don't have voting rights;

(*iv*) Payment of fixed rate of dividend to preference shares may enable a company to declare higher rates of dividend for the equity shareholders in good times;

(*v*) Preference shareholders have a preferential right of repayment over equity shareholders in the event of liquidation of a company;

(*vi*) Preference capital does not create any sort of charge against the assets of a company.

Limitations

The major limitations of preference shares as source of business finance are as follows:

(*i*) Preference shares are not suitable for those investors who are willing to take risk and are interested in higher returns;

(*ii*) Preference capital dilutes the claims of equity shareholders over assets of the company;

(*iii*) The rate of dividend on preference shares is generally higher than the rate of interest on debentures;

(*iv*) As the dividend on these shares is to be paid only when the company earns profit, there is no assured return for the investors. Thus, these shares may not be very attractive to the investors;

(*v*) The dividend paid is not deductible from profits as expense. Thus, there is no tax saving as in the case of interest on loans.

DEBENTURES[6]

Debentures are an important instrument for raising long term debt capital. A company can raise funds through issue of debentures, which bear a fixed rate of interest. The debenture issued by a company is an acknowledgment that the company has borrowed a certain amount of money, which it promises to repay at a future date. Debenture holders are, therefore, termed as creditors of the company. Debenture holders are paid a fixed stated amount of interest at specified intervals say six months or one year. Public issue of debentures requires that the issue be rated by a credit rating agency like CRISIL (Credit Rating and Information Services of India Ltd.) on aspects like track record of the company, its profitability, debt servicing capacity, credit worthiness and the perceived risk of lending. Issue of Zero Interest Debentures (ZID) which do not carry any explicit rate of interest has also become popular in recent years. The difference between the face value of the debenture and its purchase price is the return to the investor. A company can issue following types of debentures:

Types of Debentures

1. *Secured and Unsecured:* Secured debentures are such which create a charge on the assets of the company, thereby mortgaging the assets of the company. Unsecured debentures on the other hand do not carry any charge or security on the assets of the company.

2. *Registered and Bearer:* Registered debentures are those which are duly recorded in the register of debenture holders maintained by the company. These can be transferred only through a regular instrument of transfer. In contrast, the debentures which are transferable by mere delivery are called bearer debentures.

3. *Convertible and Non-Convertible:* Convertible debentures are those debentures that can be converted into equity shares after the expiry of a specified period. On the other hand, non-convertible debentures are those which cannot be converted into equity shares.

4. *First and Second:* Debentures that are repaid before other debentures are repaid are known as first debentures. The second debentures are those which are paid after the first debentures have been paid back.

Mahindra and Mahindra was the first company in India to issue convertible Zero Interest Debentures in January 1990. Recently, the board of Titan Industries has approved the issue of partly convertible debentures on a rights basis to raise around ₹ 126.83 crores. The issue will comprise 21 lakh partly convertible debentures of ₹ 600 each in the ratio of one partly convertible debenture for every 20 equity shares held in the company to the shareholders.

Merits

The merits of raising funds through debentures are given as follows:

(*i*) It is preferred by investors who want fixed income at lesser risk,

(*ii*) Debentures are fixed charge funds and do not participate in profits of the company;

(*iii*) The issue of debentures is suitable in the situation when the sales and earnings are relatively stable;

(*iv*) As debentures do not carry voting rights, financing through debentures does not dilute control of equity shareholders on management;

(*v*) Financing through debentures is less costly as compared to cost of preference or equity capital as the interest payment on debentures is tax deductible.

Limitations

A debenture as source of funds has certain limitations. These are given as follows:

(*i*) As fixed charge instruments, debentures put a permanent burden on the earnings of a company. There is a greater risk when earnings of the company fluctuate;

(*ii*) In case of redeemable debentures, the company has to make provisions for repayment on the specified date, even during periods of financial difficulty;

(*iii*) Each company has certain borrowing capacity. With the issue of debentures, the capacity of a company to further borrow funds reduces.

TRADE CREDIT[7]

Trade credit is the credit extended by one trader to another for the purchase of goods and services. Trade credit facilitates the purchase of supplies without immediate payment. Such credit appears in the records of the buyer of goods as 'sundry creditors' or 'accounts payable'. Trade credit is commonly used by business organizations as a source of short-term financing. It is granted to those customers who have reasonable amount of financial standing and goodwill. The volume and period of credit extended depends on factors such as reputation of the purchasing firm, financial position of the seller, volume of purchases, past record of payment and degree of competition in the market. Terms of trade credit may vary from one industry to another and from one person to another. A firm may also offer different credit terms to different customers.

Merits

The important merits of trade credit are as follows:

(*i*) Trade credit is a convenient and continuous source of funds;

(*ii*) Trade credit may be readily available in case the credit worthiness of the customers is known to the seller;

(*iii*) Trade credit needs to promote the sales of an organization;

(*iv*) If an organization wants to increase its inventory level in order to meet expected rise in the sales volume in the near future, it may use trade credit to, finance the same;

(*v*) It does not create any charge on the assets of the firm while providing funds.

Limitations

Trade credit as a source of funds has certain limitations, which are given as follows:

(*i*) Availability of easy and flexible trade credit facilities may induce a firm to indulge in overtrading, which may add to the risks of the firm;

(*ii*) Only limited amount of funds can be generated through trade credit;

(*iii*) It is generally a costly source of funds as compared to most other sources of raising money.

FACTORING[8]

Factoring is a financial service under which the 'factor' renders various services which includes:

(*a*) Discounting of bills (with or without recourse) and collection of the client's debts. Under this, the receivables on account of sale of goods or services are sold to the factor at a certain discount. The factor becomes responsible for all credit control and debt collection from the buyer and provides protection against any bad debt losses to the firm. There are two methods of factoring—recourse and non-recourse. Under recourse factoring, the client is not protected against the risk of bad debts. On the other hand, the factor assumes the entire credit risk under non-recourse factoring i.e., full amount of invoice is paid to the client in the event of the debt becoming bad.

(*b*) Providing information about credit worthiness of prospective client's etc., Factors hold large amounts of information about the trading histories of the firms. This can be valuable to those who are using factoring services and can thereby avoid doing business with customers having poor payment record. Factors may also offer relevant consultancy services in the areas of finance, marketing, etc. The factor charges fees for the services rendered. Factoring appeared on the Indian financial scene only in the early nineties as a result of RBI initiatives. The organizations that provide such services include SBI Factors and Commercial Services Ltd., Canbank Factors Ltd., Foremost Factors Ltd., State Bank of India, Canara Bank, Punjab National Bank, Allahabad Bank. In addition, many non-banking finance companies and other agencies provide factoring service.

Merits

The merits of factoring as a source of finance are as follows:

(*i*) Obtaining funds through factoring is cheaper than financing through other means such as bank credit;

(*ii*) With cash flow accelerated by factoring, the client is able to meet his/her liabilities promptly as and when these arise;

(*iii*) Factoring as a source of funds is flexible and ensures a definite pattern of cash inflows from credit sales. It provides security for a debt that a firm might otherwise be unable to obtain;

(*iv*) It does not create any charge on the assets of the firm;

(*v*) The client can concentrate on other functional areas of business as the responsibility of credit control is shouldered by the factor.

Limitations

The limitations of factoring as a source of finance are as follows:

(*i*) This source is expensive when the invoices are numerous and smaller in amount;

(*ii*) The advance finance provided by the factor firm is generally available at a higher interest cost than the usual rate of interest;

(*iii*) The factor is a third party to the customer who may not feel comfortable while dealing with it.

LEASE FINANCING[9]

A lease is a contractual agreement whereby one party i.e., the owner of an asset grants the other party the right to use the asset in return for a periodic payment. In other words it is a renting of an asset for some specified period. The owner of the assets is called the 'lessor' while the party that uses the assets is known as the 'lessee'. The lessee pays a fixed periodic amount called lease rental to the lessor for the use of the asset. The terms and conditions regulating the lease arrangements are given in the lease contract. At the end of the lease period, the asset goes back to the lessor. Lease finance provides an important means of modernization and diversification to the firm. Such type of financing is more prevalent in the acquisition of such assets as computers and electronic equipment which become obsolete quicker because of the fast changing technological developments. While making the leasing decision, the cost of leasing an asset must be compared with the cost of owning the same.

Merits

The important merits of lease financing are as follows:

(*i*) It enables the lessee to acquire the asset with a lower investment;

(*ii*) Simple documentation makes it easier to finance assets;

(*iii*) Lease rentals paid by the lessee are deductible for computing taxable profits;

(*iv*) It provides finance without diluting the ownership or control of business;

(*v*) The lease agreement does not affect the debt raising capacity of an enterprise;

(*vi*) The risk of obsolescence is borne by the lesser. This allows greater flexibility to the lessee to replace the asset.

Limitations

The limitations of lease financing are given as below:

(*i*) A lease arrangement may impose certain restrictions on the use of assets. For example, it may not allow the lessee to make any alteration or modification in the asset;

(*ii*) The normal business operations may be affected in case the lease is not renewed;

(*iii*) It may result in higher payout obligation in case the equipment is not found useful and the lessee opts for premature termination of the lease agreement; and

(*iv*) The lessee never becomes the owner of the asset. It deprives him of the residual value of the asset.

PUBLIC DEPOSITS[10]

The deposits that are raised by organizations directly from the public are known as public deposits. Rates of interest offered on public deposits are usually higher than that offered on bank deposits. Any person who is interested in depositing money in an organization can do so by filling up a prescribed form. The organization in return issues a deposit receipt as acknowledgment of the debt. Public deposits can take care of both medium and short-term financial requirements of a business. The deposits are beneficial to both the depositor as well as to the organization. While the depositors get higher interest rate than that offered by banks, the cost of deposits to the company is less than the cost of borrowings from banks. Companies generally invite public deposits for a period up to three years. The acceptance of public deposits is regulated by the Reserve Bank of India.

Merits

The merits of public deposits are:

(*i*) The procedure of obtaining deposits is simple and does not contain restrictive conditions as are generally there in a loan agreement;

(*ii*) Cost of public deposits is generally lower than the cost of borrowings from banks and financial institutions;

(*iii*) Public deposits do not usually create any charge on the assets of the company. The assets can be used as security for raising loans from other sources;

(*iv*) As the depositors do not have voting rights, the control of the company is not diluted.

Limitations

The major limitations of public deposits are as follows:

(*i*) New companies generally find it difficult to raise funds through public deposits;

(*ii*) It is an unreliable source of finance as the public may not respond when the company needs money;

(*iii*) Collection of public deposits may prove difficult, particularly when the size of deposits required is large.

COMMERCIAL PAPER (CP)[11]

Commercial Paper emerged as a source of short term finance in our country in the early nineties. Commercial paper is an unsecured promissory note issued by a firm to raise funds for a short period, varying from 90 days to 364 days. It is issued by one firm to other business firms, insurance companies, pension funds and banks. The amount raised by CP is generally very large. As the debt is totally unsecured, the firms having good credit rating can issue the CP. Its regulation comes under the purview of the Reserve Bank of India. The merits and limitations of a Commercial Paper are as follows:

Merits

(*i*) A commercial paper is sold on an unsecured basis and does not contain any restrictive conditions;

(*ii*) As it is a freely transferable instrument, it has high liquidity;

(*iii*) It provides more funds compared to other sources. Generally, the cost of CP to the issuing firm is lower than the cost of commercial bank loans;

(*iv*) A commercial paper provides a continuous source of funds. This is because their maturity can be tailored to suit the requirements of the issuing firm. Further, maturing commercial paper can be repaid by selling new commercial paper;

(*v*) Companies can park their excess funds in commercial paper thereby earning some good return on the same.

Limitations

(*i*) Only financially sound and highly rated firms can raise money through commercial papers. New and moderately rated firms are not in a position to raise funds by this method;

(*ii*) The size of money that can be raised through commercial paper is limited to the excess liquidity available with the suppliers of funds at a particular time;

(*iii*) Commercial paper is an impersonal method of financing. As such if a firm is not in a position to redeem its paper due to financial difficulties, extending the maturity of a CP is not possible.

COMMERCIAL BANKS[12]

Commercial banks occupy a vital position as they provide funds for different purposes as well as for different time periods. Banks extend loans to firms of all sizes and in many ways, like, cash credits, overdrafts, term loans, purchase/discounting of bills, and issue of letter of credit. The rate of interest charged by banks depends on various factors such as the characteristics of the firm and the level of interest rates in the economy. The loan is repaid either in lump sum or in installments. Bank credit is not a permanent source of funds. Though banks have started extending loans for longer periods, generally such loans are used for medium to short periods. The borrower is required to provide some security or create a charge on the assets of the firm before a loan is sanctioned by a commercial bank.

Merits

The merits of raising funds from a commercial bank are as follows:

(*i*) Banks provide timely assistance to business by providing funds as and when needed by it;

(*ii*) Secrecy of business can be maintained as the information supplied to the bank by the borrowers is kept confidential;

(*iii*) Formalities such as issue of prospectus and underwriting are not required for raising loans from a bank. This, therefore, is an easier source of funds;

(*iv*) Loan from a bank is a flexible source of finance as the loan amount can be increased according to business needs and can be repaid in advance when funds are not needed.

Limitations

The major limitations of commercial banks as a source of finance are as follows:

(*i*) Funds are generally available for short periods and its extension or renewal is uncertain and difficult;

(*ii*) Banks make detailed investigation of the company's affairs, financial structure etc., and may also ask for security of assets and personal sureties. This makes the procedure of obtaining funds slightly difficult;

(*iii*) In some cases, difficult terms and conditions are imposed by banks. for the grant of loan. For example, restrictions may be imposed on the sale of mortgaged goods, thus making normal business working difficult.

FINANCIAL INSTITUTIONS[13]

The government has established a number of financial institutions all over the country to provide finance to business organizations. These institutions are established by the central as well as state governments. They provide both owned capital and loan capital for long and medium term requirements and supplement the traditional financial agencies like commercial banks. As these institutions aim at promoting the industrial development of a country, these are also called development banks'. In addition to providing financial assistance, these institutions also conduct market surveys and provide technical assistance and managerial services to people who run the enterprises. This source of financing is considered suitable when large funds for longer duration are required for expansion, reorganization and modernization of an enterprise.

Merits

The merits of raising funds through financial institutions are as follows:

(*i*) Financial institutions provide long-term finance, which are not provided by commercial banks;

(*ii*) Besides providing funds, many of these institutions provide financial, managerial and technical advice and consultancy to business firms;

(*iii*) Obtaining loan from financial institutions increases the goodwill of the borrowing company in the capital market. Consequently, such a company can raise funds easily from other sources as well;

(*iv*) As repayment of loan can be made in easy installments, it does not prove to be much of a burden on the business;

(*v*) The funds are made available even during periods of depression, when other sources of finance are not available.

Limitations

The major limitations of raising funds from financial institutions are as given below:

(*i*) Financial institutions follow rigid criteria for grant of loans. Too many formalities make the procedure time consuming and expensive;

(*ii*) Certain restrictions such as restriction on dividend payment are imposed on the powers of the borrowing company by the financial institutions;

(*iii*) Financial institutions may have their nominees on the Board of Directors of the borrowing company thereby restricting the powers of the company.

The major financial institutions set up in our country for business financing are as follows:

1. ***Industrial Finance Corporation of India (IFCI):*** It was established in July 1948 as a statutory corporation under the Industrial Finance Corporation Act, 1948. Its objectives include assistance towards balanced regional development and encouraging new entrepreneurs to enter into the priority sectors of the economy. IFCI has also contributed to the development of management education in the country.

2. ***State Financial Corporations (SFC):*** The State Financial Corporations Act, 1951 empowered the State Governments to establish State Financial Corporations in their respective regions for providing medium and short term finance to industries which are outside the scope of the IFCI. Its scope is wider than IFCI, since the former covers not only public limited companies but also private limited companies, partnership firms and proprietary concerns.

3. ***Industrial Credit and Investment Corporation of India (ICICI):*** This was established in 1955 as a public limited company under the Companies Act. ICICI assists the creation, expansion and

modernization of industrial enterprises exclusively in the private sector. The corporation has also encouraged the participation of foreign capital in the country.

4. ***Industrial Development Bank of India (IDBI):*** It was established in 1964 under the Industrial Development Bank of India Act, 1964 with an objective to coordinate the activities of other financial institutions including commercial banks. The bank performs three types of functions, namely, assistance to other financial institutions, direct assistance to industrial concerns, and promotion and coordination of financial-technical services.
5. ***State Industrial Development Corporations (SIDC):*** Many state governments have set up State Industrial Development Corporations for the purpose of promoting industrial development in their respective states. The objectives of the SIDCs differ from one state to another.
6. ***Unit Trust of India (UTI):*** It was established by the Government of India in 1964 under the Unit Trust of India Act, 1963. The basic objective of UTI is to mobilize the community's savings and channelize them into productive ventures. For this purpose, it sanctions direct assistance to industrial concerns, invests in their shares and debentures, and participates with other financial institutions.
7. ***Industrial Investment Bank of India Ltd.:*** It was initially set up as a primary agency for rehabilitation of sick units and was known as Industrial Reconstruction Corporation of India. It was reconstituted and renamed as the Industrial Reconstruction Bank of India in 1985 and again in 1997 its name was changed to Industrial Investment Bank of India. The Bank assists sick units in the reorganization of their share capital, improvement in management system, and provision of finance at liberal terms.
8. ***Life Insurance Corporation of India (LIC):*** LIC was set up in 1956 under the LIC Act, 1956 after nationalizing 245 existing insurance companies. It mobilizes the community's savings in the form of insurance premia and makes it available to industrial concerns, both public as well as private, in the form of direct loans and underwriting of and subscription to shares and debentures.

INTERNATIONAL FINANCING[14]

In addition to the sources discussed above, there are various avenues for organizations to raise funds internationally. With the opening up of an economy and the operations of the business organizations becoming global, Indian companies have an access to funds in global capital market. Various international sources from where funds may be generated include:

(i) ***Commercial Banks:*** Commercial banks all over the world extend foreign currency loans for business purposes. They are an important source of financing non-trade international operations. The types of loans and services provided by banks vary from country to country. For example, Standard Chartered emerged as a major source of foreign currency loans to the Indian industry.

(ii) ***International Agencies and Development Banks:*** A number of international agencies and development banks have emerged over the years to finance international trade and business. These bodies provide long and medium term loans and grants to promote the development of economically backward areas in the world. These bodies were set up by the Governments of developed countries of the world at national, regional and international levels for funding various projects. The more notable among them include International Finance Corporation (IFC), EXIM Bank and Asian Development Bank.

(iii) ***International Capital Markets:*** Modern organizations including multinational companies depend upon sizeable borrowings in rupees as well as in foreign currency.

Choosing the Best Source of Finance[15]

Financial needs of a business are of different types—long term, short term, fixed and fluctuating. Therefore, business firms resort to different types of sources for raising funds. Short-term borrowings offer the benefit of reduced cost due to reduction of idle capital, but long-term borrowings are considered a necessity on many grounds. Similarly equity capital has a role to play in the scheme for raising funds in the corporate sector. As no source of funds is devoid of limitations, it is advisable to use a combination of sources, instead of relying only on a single source. A number of factors affect the choice of this combination, making it a very complex decision for the business. The factors that affect the choice of source of finance are briefly discussed below:

(i) ***Cost:*** There are two types of cost viz., the cost of procurement of funds and cost of utilizing the funds. Both these costs should be taken into account while deciding about the source of funds that will be used by an organization.

(ii) ***Financial strength and stability of operations:*** The financial strength of a business is also a key determinant. In the choice of

source of funds business should be in a sound financial position so as to be able to repay the principal amount and interest on the borrowed amount. When the earnings of the organization are not stable, fixed charged funds like preference shares and debentures should be carefully selected as these add to the financial burden of the organization.

(iii) ***Form of organization and legal status:*** The form of business organization and status influences the choice of a source for raising money. A partnership firm, for example, cannot raise money by issue of equity shares as these can be issued only by a joint stock company.

(iv) ***Purpose and time period:*** Business should plan according to the time period for which the funds are required. A short-term need for example can be met through borrowing funds at low rate of interest through trade credit, commercial paper, etc. For long term finance, sources such as issue of shares and debentures are more appropriate. Similarly, the purposes for which funds are required need to be considered so that the source is matched with the use. For example, a long-term business expansion plan should not be financed by a bank overdraft which will be required to be repaid in the short term.

(v) ***Risk profile:*** Business should evaluate each of the sources of finance in terms of the risk involved. For example, there is a least risk in equity as the share capital has to be repaid only at the time of winding up and dividends need not be paid if no profits are available. A loan on the other hand, has a repayment schedule for both the principal and the interest. The interest is required to be paid irrespective of the firm earning a profit or incurring a loss.

(vi) ***Control:*** A particular source of fund may affect the control and power of the owners on the management of a firm. Issue of equity shares may mean dilution of the control. For example, as equity share holders enjoy voting rights, financial institutions may take control of the assets or impose conditions as part of the loan agreement. Thus, business firm should choose a source keeping in mind the extent to which they are willing to share their control over business.

(vii) ***Effect on credit worthiness:*** The dependence of business on certain sources may affect its credit worthiness in the market. For example, issue of secured debentures may affect the interest of unsecured creditors of the company and may adversely affect their willingness to extend further loans as credit to the company.

(viii) ***Flexibility and ease:*** Another aspect affecting the choice of a source of finance is the flexibility and ease of obtaining funds. Restrictive provisions, detailed investigation and documentation in case of borrowings from banks and financial institutions for example may be the reason that a business organization may not prefer it, if other options are readily available.

(ix) ***Tax benefits:*** Various sources may also be weighed in terms of their tax benefits. For example, while the dividend on preference shares is not tax deductible, interest paid on debentures and loan is tax deductible and may, therefore, be preferred by organizations seeking tax advantage.

Thus, in choosing the best source of finance, it is essential to know the merits and demerits of all the sources. The primary advantage of debt financing is that it allows the founders to retain ownership and control of the company. In contrast to equity financing, the entrepreneurs are able to make key strategic decisions and also to keep and reinvest more company profits. Another advantage of debt financing is that it provides small business owners with a greater degree of financial freedom than equity financing. Debt obligations are limited to the loan repayment period, after which the lender has no further claim on the business, whereas equity investors' claim does not end until their stock is sold. Debt financing is also easy to administer, as it generally lacks the complex reporting requirements that accompany some forms of equity financing. Finally, debt financing tends to be less expensive for small businesses over the long term, though more expensive over the short term, than equity financing.

The main disadvantage of debt financing is that it requires a small business to make regular monthly payments of principal and interest. Very young companies often experience shortages in cash flow that may make such regular payments difficult, and most lenders provide severe penalties for late or missed payments. Another disadvantage associated with debt financing is that its availability is often limited to established businesses. Since lenders primarily seek security for their funds, it can be difficult for unproven businesses to obtain loans.

The main advantage of equity financing for small businesses, which are likely to struggle with cash flow initially, is that there is no obligation to repay the money. Equity financing is also more likely to be available to concept and early stage businesses than debt financing. Equity investors primarily seek growth opportunities, so they are often willing to take a chance on a good idea. But debt financiers primarily seek security, so they usually require the business to have some sort of track record before they will consider making a loan. Another advantage of equity financing is that investors often prove to be good sources of advice and contacts for small business owners.

The main disadvantage of equity financing is that the founders must give up some control of the business. If investors have different ideas about the company's strategic direction or day-to-day operations, they can pose problems for the entrepreneur. In addition, some sales of equity, such as initial public offerings, can be very complex and expensive to administer. Such equity financing may require complicated legal filings and a great deal of paperwork to comply with various regulations. For many small businesses, therefore, equity financing may necessitate enlisting the help of attorneys and accountants.

Major sources of Finances for Indian Companies[16]

Raising of funds to finances the firm's investments is an important function of the financial manager. In practice, it is observed that financial managers use different combinations of debt and equity. The study conducted by I.M.Pandey (1984) about the corporate managers' attitude towards use of borrowings in India revealed that the practicing managers generally preferred to borrow instead of using other sources of funds because of low cost of debt due to the interest tax deductibility and the complicated procedures for raising the equity capital. In the light of the finding, Pandey (1985) conducted another empirical study examining the industrial trail patterns, trend, and volatilities of leverage and the impact of size, profitability, and growth of leverage. For this purpose, data of 743 companies in 18 industrial groups for the period 1973-74 to 1980-81 were analyzed. It was found that about 72 to 80 per cent of assets of sample companies were financed by external debt including current liabilities. Companies trade credit as much as bank borrowings. The level of leverage for all industries showed a noticeable increase after 1973-74. The study also indicated that classifying leverage percentages by the type of industry dies not produce any patterns which may be regarded as systematic and significant. The trends and volatilities associated with the leverage percentages also did not give any support to the belief and the type of industry impact on the degree of leverage. It also revealed that there was some evidence of the tendency of large size companies to concentrate on the higher level of leverage .But it was difficult to say conclusively that size has an impact on the degree of leverage since a large number of small firms were also found employing high level of debt. The study also did not show a definite structural relationship between the degrees of leverage, on the one hand and profitability and growth, on the other hand; although over time, profitability and growth have improved and so has the degree of leverage. The majority of the profitability and growth groups of companies were concentrated with narrow bands of leverage.

Chakraborty (1977) has also conducted a study to investigate debt-equity ratio in the private corporate sector of India. He tested the relation of debt-equity ratio with age, total assets, retained earnings, profitability and capital intensity. He found that age, retained earnings and profitability were negatively correlated while total assets and capital intensity were positively correlated to debt-equity ratio. He also provided a glimpse of the regional patterns of debt-equity ratios in different industrial centers in India. He also attempted a prediction equation for debt-equity ratio for each industry. Chakraborty also used a very simple methodology for calculating the cost of capital. He showed calculation of cost of capital for 22 firms. He found that cost of capital increased from 7.36 per cent to 12.36 per cent over years. The average cost of capital for the entire consumer good industry taken together was highest while, it was lowest for the intermediate goods firms. One of the reasons for this was attributed to relatively low amount of debt used in the former industry than in the latter.

In his Doctoral Thesis "Financing of Private Corporate Sector in India: Trends and Determinants During 1966-67 to 2000-01", L.M.Bhole conducted an analysis of the trends in corporate capital structure and the various sources of finance (i.e. retained earnings, bank capital, trade credit, equity capital and foreign capital) of Public Limited Companies (PULCos), Private Limited Companies (PRLCos), and Foreign Companies (FRCos) in India during the period of 1966-67 to 2000-01. He has also conducted period analysis to gauge the impact of liberalization on the determinants of corporate capital structure as well as other sources of financing of private corporate sector in India. The study finds that the leverage ratios of all the three types of companies have increased significantly during 1966-67 to 2000-01, and the dependence on debt is more in the case of public limited companies as compared to the private limited and foreign companies. Unlike in countries like USA, UK, Australia, the pecking order of funds in India broadly has been borrowings, trade dues, external equity, and reserves and surplus. From the empirical analysis it is found that cost of borrowing, the cost of equity, size of firm, collateral value of assets, liquidity, and the non-debt tax shields are the major determinants of corporate capital structure in India. Corporate saving rate in India has not increased much and it has remained at a relatively low level through out a long period of 1966-67 to 2000-01. The savings of this sector have not kept pace with its capital formation. The econometric analysis shows that the profits after tax, investment opportunities, availability of external funds, cost of borrowings, and cost of equity have been the major determinants of retained earnings of the Indian joint-stock companies. There are decreasing trends in bank financing in the case of PULCos during the period 1966-67 to 2000-01. The dependence on bank borrowings is high in the case of PRLCos than PULCos and FRCos in India. The supply of long-term loans by banks to the private corporate sector is increasing throughout the period. The phenomenon of over financing of private corporate sector by banks continues to exist and the availability of other domestic debt, size of the firm, liquidity, rate of interest, and profitability are the major determinants of demand for bank credit of the private corporate sector in India. It has been found that the government sector has remained a substantial user of trade credit throughout the entire period. There has been a mild tendency towards the substitution between trade dues and bank credit in India. The relationship between trade credit and inventories concluded that it is highly unlikely that the use of trade credit has been inflationary in India. The nature of behaviour of trade credit and the changes in it over the years clearly depend upon the type / ownership of companies. It has been found that availability of external credit, rate of interest, volume of business, size of firms, high powered money, liquidity, rate of profit, and inventories are the determinants of the demand for and supply of trade credit, and that the trade credit functions are stable in India. The trend analysis shows that the stock market is an important but only one among many sources of funds for the Indian corporate sector. The role of equity capital financing is more in the case of PRLCos than PULCos and FRCos. It has been found that the stock market is a source of funds primarily for the existing companies, and not so much for the new companies. The study concludes that total long term borrowings, size of the firm, profitability, growth rate of the firm, liquidity and cost of equity are the major determinants of the demand for equity capital of the private corporate sector in India. There is a very limited role of foreign capital financing for the private corporate sector in India. India's share in total FDI inflows of developing economies of Asia has increased from 2.7 per cent to 3.3 per cent during 1996-97 to 2000-01. All the components of foreign investments have been subject to a high degree of volatility, and foreign debt has increased more rapidly than other components. The domestic long-term borrowings ratio, size of the firm, profitability, and liquidity are the major determinants of the foreign capital financing in India.[17]

A recent study on the financing sources of Indian Corporate shows that:

- Companies have slowly moved towards internal sources as a preferred mode of capital. It was just about 30 per cent initially of total capital and has doubled to 60 per cent now;

- The debt equity ratio has become lower from 88.4 per cent in mid 80's to to 61.6 now per cent;
- Within external sources, Bank borrowing increased and reliance on equity capital is lower;
- Debentures which found huge favor earlier in 90s is an absolute no-no;
- Borrowing from FI (IDBI, IFCI etc.) has also come down;
- Overall summary is that reliance on both bank and bank financing has come down.

The following table shows the trend of corporate finance of Indian companies:

Table 3.1 : Pattern of Sources of Funds for Indian Corporate

(Per cent to total)

	1970-80	1980-90	1990-2000	After 2000
1. Internal Sources	31.9	29.9	37.1	60.7
2. External Sourcesof which:	68.1	70.1	62.9	39.3
(*a*) Equity capital	7.2	18.8	13.0	9.9
(*b*) Borrowingsof which:	37.9	32.7	35.9	11.5
(*i*) Debentures	11.0	7.1	5.6	−1.3
(*ii*) From Banks	13.6	8.2	12.3	18.4
(*iii*) From FIs	8.7	10.3	9.0	−1.8
(*c*) Trade dues & other current liabilities	22.8	18.4	13.7	17.3
Total	**100.0**	**100.0**	**100.0**	**100.0**
Memo:				
(*i*) Share of Capital Market Related Instruments (Debentures and Equity Capital)	18.2	26.0	18.6	8.6
(*ii*) Share of Financial Intermediaries (Borrowings from Banks and FIs)	22.2	18.3	21.3	16.6
(*iii*) Debt-Equity Ratio	88.1	85.5	65.2	61.6

Note: Data pertain to a sample of non-government non-financial public limited companies.
Source: Article on 'Finances of Public Limited Companies', RBI Bulletin (various issues).

The study says that Indian companies prioritize their sources of financing (from internal financing to equity) according to the law of least effort, or of least resistance, preferring to raise equity as a financing means "of last resort". Hence internal funds are used first, and when that is depleted debt is issued, and when it is not sensible to issue any more debt, equity is issued.[18]

Conclusion and Promising Research Ideas

A company's reasonable, proportional use of debt and equity to support its assets is a key indicator of balance sheet strength. A healthy capital structure that reflects a low level of debt and a corresponding high level of equity is a very positive sign of investment quality. Since capital is expensive for small businesses, it is particularly important for small business owners to determine a target capital structure for their firms. Capital structure decisions are complex ones that involve weighing a variety of factors. In general, companies that tend to have stable sales levels, assets that make good collateral for loans, and a high growth rate can use debt more heavily than other companies. On the other hand, companies that have conservative management, high profitability, or poor credit ratings may wish to rely on equity capital instead.

REFERENCES

1. http://www.scribd.com/doc/22615511/Financial-Management-Notes.
2. http://www.elearning.strathmore.edu/file.php/582/Financing.docx.
3. http://www.bized.co.uk/learn/accounting/financial/sources/capital.htm.
4. http://wiki.answers.com/Q/Types+of+long+term+sources.
5. http://www.scribd.com/doc/22615511/Financial-Management-Notes.
6. http://www.scribd.com/doc/22615511/Financial-Management-Notes.
7. http://www.scribd.com/doc/22615511/Financial-Management-Notes.
8. http://www.scribd.com/doc/22615511/Financial-Management-Notes.
9. http://www.scribd.com/doc/22615511/Financial-Management-Notes.
10. http://www.scribd.com/doc/22615511/Financial-Management-Notes.
11. http://www.scribd.com/doc/22615511/Financial-Management-Notes.
12. http://www.scribd.com/doc/22615511/Financial-Management-Notes.
13. http://www.scribd.com/doc/22615511/Financial-Management-Notes.
14. http://www.scribd.com/doc/22615511/Financial-Management-Notes.
15. http://www.scribd.com/doc/22615511/Financial-Management-Notes.
16. http://www.coolavenues.com/forums/showthread.php?t=11359
17. Bhole L M "Financing of Private Corporate Sector In India: Trends and Determinants During 1966-67 to 2000-01".
18. http://mostlyeconomics.wordpress.com/2007/06/06/capital-structure-of-indian-companies.

4 Liberalization and Capital Structure of Indian Corporate

Introduction

The Government of India started the economic liberalization policy in 1991. Even though the power at the centre has changed hands, the pace of the reforms has never slackened till date. Before 1991, changes within the industrial sector in the country were modest to say the least. The sector accounted for just one-fifth of the total economic activity within the country. The sectoral structure of the industry has changed, albeit gradually. Most of the industrial sector was dominated by a select band of family-based conglomerates that had been dominant historically. Post 1991, a major restructuring has taken place with the emergence of more technologically advanced segments among industrial companies. Nowadays, more small and medium scale enterprises contribute significantly to the economy.

By the mid-90s, the private capital had surpassed the public capital. The management system had shifted from the traditional family based system to a system of qualified and professional managers. One of the most significant effects of the liberalization era has been the emergence of a strong, affluent and buoyant middle class with significant purchasing powers and this has been the engine that has driven the economy since. Another major benefit of the liberalization era has been the shift in the pattern of exports from traditional items like clothes, tea and spices to automobiles, steel, IT etc. The 'made in India' brand, which did not evoke any sort of loyalty has now become a brand name by itself and is now known all over the world for its quality.[1]

Capital Structure of Indian Corporate Before Liberalization

Studies on capital structure of Indian Industries are inconclusive and often conflicting. A study by Sharma and Rao (1968) on 30 Engineering firms for three years concludes that debt due to its tax-deductibility is a prominent determinant of the cost of capital. A study by I. M. Pandey (1981) on cotton textiles, chemicals, engineering and electricity generations lends support to the traditional approach. Bhatt (1980) in his paper concludes that the leverage ratio is very much influenced by business risks measured in term of variability in earnings, profitability, debt service capacity, and dividend-payout ratio. I. M. Pandey (1984) in another study found that during 1973-81 about 80 per cent of the assets of the companies sampled were financed by external debt and current liabilities. Large sized companies were more levered though a large number of small firms also courted more debt capital. Leverage did not exhibit a definite relationship with growth and profitability, although all the three variables moved in the same direction. He also found that a majority of the profitability and growth oriented companies were within the narrow bands of leverage. S. K. Chakraborty (1977) in his study found that age, retained earnings, and profitability were negatively correlated with the debit equity ratio, while total assets and capital intensity were directly related to it. He felt that a high cost of capital for all the consumer industries was due to their low debt component. His indirect attempt to test the MM hypothesis for 22 firms showed that cost of capital was almost invariant to the debt equity ratios.

Before 1980s Indian financial managers courted debt due to its low cost, tax advantages and the complicated procedures to be observed in garnering equity capital. The substitutability of short term debt for long term loan was another attraction. However, with the waves of liberalization, privatization and globalization sweeping the capital market in recent years, the corporate world has started wooing equity capital in a big way. The arrival of a matrix of new financial instruments such as commercial papers, asset securitization, factoring and forfeiting services, and the market related interest rate structure and their stringent conditions for lending, force modern enterprises to court equity finance.

In the study conducted by Chhabi Majumdar in 1992 for his Doctoral Thesis titled, "Borrowing as a Source of Financing Working Capital in The Corporate Sector in India: An Empirical Analysis"[2] on Working Capital Financing Sources of Indian Corporate before liberalization, for the period 1981 to 1990, he analyzed the balance sheets of 20 companies, 10 from private sector and 10 from public sector. In addition, he has processed the relevant figures of a good number (ranging from 534 to 641 units) of public limited companies whose results have been published in the RBI (Reserve Bank of India) Bulletins during the period under study. While processing the figures so obtained, he has taken help of some accounting as well as statistical tools e.g. current ratio, debt-equity ratio, standard deviation, co-efficient of variation and test of significance.

In the process of the study he has seen that the working capital of each firm is constituted by several types of sources like bank borrowings, public deposits, trade credit, long-term borrowings and equity capital. At the outset, he has tried to find out the reasons behind utilizing several sources instead of relying upon one or two best-suited sources. What appears there from is that, since working capital needs are partly fixed and partly fluctuating, the companies cannot but resort to sources of different types and terms. Moreover, whereas short-term borrowings offer the benefit of reduced cost due to reduction of idle capital, the use of long-term borrowings has also the necessity on many grounds. Long-term borrowings are less risky than short-term borrowings and the firms would not have to meet the cash obligations off and on. Not only the long-term borrowings, but the equity capital has also its role to play in the financing of working capital in Indian corporate sector. At the initial stage of a firm, fixed assets as well as current assets have to be financed by this equity capital, since other sources may not be easily available at that time. Subsequently, when the firms get momentum, several lenders may stretch their hands for advancing loan, but the importance of equity capital does not end altogether. On the ground of stability and security, each firm is to maintain 'equity-cushion' throughout its life time. In view of this, it has been deduced in his study that there is need for financing working capital from various sources.

Of different sources, bank credit has been working since long as a major source of working capital in India and abroad. In 1970s the use of bank credit in Indian corporate sector became so excessive that the desired correlation between bank credit and the holding of inventory and book debt was hampered in most cases. Hence, attempt was initiated to bring in a 'check' on the use of bank credit and several study groups (Dehejia Study Group, Tandon Study Group, Chore Study Group, Marathe Committee, Chakraborty Committee etc.) were set to find out a way in this regard. All the study Groups gave recommendations in favour of providing a 'restraint' on the use of bank credit, and the Tandon Study Group prescribed some definite norms to that effect. Suggesting a limit on the holding of inventory and book debt, the Tandon Study Group prescribed three methods (methods I, II &III) to be implemented one after another, with a view to reducing the share of bank credit in the working capital. Applying the prescribed (prescribed by Tandon Study Group) norms for holding inventory and bank credit he has seen in his study that there has been a positive impact of the Tandon Study Group recommendations on the use of bank credit by Indian companies. That means the desired correlation between bank credit and the holding of inventory and receivables has now been mostly established. Notwithstanding, the share of bank borrowings to total borrowings in public limited companies is 20 per cent in average during the period 1981-90, and that to current assets is 22-25 per cent. The yearly scores during the decade of eighty are also in agreement with the average results, and hence the standard deviations calculated thereon have been very low. In government companies, the combined scores in relation to total borrowings as well as to current assets are only 5-6 per cent no doubt, but in six out of ten government companies the individual scores range from 17 per cent to 31 per cent. In view of this, it may be said that the role of bank borrowings in working capital financing in Indian corporate sector is still immense. Then, he has analyzed the role of public deposit as a source of working capital in Indian corporate sector. This source emerged in India in 1930s. In 1950s, there became a downfall in the use of it. In 1970s it again came into prominence. Use of public deposit may frustrate the Government's policy of canalizing the flow of funds to industrial sector according to planned priorities. Moreover, it is said that the unwary depositors may come into the trap of unscrupulous depositee companies, by lending their hard-earned money as public deposit. But from the standpoint of depositee companies, public deposit can be said to be a viable source of finance in many respects. The most important argument in favour of its use is that it is cheaper than bank borrowings and many other sources of finances. Now, government has imposed some regulation and as a result the interest of innocent investors has been protected to an extent and the flow of public deposit has also been restrained in the interest of planned economy. It is thus expected that the investors will now accept the offer for public deposit more freely and the firms, due to its cost advantage, will utilize this source up to at least the permissible limit. But what he has observed is that the share of public deposit to total borrowings is, on an average, only 6 per cent in public limited companies, and this is as meager as 0.08 per cent in government companies. Share of public deposit to current assets is also only 7 per cent in public limited companies and 0.08 per cent in government companies. The individual results as to the use of public deposit are, however, widely scattered, and this is substantiated by the high co-efficient of variation (108%) of the scores. Nevertheless, it is evident from the combined results that the role of public deposit as a source of working capital is not significant in the decade of eighty, though in 1970s its role had been better to some extent.

Long-term borrowings like debenture, institutional loan and government loan have also a contribution to working capital financing, since, a part of current assets is usually covered by long-term funds. The corporate practices as to these of different types of long-term sources reveal that the position of debenture in corporate finance is almost equal to that of institutional loan. In RBI sample, both hold individually 14 per cent of total borrowings. In case of ten selected public limited companies their individual scores are seven per cent and in case of government companies their scores are only 0.1 per cent – 0.3 per cent. Government loan, on the other hand, occupies as much as 66 per cent share of total borrowings in government companies, though its position in public limited companies is really insignificant.

Sometimes long-term borrowings may occupy important role in total borrowings, but that does not mean that contribution of long-term borrowings to working capital will also be significant. If current liabilities cover the current assets in full, the long-term sources, whatever may be their position to total borrowings, will have to be presumed to be used for financing the fixed assets only. From this view point, he has computed the extent of gap between current assets and current liabilities of the selected companies, and has presumed that the gap has been financed by long-term sources as a whole. Multiplying the gap with the ratio of each long-term source to total long-term funds, he has estimated the share of different companies of long-term borrowings, viz, debenture, institutional loan and government loan, in the context of working capital. The results so obtained reveal that the individual share of institutional loan and debentures towards financing working capital is two per cent – five per cent in case of public limited companies and 0.05 per cent – 0.16 per cent in case of government companies. Thus, it appears that the role of debenture and institutional loan in working capital finance is almost an exercise of paper only. Position of government loan is also disappointing in public limited companies. But in government companies its contribution is remarkable. This is quite expected as government companies have developed a practice of banking upon 'easily-available' government loans. However, the position of government loan as a source of finance is gradually decreasing even in government companies. On the other hand the position of debenture is gradually improving both in private as well as in public sector. Institutional loan exhibits a fluctuating trend during the decade of eighty, although ultimately its position has improved to an extent.

Another viable source of working capital is trade credit, which is considered to be a formality-free, security-free and interest-free source of finance. Due to the above advantages, trade credit has been practically a common source of working capital to almost all enterprises;

notwithstanding the fact that there is some implicit cost associated with trade credit and the explicit cost is also originated when cash discount offered is foregone. During 1980s, 30 per cent of current assets and 25 per cent of total borrowings of public limited companies have come from trade credit and in case of government companies the scores have respectively been 8.3 per cent and 8.8 per cent. As such, it may be stated that the role of trade credit is equally important during the period under study. However, its contribution in public limited companies is higher in comparison with that in government companies.

One of the important factors determining the feasibility or otherwise of a particular source of finance is stated to be the cost. Hence, he has attempted to see thereafter how far the cost actually plays the decisive role in the selection of sources.

With an attempt to estimate the effect of cost on their selection, he has computed the specific costs of some sources. Trade credit has been taken to be less costly source of finance, although there are some implicit costs of trade credit over and above the cost of foregoing cash discount. Bank borrowings, on the other hand, appear to be costliest of the three sources. Thus, on cost consideration, it is natural that share of bank borrowing in working capital finance will be much lower than that of trade credit. But the corporate practices reveal that ratio of bank borrowings, to trade credit is, on an average, 88 per cent, that is, bank borrowings do not lag as much behind the trade credit as it should be from the view point of cost of finance. Then, coming to the comparative position of bank borrowings and public deposit he found that, throughout the decade of eighty, the cost of public deposit had always been lower than that of bank borrowings. But during the period, the use of bank borrowings was approximately four times of public deposit. Moreover, it has been revealed that the cost of public deposit, contrary to general expectation, has gradually come down. Had the cost been a factor for the use of public deposit, its share to current assets would have been higher over time due to gradual reduction in cost. Reversely, he has observed a decreasing trend in the use of this source. In view of all these, he concluded that effect of cost on the selection of sources of working capital is not at all significant.

Liberalization and Its Impact on Capital Structure of Indian Corporate

Until the early nineties, corporate financial management in India was a relatively drab and placid activity. There were not many important financial decisions to be made for the simple reason that firms were given very little freedom in the choice of key financial policies. The government regulated the price at which firms could issue equity, the rate of interest which they could offer on their bonds, and the debt equity ratio that was permissible in different industries. Moreover, most of the debt and a significant part of the equity were provided by public sector institutions. At the beginning of the reform process, the Indian corporate sector found it significantly over-levered. This was because of several reasons:

- Subsidized institutional finance was so attractive that it made sense for companies to avail of as much of it as they could get away with. This usually meant the maximum debt-equity ratios laid down by the government for various industries;
- In a protected economy, operating (business) risks were lower and companies could therefore afford to take more risks on the financing side;
- Most of the debt was institutional and could usually be rescheduled at little cost.

The liberalization changed all of this. The corporate sector was exposed to international competition and subsidized finance gave way to a regime of high real interest rates. One of the first tasks for the Indian companies was substantial deleveraging. Fortunately, a booming equity market and the appetite of foreign institutional investors for Indian paper helped companies to accomplish this to a great extent in 1993 and 1994. The downturn in the stock market that has followed since then has stopped this process from going any further and has probably left many companies still excessively levered. According to the figures compiled by the Centre for Monitoring the Indian Economy, the average debt-equity ratio of private sector manufacturing companies in India fell from 1.72 in 1990-91 to 1.05 in 1996-97, and more than half of this reduction took place in one single year—1994-95. And consequently, the post-liberalized era has started observing the following changes in the sources of Industrial finance:

(a) Domestic Capital Formation : The planners, in the fifties, had recognized that the material shortage of capital in relation to labour was the principal constraint to the industrial growth. It was envisioned that increased capital formation would contribute for more industrial output and a 'virtuous circle' of growth. Gross Capital Formation (GCF) is estimated across three types of assets, viz., construction, machinery and equipment. The GCF, adjusted for errors and omissions, is termed as aggregate investment or Gross Domestic Capital Formation (GDCF). A positive association is hypothesized between the capital formation and the industrial production.

(b) Foreign Direct Investment : Foreign investment can be classified as foreign direct investment (FDI) and foreign portfolio investment.

International investment in financial assets such as shares, debentures and bonds, is called portfolio investment. Foreign investment in real assets is called foreign direct investment (FDI). Multinational corporations (MNCs) are the chief source of foreign direct investment in real assets. Real assets consist of physical things such as factories, land, capital goods, infrastructure and inventories. Multinational may collaborate in joint ventures with host country enterprises or may have fully owned subsidiaries in host countries. Such investments are called foreign direct investments.

A few decades ago, many countries considered FDI as the source of economic imperialism. But things are quite different now. The argument is that FDI contribute to the growth of host economies in many ways. e.g. physical capital formation, technology transfer, human formation, stimulation of productivity, augmentation of output, promotion of foreign trade and improvement of competitiveness of indigenous entrepreneurs. After weighing the prospects and consequences, Government of India seems keen to attract ever-increasing amount of FDI, which can be evidenced by its efforts aimed at deregulation, transparency and globalization. In brief, it can be regarded as a source of industrial growth. As part of the economic reforms introduced in 1991, in the wake of a sharp external payments crisis, policies relating to foreign investment and foreign technology agreements were radically changed. Foreign Investment Promotion Board (FIPB) was specifically created to invite and negotiate for substantially large investment by international companies.

(c) Primary Issues in the Capital Market : Capital market constitutes primary (new issues market) and secondary (stock) market. The primary market helps the public and private sector companies in raising finance mainly for their new projects, expansion, modernization, acquisition etc. The secondary market provides liquidity for the financial instruments (equity, preference shares and debentures/bonds) through adequate marketability and price continuity. The array of financial institutions also have played crucial role in meeting long-term credit needs of the industrial sector.

With the liberalization of the Indian economy since 1991, the Government has provided a number of additional fiscal and other incentives to foster capital market development. The result has been an explosive growth of the market. The magnitude of the growth has been rapid and vivid in terms of fund mobilized, the amount of market capitalization and the expansion of investor population. The Indian market was opened up for investment by the foreign institutional investors (FIIs) in Sept. 1992 and the Indian companies were allowed to raise resources abroad through Global Depository Receipts (GDR) and Foreign Currency Convertible Bonds (FCCB). Both the primary and secondary segments of the capital market displayed rapid expansion and growth accompanied by greater institutionalization and larger participation of individual investors during the post-reform period.

Despite the structural transformation of the Indian capital market, there are many problems which often come on the way of its efficiency. These relate to investor protection, consolidation (after massive expansion), integration with other market segments, product innovation and technology, etc. which are critical and need to be addressed. Reserve Bank of India has expressed concern over continued sluggishness in the primary capital market for the last two years (1996-97 and 1997-98), as long term prospects for industrial development are critically dependent on the revival of primary market.

(d) Bank Credit : Banks are the dominant financial intermediaries in developing countries including India. Bank credit is considered as an important source of industrial finance. The dependence on bank for finance could vary according to the size of the companies. The small-scale industrial units have increased their dependence on banks for loans because they have virtually no access to the capital markets.

The Reserve Bank of India's attempt at reforming the financial sector was visible from the recommendations of the Committee to Review the Working of the Monetary System (1985) (referred to as Chakraborthy Committee Report).The Committee advocated the necessity of moving away from quantitative controls which, it felt, led to distortions in the credit market and resulted in curbing the growth of the economy. But the impetus to reforms in the financial sector was given by the Report of the Committee on the financial system (Narasimham Committee). The financial sector reforms, based on this report were mainly aimed to provide credit to the industrial sector by reducing the Cash Reserve Ratio and Statutory Liquidity Ratio. The liberalization policy also called for increased efficiency of commercial banks by encouraging them to compete in the market. The public sector banks were given autonomy to frame their policies including interest rate fixation. It may be noted that the bank credit to the industrial sector has not increased during the post-reform period in spite of the various attempts.[3]

Capital Structure of Indian Companies After Liberalization

Capital Structure management has been impacted by a number of the developments discussed above—operational reforms in the area of credit assessment and delivery, interest rate deregulation, changes in the competitive structure of the banking and credit systems, and the emergence of money and debt markets. Some of the important implications of these changes for short term financial management in the Indian corporate sector are:

1. ***Creditworthiness:*** The abolition of the notion of maximum permissible bank finance has given banks greater freedom and responsibility for assessing credit needs and creditworthiness. Similarly commercial paper and other disintermediated forms of short term finance are very sensitive to the company's credit rating and perceived creditworthiness. Companies are suddenly finding that their creditworthiness is under greater scrutiny than ever before. Over a period of time, companies will have to strengthen their balance sheets significantly to ensure a smooth flow of credit. In the meantime, many borrowers' especially small and medium businesses have seen their source of credit dry up.
2. ***Choice:*** Top notch corporate borrowers are seeing a plethora of choices. The disintegration of the consortium system, the entry of term lending institutions into working capital finance, and the emergence of money market borrowing options gives them the opportunity to shop around for the best possible deal. Some borrowers indeed appear to have moved to a highly transaction oriented approach to their bankers. Over time, however, we would probably see the re-emergence of relationship banking in a very different form.
3. ***Maturity Profile:*** The greater concern for interest rate risk makes choice of debt maturity more important than before. Short term borrowings expose borrowers to roll-over risk and interest rate risk.
4. ***Cash Management:*** Cash management has become an important task with the phasing out of the cash credit system. Companies now have to decide on the optimal amount of cash or near-cash that they need to hold, and also on how to deploy the cash. Deployment in turn involves decisions about maturity, credit risk and liquidity. In the mid-nineties, many corporate found that they had got these decisions wrong. During the tight money policy of this period, some companies were left with too little liquid cash, while others found that their 'cash' was locked up in unrealizable or illiquid assets of uncertain value.

In quantitative terms, the growth of the Indian capital markets since the advent of reforms has been very impressive. The market capitalization of the Bombay Stock Exchange (which represents about 90 per cent of the total market capitalization of the country) has quadrupled from ₹ 1.1 trillion at the end of 1990-91 to ₹ 4.3 trillion at the end of 1996-97. As a percentage of GDP, market capitalization has been more erratic, but on the whole this ratio has also been rising. Total trading volume at the Bombay Stock Exchange and the National Stock Exchange (which together account for well over half of the total stock market trading in the country) has risen more than ten-fold from ₹ 0.4 trillion in 1990-91 to ₹ 4.1 trillion in 1996-97. The stock market index has shown a significant increase during the period despite several ups and downs, but the increase is much less impressive in dollar terms because of the substantial depreciation of the Indian rupee. It may also be seen from the chart that after reached its peak in 1994-95, the stock market index has been languishing at lower levels apart from a brief burst of euphoria that followed an investor friendly budget in 1997. For the primary equity market too, 1994-95 was the best year with total equity issues (public, rights and private placement) of ₹ 355 billion. Thereafter, the primary market collapsed rapidly. Equity issues in 1996-97 fell to one-third of 1994-95 levels and the decline appears to be continuing in 1997-98 as well. More importantly, most of the equity issues in recent months have been by the public sector and by banks. Equity issues by private manufacturing companies are very few.

A study conducted by Justin Paul, A. Ramanathan, reveals that bank credit constitutes two-third of the total credit to the industrial sector and still continues as the important source of finance for small-scale industries. More attention has to be paid for providing as much as bank credit for the industrial sector. Reserve Bank of India's efforts to reduce the Cash Reserve Ratio and withdrawal of adhoc treasury bills (abolition of automatic monetization of fiscal deficit) will be helpful to pump more credit to the banking sector. But commercial banks are required to take steps for providing more credit to the industrial sector, rather than investing in government securities. Priority should be given for small-scale units and new entrepreneurs. Bank rate has to brought down in order to reduce the cost of funds (interest rate) in India. Similarly, certain measures have to be adopted immediately in the financial sector to recover the buoyancy in the stock market.[4]

Conclusion and Promising Research Ideas

So far as India is concerned, much remains to be done for industrialization. There exists the need to develop a synergic relation between the government and the private sector. State will have to keep constant dialogue with the entrepreneurs and their representatives to revive their confidence. To overcome the severe demand contraction in the economy,

India has to rely on higher government spending and tax cuts. The government has to play a dominant role for allocating the limited resources and for more public investments. In sum, the study leads to the conclusion that India has to concentrate on domestic capital formation. In order to achieve this goal, we have to promote the private corporate investment from Indian nationals as well as non-resident Indians. Despite the relaxations in some regulatory acts, India continues to repel investors with interminable delays. Indians abroad have demonstrated to the world that its entrepreneurial and professional skills are as good as best. Corporate sector has entered into a world where only the fittest can survive. To be able to do so, Indian industry must become more quality conscious, invest in human capital and encourage professional management.

REFERENCES

1. http://www.chillibreeze.com/articles/India-liberalization.asp
2. M. Chhabi, "Borrowing as a Source of Financing Working Capital in The Corporate Sector in India: An Empirical Analysis".
3. Paul Justin, Ramanathan. A "Sources of Industrial Finance: Some Econometric Evidence"
4. Paul Justin, Ramanathan. A "Sources of Industrial Finance: Some Econometric Evidence".

5 Review of Literature

Introduction

In the light of the vast literature on capital structure issues, we do not try to provide a comprehensive review, and we do not discuss theory in detail. Rather, as a starting ground, we will give a brief outline of the major theoretical ideas and the corresponding empirical implications and present some empirical studies on capital structure issues. The focus of our discussion is on (subjectively) selected recent empirical studies.

Review of Selected Empirical Studies[1]

Sound financing decisions of a firm basically should lead to an optimal capital structure. Capital structure represents the proportion in which various long-term capital components are employed. Over the years, these decisions have been recognized as the most important decisions that a firm has to take. This is because of the fact that capital structure affects the cost of capital, net profit, earning per share, dividend payout ratio and liquidity position of the firm. These variables coupled with a number of other factors determine the value of a firm. So, capital structure is a very important determinant of the value of a firm.

Franco Modigliani and Merton Miller (hereafter called M-M) were the first to present a formal model on valuation of capital structure. In their seminal papers (1958, 1963), they showed that under the assumptions of perfect capital markets, equivalent risk class, no taxes, 100 per cent dividend-payout ratio and constant cost of debt, the value of a firm is independent of its capital structure. When corporate taxes are taken into account, the value of a firm increases linearly with debt-equity (D/E) ratio because of interest payments being tax exempted. M-M's work has been at the centre stage of the financial research till date. Their models have been criticized, supported, and extended over the last 35 years.

David Durand (1963) criticized the model on the ground that the assumptions used by M-M are unrealistic. Solomon (1963) argued that the cost of debt does not always remain constant. When the leverage level exceeds the accepted level, the probability of default in interest payments increases thus raising the cost of debt. Stiglitz (1969, 1974) proved the validity of the M-M model under relaxed assumptions whereas Smith (1972), Krause and Litzenberger (1973), Baron (1974, 1975), and Scott (1976, 1977), supported the M-M model, but only under the conditions of risk free debt and costless bankruptcy. When bankruptcy has positive costs, there exists an optimal capital structure which is a trade-off between tax advantage of debt and bankruptcy costs.

This trade-off theory was challenged by Miller (1977). He argued that bankruptcy and agency costs are too small to offset the tax advantage of debt. But when personal taxes are taken into account, this advantage is completely offset by the disadvantage of personal tax rate. Thus, in equilibrium, the value of a firm is independent of its capital structure, even when the market is imperfect. But Miller's model was rejected by DeAngelo and Masulis (1980). They argued that even if bankruptcy, agency and related costs are ignored, introduction of non-debt tax shields is enough for a firm to have an optimal capital structure. And even if these costs are taken into account, an optimal capital structure exists, irrespective of availability of non-debt tax shields. Masulis (1980, 1983), Brennen and Schwartz (1978), and Jensen and Meckling (1976) also advocated the existence of an optimal capital structure in an imperfect market, while using different mechanisms. Besides, a lot more work has been done on this problem till now, but a formal model, showing the mechanism for determining an optimal capital structure in an imperfect market, is yet to be developed.

In the Indian context, one comes across two works, one by Sharma and Rao (1969) and the other by Pandey (1992). The former tested the M-M model using cross-sectional analysis for engineering companies, wherein the value of a firm was found to be independent of its capital structure after allowing for tax advantage. But the results could not be generalized as the sample was homogeneous. The other work by Pandey (1992) observed that the M-M theory is not fully valid under Indian conditions. He concluded that, initially, cost of capital and value of a firm are independent of the capital structure changes, but they rise after a certain level. All these studies have helped understand the dynamics of this crucial issue better but have not been able to come to a definite conclusion as to how firms determine their optimal capital structure. So, the present study was planned to make another attempt to resolve this contentious issue. It may be pointed out that the study has not included the effect of factors like agency and bankruptcy costs, as they are difficult to measure in the Indian scenario.

As Myers (2001, p. 81) declares : "There is no universal theory of the debt-equity choice, and no reason to expect one." However, there are several useful conditional theories, each of which helps to understand the debt-to-equity structure that firms choose. There are three perspectives on capital structure that are particularly prominent. Since these three perspectives are influential we provide some discussion here about what patterns in the data might be expected under each theory. We do not do this to provide a definitive test of one theory against another. Instead our point is to help clarify the extent to which each of these points of view helps us to organize the patterns that we see in the data. In this way we can suggest places where each of the theories might be productively further developed. The three ideas are as follows:

(1) *The trade-off theory*. Firms' trade-off between the benefits of leverage such as tax savings or mitigation of agency problems against the costs of leverage such as the expected deadweight costs of bankruptcy;

(2) *The pecking order theory*. Due to adverse selection, firms prefer to finance their activities using retained earnings if possible. If retained earnings are inadequate, then they turn to the use of debt. Equity financing is only used as a last resort;

(3) *The market timing theory*. Firms try to time the market by using debt when it is cheap and equity when it seems cheap.

These theories can be divided into two groups—either they predict the existence of the optimal debt-equity ratio for each firm (so-called static trade-off models) or they declare that there is no well-defined target capital structure (pecking-order hypothesis). Static trade-off models understand the optimal capital structure as an optimal solution of a trade-off, for example the trade-off between a tax shield and the costs of financial distress in the case of trade-off theory. According to this theory the optimal capital structure is achieved when the marginal present value of the tax shield on additional debt is equal to the marginal present value of the costs of financial distress on additional debt. The trade-off between the benefits of signalling and the costs of financial distress in the case of signalling theory implies that a company chooses debt ratio as a signal about its type. Therefore in the case of a good company the debt must be large enough to act as an incentive compatible signal, i.e., it does not pay off for a bad company to mimic it. In the case of agency theory the trade-off between agency costs stipulates that the optimal capital structure is achieved when agency costs are minimized. Finally, the trade-off between costs of financial distress and increase of efficiency in the case of free cash-flow theory, which is designed mainly for firms with extra-high free cash-flows, suggests that the high debt ratio disciplines managers to pay out cash instead of investing it below the cost of capital or wasting it on organizational inefficiencies. On the other hand, the pecking-order theory suggests that there is no optimal capital structure. Firms are supposed to prefer internal financing (retained earnings) to external funds. When internal cash-flow is not sufficient to finance capital expenditures, firms will borrow, rather than issue equity. Therefore there is no well-defined optimal leverage, because there are two kinds of equity, internal and external, one at the top of the pecking order and one at the bottom.

Details of Research and Publications on This Topic

How do firms finance their investments? How does financing interact with investment? And, most generally, do financing decisions affect firm value? These essential questions in corporate finance are still contended, and the theoretical and empirical literature is far from reaching consensus even on some of the most basic issues. Some of the recent researches and publications on this topic are given below:

Gorden (1962)[2] found that as gearing increased with size, return on investment was negatively related to debt ratio. He also confirmed the negative association between operating risk and debt ratio.

Baxter (1967)[3] reported that leverage would depend on the variance of net operating earnings. Since business with relatively stable income streams are less subject to the possibility of ruin, they may find it desirable to rely relatively heavily on debt financing. On the other hand, firms with risky income streams are less able to assume fixed charge sources of finance. Hence he concluded negative association between variance of net operating earnings and leverage.

Gupta (1969)[4] conducted a study on the financial structure of American Manufacturing Enterprises. The focus of the study was analyzing the industry effect and the growth effect on the financial structural relationship of American Manufacturing Enterprises. It was a cross sectional study for the year 1961-62. The study confirmed that total debt ratios were positively related to growth and negatively related to size. He also found significant industry effect on debt ratio. He further observed that "family pattern of ownership" is an important determinant of leverage in the paper and allied product industry.

Toy et al. (1974)[5] reported that higher the operating risk companies showed, higher is the debt ratio. They found that debt ratios were positively related to growth typically measured as sales growth and return on investment was negatively related to debt ratio. They also concluded that the corporation size and the industry class do not appear to be determinants of debt ratio.

Carelton and Siberman (1997)[6] concluded that higher the variability in rate of return on invested capital, lower will be the degree of financial leverage adopted. Hence it is the variance, not the rate of return that is the ultimate determinant of leverage. They also found return on investment to be negatively related to debt ratio.

Ferri and Jones (1979)[7] examined the determinants of financial structure. The objective of their study was to investigate the relationship between a firm's financial structure and its industrial class, size, variability of income and operating leverage. They found that the industry class was linked to the firm's leverage, but not in a direct manner as was suggested in other researches. Secondly, a firm's use of debt is related to its size, but the income could not be shown to be associated with the firm's leverage. Finally, operating leverage does influence the percentage of debt in a firm's financial structure and the relationship between these two types of leverage is similar to the negative linear form which financial theory suggests.

Bhat (1980)[8] studied the impact of size, growth, business risk, dividend policy, profitability, debt service capacity and the degree of operating leverages on the leverage ratio of the firm. He used multiple regression models to find out the contribution of each characteristic. Business risk (defined as earning instability), profitability, dividend payout and debt service capacity were found to be significant determinants of the leverage ratio. He used a sample of 63 companies from engineering industry.

Venkatesan (1983)[9] investigated the determinants of financial leverage by analyzing the relationship between seven different variables and the financial structure of the firms. The variables included industry categorization, size, operating leverage, debt coverage, cash flow coverage, business risk, and growth ratio. Industry influence has been examined on the grouping of firms in various leverages classes and he found a statistical relationship between industry class and leverage, but the relationship could not be significant and conclusive. The impact of the remaining independent variables on the dependent variable was examined in two sample classifications, viz. Intra-industry and Inter-industry through multiple regression analysis. In summation, only debt coverage ratio was found to be the important variable significantly affecting the financial structure of the firm. Mathew (1997)[10] has made an attempt to analyze the relationship between ownership structure and financial structure with a view to know whether the former has any impact on the latter. The analysis was based on three hypothetical relationships that exist between ownership structures on one hand and unsystematic risk, non-manufacturing expenses and profit appropriation policies on the other hand. He concluded that wherever the management stake is high, leverage will be low and vice versa and there exists a significant relationship between ownership structure and financial structure of firms.

Ram Kumar Kakani (1999)[11] in his paper entitled "Determinants of Capital Structure" attempted to find out the determinants of the capital structure and its maturity in India and he has analyzed measure of short-term and long-term debt rather than an aggregate measure of total debt. And he also analyzed the empirical implications of liberalizations of the Indian Economy 'on the determinants of capital structure of the firms'.

Kotrappa (2000)[12] slacked that the success of a corporation greatly depends upon sound financing. When the original financing has been sound, a co-operation has less fear for the future, provided it is given by a competent management. In this write-up, he attempts to sketch the factories responsible for reduced proportion of debt capital in the total capital employed. However, the choice between debt and equity sources of capital for a corporate borrower is greatly influenced by these factors: (1) Taxes on Corporate Incomes; (2) Inflation; (3) Controlling Interest; (4) Capital Market Reforms. Bradley, Jarroll and Kim (2002)[13] found that debt to asset ratio is negatively related to both the volatility of annual operating earnings and advertising and Research and Development expenses.

Conclusion and Promising Research Ideas

The discussion of empirical studies on additional determinants of corporate leverage, which have gained only recently attention in the literature, illustrates that apart from adjustment behaviour, there is still room for future theoretical and empirical work. Only recently, the role of rating agencies for capital structure decisions has been analyzed, despite the obvious relevance in modern capital markets. There is probably much future research to do, to really understand the impact of this and other corporate governance mechanisms on capital structure choices. Also, the emerging empirical literature inspired by motives from behavioural finance has revealed that problems other than asymmetric information and agency costs, which are the dominating arguments leading to the classic trade-off or pecking order theories, seem to be of empirical relevance.

With respect to these classical theories, the available evidence is still contradictory, finding empirical results consistent with adjustment behaviour and some preference of firms for cash flow financing. But, patterns like the pronounced usage of equity financing for smaller firms remain puzzling in the pecking order context. Quite consistently, however, the evidence suggests that market-timing behaviour to some extent explains observed capital structure patterns.

In conclusion, it remains an interesting challenge for future (empirical) research, to improve our understanding of circumstances, where certain capital structure determinants are relevant, and to identify (further) reliable empirical patterns and core factors of systematic variation in corporate leverage.

REFERENCES

1. Dhankar Raj S and Boora Ajit S "*Cost of Capital, Optimal Capital Structure, and Value of Firm: An Empirical Study of Indian Companies*".
2. Gorden. M. J.; "*The Investment, Financing and Valuation of Corporation*"; Homewood Ill; Irwin; 1962.
3. Baxter, N.D.; "Leverage, Risk of Ruin and the Cost of Capital"; *Journal of Finance*; Vol. 22; Sep.1967; pp. 395-403.
4. Gupta, M.C.,; "The Effect of Size, Growth and Industry on Financial Structure of Manufacturing Companies"; *Journal of Finance*; Vol. 24; No. 3; June 1969; pp. 517-529.
5. Toy.N., Stonehill A., Rammers, L. and Beekhuisen.T.; "A Comparative International Study of Growth, Profitability and Risk as Determinants of Corporate Debt Ratio in the Manufacturing Sector"; *Journal of Financial and Quantitative Analysis*; Vol.9; No. 1974. pp. 875-886.
6. Carelton. W.T. and Siberman, I.H.; "Joint Determination of Rate of Return and Capital Structure; An econometric analysis"; *Journal of Finance*; Vol.32; June 1977; pp. 811-821.
7. Ferri. M.G. and Jones.W.H. "Determinants of Financial Structure; A New Methodological Approach"; *Journal of Finance*; Vol. 34; No. 3; June 1979; pp. 031-044.
8. Bhat. K. and Ramesh. K. "Determinants of Financial Leverage: Some Further Evidence"; *The Chartered Accountant*; Vol. 9; No. 9; 1980; pp. 451-456.
9. Venketesan. S; "Determinants of Financial Leverage: An Empirical Extension"; *The Chartered Accountant*; 1983; pp. 519-527.
10. Mathew T. "*Optional Financial Leverage the Ownership Factor Finance India*", Vol. 5; No 2; June 1991; pp. 195-201.
11. Ram Kumar Kakani. "The Determinants of Capital Structure—An Econometric Analysis"; *Finance India*; Vol. XII; No. 1; March 1000; pp. 51 60.
12. Kotrappa. G; "Contemporary in Business Finance" by Omprakash Kajipet; Discovery Publishing House; New Delhi; 1st Edn; 2000; pp. 70-75.
13. Bradley, Jarell and Kim; "A Review of Research on the Practices of Corporate Finance"; *South Asian Journal of Management*; Vol. 9; No. 4; July-Sep 2002; pp. 29.

6 Methodology and Tools for Analysis

Introduction

This chapter contains the methodology adopted in collection and analysis of data for the study. The scope of the study, procedure followed for selection of samples, collection of data, classification and analysis of the data are elaborated in the following paragraphs. The chapter also discusses the format used for the historical Funds Flow Analysis and other techniques used for the analysis and interpretation of the total sample and also the variables. The hypotheses to be tested in the course of the analysis and the various limitations which are associated with the study have also been discussed in this chapter. The basic purpose of this chapter is to discuss about the different methods available top analyze the capital structure. In the way of analysis, one may be tempted to analyze the financial statements, which provide organized and detailed information for the study. Among all the techniques, two important techniques, i.e. Ratio Analysis and Funds Flow Statement Analysis have been selected to study the capital structure; as these two methods are widely used. The present chapter is concerned with a detailed account of mainly these two tools for analysis of the capital structure.

Scope of the Study

The proposed research is intended to examine the trend and pattern of financing the capital structure of Indian companies. The central issue we will address is to examine empirically the existence of inter-firm and inter-industry differences in the capital structure of Indian firms and identify the possible sources of such variation in capital structure. We will also try to find out the factors that determine the financing pattern of capital structure of Indian companies, particularly in the private sector.

Nature of the Data

The nature of the data required for the purpose of study are information relating to corporate growth, mobilization of corporate finance at the national and state levels. Further, information relating to nature of industry, size and age of sample companies and their annual financial statements from 1999-2000 to 2007-08 are also needed.

Source of the Data

For our study purpose, only secondary data is used which is sourced from the website *www.moneycontrol.com.* The information relating to nature of industry, size, age, state and region, company background, value of total assets and annual financial statements of sample companies for the period 1999-2000 to 2007-2008 have been obtained from the same. Information relating to industrial and corporate growth and mobilization of corporate finance has been collected from various books, periodicals, government reports and RBI Bulletins. In some cases we have also collected the required information directly from the sampled company.

Selection of Sample

Keeping in view the scope of the study, it was decided to select companies on the basis of purposive sampling rather than taking the whole thing. Our sample consists of 300 firms from a heterogeneous set of 20 different sectors. For our study purpose we have taken the data of top 15 companies of each sector selected on the basis of their total assets value as on 31st March 2008. The study excludes financial and securities sector companies, as their financial characteristics and use of leverage are substantially different from other companies. As continuity and the homogeneity in the available data is a prerequisite for studying the trend of capital formation in the corporate sector, hence we had to exclude those companies whose data was not available for the entire study period or whose financial years were not in uniform.

Classification of Sample

The sample has been classified in terms of age, size, region and industry wise. These different classifications are discussed below:

Age

The sample is classified under this variable according to the period of operation of the companies, which has been divided into three phases.

First, companies incorporated before independence i.e. prior to 1947 are treated as very old. The companies incorporated after 1947 but before 1980 are treated as old. The companies incorporated after 1980 has been treated as new companies. The number of companies under each category is mentioned below:

Year of Incorporation	Age Group	No. of Companies	% to Total Sample
Prior to 1947	Very Old	44	14.67
1947 - 1980	Old	95	31.67
After 1980	New	161	53.66
Total		**300**	**100**

The very old companies constitute 14.67 per cent of the sample, whereas old and new companies respectively comprise 31.67 and 53.66 per cent of the total number of sample companies.

Region

It is necessary to classify the sample companies into different regions. Although in India the need for dispersal industries as a means of attaining a balanced development of economy has been emphasized in different plan periods, yet some regions/states achieve higher rate of industrial growth, whereas other regions/states lagged far behind. This is due to historical and political reasons. Under this variable, the sample companies are classified into four regions. The region of a company is determined taking into account the geographical area. The companies registered in the States/Union Territories—Bihar, Assam, West Bengal, Orissa, other North Eastern States and Andaman Nikobar Islands belong to Eastern Region. The companies registered in the States/Union Territories—Maharastra, Gujarat, Madhya Pradesh, Goa, Dadar and Nagar Haveli, Damon and Diu relate to Western Region. The companies registered in the States/Union Territories—Andhra Pradesh, Karnataka, Kerala, Tamil Nadu, and Pondicherry belongs to Southern Region. And, the companies registered in the States/Union Territories—Haryana, Punjab, Rajasthan, Delhi, Himanchal Pradesh, Uttar Pradesh, Jamu and Kashmir is called Northern Region Companies. The number of companies covered under each region is given below:

Region/Group	Eastern	Western	Southern	Northern	Total
No. of Companies	34	135	85	46	300
% of Total Sample	11.33	45	28.33	15.34	100

The Western region companies constitute 45 per cent of the total sample, which is the highest while the number of companies registered in Southern and Northern are 28.33 and 15.34 per cent respectively. Rest of the companies belongs to Eastern region which is only 11.33 per cent of total sample.

Size

The total sample of 300 companies has been classified into three categories as Small, Medium and Large on the basis of their Total Assets as on 31st March, 2008. Companies having total assets less than ₹ 100 Crores are termed as small, companies having the total assets in between ₹ 100 crores and ₹ 500 crores are regarded as medium and companies having the value of total assets more than ₹ 500 crores are categorized as large size companies. The following table shows the classification details:

Size of the Company	Total Assets as on 31st March 2008 (Rs. in Crores)	No. of Companies	% to Total Sample
Small	Below ₹ 100 Crores	75	25
Medium	₹ 100 Crores to ₹ 500 Crores	98	32.67
Large	Above ₹ 500 Crores	127	42.33
Total		**300**	**100**

Industry

The necessacity to classify the companies into different industrial groups has also been realized because the trend and source of financing differ from one industrial group to another. As it has been already mentioned earlier, we have taken our samples from 20 different sectors, and for the purpose of analysis we have grouped those twenty different sectors into four broad industrial groups.

Industries those obtain their raw-materials from agriculture are groups under 'Agro Based Manufacturing Industries'. Similarly, the industries those obtain their raw-materials from mining or from minerals are grouped as 'Mineral Based Manufacturing Industries'. The third category is the 'Service Industries' and the fourth one is 'Plantation Industries' A brief description of the classification of industries according to their industrial group is shown in the following table:

Industrial Group	Name of the Industry/Sector	No. of Companies	Percentage to total Sample
Agro-based Manufacturing Industries	Textiles Man-made, Food Processing, Edible Oil, Cotton Textiles, Paper, Sugar	90	30
Mineral-based Manufacturing Industries	Chemicals, Cement, Fertilizer, Construction & Housing, Mining, Fabricated Metal, Electric Equipment, Pharmaceuticals, Plastic,	135	45
Service Industries	Computer Software, Hotel, Transport	45	15
Plantation Industries	Rubber, Tea & Coffee,	30	10
Total		**300**	**100**

Period of Study

The time period under consideration is a long time span of nine years i.e. 1999-2000 to 2007-08. The idea behind selecting a period of recent past was because the corporate performance in India has under gone rapid changes during this period because the Indian economy has experienced strong growth during recent times. The acceleration in real gross domestic product (GDP) has been contributed by the sustained expansion in industry and services sector. The improvement was widespread, touching all sub-sectors of manufacturing as well as service. Higher investment in power and transport sectors with increased efficiency and trade and industrial policy reforms had resulted in turnaround. This is well reflected in the performance of the manufacturing sectors during the post reform period, especially after 2000. For example, gross profits of the companies have registered an increase of 17 per cent per annum during 2000-2006[1]. Recent phase of enhanced profitability has raised the capital intensity of Indian companies even more. Rapid growth in the size and operation of Indian companies during the current decade was much more as compare to the previous decade. This ultimately resulted into an increased requirement of capital, which is raised through both debt and equity. The present study is purely intended to examine whether during the period 1999-2000 to 2007-2008, companies preferred to raise the capital through equity or debt and the reason for it. Going beyond to this we will also examine whether during this period there is any change in the capital structure of Indian companies or not.

Design of the Study

The proposed research is intended to find out the different types of capital structure that prevails in Indian companies' particularly in private sector and to investigate the reasons for such variation during the period 1999-2000 to 2007-2008. This study makes a humble attempt to examine whether the capital structure of Indian companies are similar with those of others in the industry and also with the firms across different industries. The methodology that we have designed for our study consists of five major steps namely: review of the literature; construction of hypothesis or theory or model; data collection; estimation and testing; and interpretation of findings to generate conclusions and relate them to the literature and theory. Some operating performance variables which have close interaction with capital structure decisions viz., size of investment(represented by the sum of gross fixed assets and current assets), asset structure(represented by fixed assets as a proportion of total assets), liquidity(represented by the current assets proportion over the current liabilities) are selected for analysis. The behaviour of all these variables (including debt-equity ratio) is examined by computing index number of the relevant data for the study period. Their inter-relationship is studied with the help of Karl Pearson's Coefficient of Correlation technique. Finally, the correlation of each of the selected variables vis-à-vis debt-equity ratio is analyzed for understanding the impact of the latter on the former and vice versa. Inferences are drawn based on the result of the analysis.

Objectives of the Study

The research output will help us to know:

1. Whether there exist any significant variations in the capital structures of Indian companies and if yes, the reason for it.
2. Whether the age, size, nature and region of a company has a bearing on the capital structure of a company.
3. Whether Indian companies rely more on external sources to meet the financial requirements.
4. Which is the most preferred source of capital of Indian companies i.e. Debt or Equity?

Hypothesis of the Study

In the course of analysis, we propose to test the following hypothesis for our study purpose. However, the testing of hypothesis is applied only to the sample, the study is confined to. Proper significance tests are not possible due to inadequate data, limited period of study and small size of the sample. The hypotheses are :

Hypothesis 1 : There exists the variation in the capital structure of firms of a particular industry or among the firms in different industries.

Hypothesis 2 : Indian companies prefer internal sources of finance rather than external to meet their financial requirement.

Hypothesis 3 : The region to which the company belongs to influences the quantum of inflow of funds (both debt and equity).

Hypothesis 4 : Age of the company has a bearing on its ability to generate internal funds and to attract funds from outside.

Hypothesis 5 : Size of the company has a bearing on its capital structure.

Hypothesis 6 : Nature of the company i.e. the industry to which it belongs to plays an important role in deciding the capital structure of the company.

Tools and Techniques of Analysis

The data collected from the financial statements of the companies are analyzed with the help of the following accounting and statistical tools each of which is discussed below:

(*i*) Funds Flow Analysis

(*ii*) Ratio Analysis

(*iii*) Correlation Analysis

FUNDS FLOW ANALYSIS

The funds flow statement is a statement which shows the movement of funds and is a report of the financial operations of the business undertaking. It indicates various means by which funds were obtained during a particular period and the ways in which these funds were employed. In simple words, it is a statement of sources and applications of funds.[2] The funds flow statement is condensed report of how the activities of the business have been financed and the financial resources have been used during the period covered by the statement. If a transaction results in the increase of funds, it is called source of funds and if it results in the decrease of funds, it is known as application of funds.

IMPORTANCE OF FUNDS FLOW STATEMENT

A funds flow statement is an essential tool for the financial analysis and is of primary importance to the financial management. Now-a-days, it is being widely used by financial analysis, credit granting institutions and financial managers. The basic purpose of a funds flow statement is to reveal the changes in the working capital on the two balance sheet dates. It also describes the sources from which additional working capital has been financed and the uses to which working capital has been applied. Such a statement is particularly useful in assessing the growth of the firm, its resulting financial needs and in determining the best way in financing these needs. By making use of projected funds flow statements, the adequacy or inadequacy of working capital can be assessed even in advance. One can plan the intermediate and long-term financing of the firm, repayment of long-term debts, expansion of the business, allocation of resources etc.

In our study, the information obtained from the financial statements of the companies is analyzed with the help of historical funds flow analysis technique. From the balance sheets of sample companies, year wise funds flow statements are prepared for each company. These gives source-wise details of the funds raised by the companies for asset formation under various heads during the accounting year. By and large, the increase in various items of assets and liabilities during the year represent the sources and uses of funds under respective heads. As such this statement can be compiled from the balance sheets for two consecutive years. This statement is intended to show the accretion to total funds of the companies and the assets in which these funds are invested. The format used for the funds flow statement is given below:

PROFORMA OF FUNDS FLOW STATEMENT

Sources of Funds

EXTERNAL SOURCES	*₹ in Crores*
Equity Share Capital	XXXXXX
Preference Share Capital	XXXXXX
Share Application Money	XXXXXX
Secured Loans	XXXXXX
Unsecured Loans	XXXXXX
Current Liabilities	XXXXXX
Deferred Credit	XXXXXX
INTERNAL SOURCES	
General Reserves	XXXXXX
Revaluation Reserves	XXXXXX
Provisions	XXXXXX
Accumulated Depreciation	XXXXXX
Total Sources of Funds	**XXXXXX**

(Contd...)

Application of Funds	
Gross Block	XXXXXX
Capital Work in Progress	XXXXXX
Investments	XXXXXX
Current Assets	XXXXXX
Loans and Advances	XXXXXX
Fixed Deposits	XXXXXX
Miscellaneous Expenses	XXXXXX
Total Application of Funds	**XXXXXX**

We would like to mention here that the above format of funds flow statement has been designed purely for our study purpose, as it will help us to analyze the things in a better way. In general, all the sources of funds can be categorized into external sources and internal sources. External sources include equity share capital, preference share capital, share application money, secured loans, unsecured loans, deferred credit and current liabilities. The internal sources include general reserves, revaluation reserve, accumulated depreciation and provisions.

Similarly the application of funds can be categorized as application for fixed tangible assets i.e. gross block and capital work in progress, application of funds in acquiring financial and intangible assets are covered under the head investments. Amounts invested in inventories, sundry debtors, cash and bank balance are included under the head current assets. Loans and advances, fixed deposits and miscellaneous expenses are other heads of application of funds.

The different heads of accounts under which sources and uses of funds are presented in the funds flow statement represents the changes taken place during the current year as compared to the balances of the previous year. In other words the statement simply shows the changes in the position of different assets and liabilities of two years i.e. current year and previous year. A positive change in any of the heads of the sources of funds indicates an inflow of the funds to the organization during the year whereas, a negative change indicates an outflow of funds. Similarly, a positive change in any of the heads of the application of funds indicates an outflow of funds from the organization where as, a negative change indicates an inflow of funds to the organization.

The meaning, description and implication of each and every head of the accounts appeared in the funds flow statements, for the purpose of analysis are discussed below:

Sources of Funds

Issue of Share Capital: If during the year there is any increase in the share capital, whether preference or equity, it means capital has been raised during the year. Issue of shares is a source of funds, as it constitutes inflow of funds. Even the call received from partly paid shares constitutes an inflow of funds. It should also be remembered that it is the net proceeds from the issue of share capital which amounts to a source of funds and hence in case of shares are issued at premium, even the amount of premium collected shall become a source of fund. It is also true when shares are issued at discount; it will not be the nominal value of shares but the actual realization after deducting discount that will amount to inflow of funds. But sometimes shares are issued otherwise than cash. In that case the following rules must be followed:

1. Issue of shares or making of partly paid shares as fully paid shares out of accumulated profits in the form of bonus shares are excluded from equity shares;
2. Issue of shares for consideration other than current assets such as issue against purchase of land, machineries etc. does not amount to inflow of funds;
3. Conversion of debentures or loans into shares also does not amount to inflow of funds.

Equity Share Capital: This item represents additional issue of equity share capital, excluding bonus issue of shares during the year.

Preference Share Capital: This item represents the total funds raised by the company by further issue of preference shares during the accounting year.

Share Application Money: It is that money received by a company during an IPO. Payments received for a subscription of stock is normally received over the IPO life. For example: Widgets Limited has been registered with an authorized capital of ₹ 2,00,000 divided into 2,000 shares of ₹ 100 each of which, 1,000 shares were offered for public subscription at a premium of ₹ 5 per share, payable as: on application ₹ 10 on allotment ₹ 25 (including premium) on first call ₹ 40 on final call ₹ 30 for a total of ₹ 105/share. The amounts received would be carried as a current liability until such time as the stock is issued, then it would be considered as part of equity.

General Reserve: These are the funds set aside from company profits not distributed to shareholders in the form of dividends. This is otherwise known as retained earnings. Reserves are appropriations of profit which is ascertained after deducting all expenses including provision and others.

Reserves are residual earnings after all expenses and taxation which belongs to the owners namely the shareholders. This item includes retained earnings from prior business years.

Revaluation Reserve: Revaluation reserves (or, more precisely, revaluation surplus reserves) arise when the value of an asset becomes greater than the value at which it was previously carried on the balance sheet, increasing shareholders funds. In other words, it is the amount arising from the appreciated value of property; the difference between the former book value of property on the balance sheet and the present (revalued) book value of the property.

Secured Loans: A loan which is backed by assets belonging to the borrower in order to decrease the risk assumed by the lender. The assets may be forfeited to the lender if the borrower fails to make the necessary payments. The difference figure in the balances of secured loans on two balance sheet dates represents the amount raised or paid during the year for secured loans, which forms part of the funds flow statement.

Unsecured Loans: An unsecured loan is a loan that is not backed by collateral. It is also known as a signature loan or personal loan. Unsecured loans are based solely upon the borrower's credit rating. As a result, they are often much more difficult to get than a secured loans, which also factors in the borrower's income. An unsecured loan is considered much cheaper and carries less risk to the borrower. The difference figure in the balances of secured loans on two balance sheet dates represents the amount raised or paid during the year for secured loans, which forms part of the funds flow statement.

Accumulated Depreciation: It is the total amount of depreciation that has been recorded for an asset since its date of acquisition. Here the difference in accumulated depreciation between two balance sheet dates under review is found out which gives the figure of depreciation charged during the year. It represents the sum total of depreciation charges and amortization of heavy organization costs, development expenditure etc. charged to income statement during the accounting period. Depreciation may be regarded as the capital cost of an asset allocated over the life of the asset. It is the gradual decrease in the value of an asset due to wear and tear, use and passage of time. Depreciation is simply a book entry having the effect of reducing the book value of the asset and the profits of current year for the same amount. It does not affect the current assets or current liabilities and does not result in the flow of funds. It is a non-fund item. Hence, although depreciation is regarded as operating expenses, but there is no real out flow of cash.[3]

There exists a controversy whether depreciation should be taken as a source of funds. Whatever may be the outcome of such controversy, the fact remains that the depreciation is a sum that is set apart out of profits and retained within the business and finance the capital needs in the normal business routine, and as such depreciation in true academic sense be deemed as a source of internal finance.

Deferred Credit: Borrowing through flotation of debentures, mortgage of fixed assets from banks, from term lending institutions, from public deposits, from State and Central Government and deferred payment schemes during the year are included in this item. Issue of debentures and raising of long-term loans are covered under this head of deferred liability. It results in the flow of funds into the business. The inflow of funds is the actual proceeds from the issue of such debentures or raising of long term loans.

Current Liabilities: This includes all borrowings from banks, except against mortgage of fixed assets, and the increase in total credits and payables during the year.

Provisions: It represents the money set aside to meet specific service liabilities, and to meet spending. A provision is a charge against profit for the purpose of providing for any liability or loss.

Application of Funds

Gross Block: Gross block is the sum total of all tangible fixed assets of the company valued at their cost of acquisition. This is inclusive of the depreciation that is to be charged on each asset i.e. cost of the total fixed assets owned by the company before deducting depreciation. For our study purpose, this item represents investment made in additional fixed assets namely land and building, plants and machinery and other tangible fixed assets during the year. Ascertaining the difference between the two gross fixed assets i.e. gross blocks of two balance sheet dates under review determine this.

Capital Work in Progress: Capital work in progress means the stage of assets which is at present not ready for use for which it is intended because of some further processing is required. It includes all tangible assets which are under course of construction and the type of investment is long term (capital) in nature. In funds flow statement this figure represents the addition made during the year to capital work in progress as the item shows the difference between the balances of two capital work in progress of two balance sheet dates under study.

Investments: It represents the purchases of financial assets like shares, debentures, bonds, etc. purchased during the year for a long term purpose as well as investment in intangible assets like patent, trade mark, goodwill etc. and also investments in subsidiaries.

Current Assets: It includes the investments made during the year in purchasing inventories, sundry debtors, and cash and bank balances. The term inventory implies the stock of raw materials, work in process, and finished goods being held for sale at a given time. The term sundry debtor represents the persons from who amounts are due for goods sold or services rendered or in respect of contractual obligations. Also termed as debtor, trade debtor, and account receivable. Cash and bank balance is the sum total of cash in hand, with bank and money at call short notices.

Loans and Advances: It represents the money lent to outsiders as well as employees of the organization as loans or advances which will be recovered in future.

Fixed Deposits: It represents the amount deposited with some banks or any other financial institutions for a fixed period.

Miscellaneous Expenses: It represents the incidental expense of a business, not classified as manufacturing, selling, or general and administrative expenses. It includes preliminary expenses, issue expenses, deferred revenue expenses etc.

The funds flow statement of the sample companies are prepared for nine years starting from 1999-2000 to 2007-2008. We have used the statement of balance sheet changes for the preparation of the funds flow statement. The year wise changes in each item discussed above are presented in these statements.

RATIO ANALYSIS

A ratio is a simple arithmetical expression of the relationship of one number to another. According to Wixon, Kell and Bedford, a ratio is an expression of the quantitative relationship between two numbers.[4] A ratio is a relation of the amount 'a' to amount 'b' (a is to b); or as a simple fraction integer, decimal, fraction or percentage.[5] The universally used technique for analysis of financial statement in modern times is the 'Ratio Analysis'. It is the principal technique used in judging the condition portrayed by the financial statements. The analyst can judge by the use of this technique the financial growth and development and the present condition of a business enterprise.[6] Ratios are a simple means of highlighting in arithmetical term the relationship between figures drawn from financial statement.[7] In financial analysis a ratio is used as an index or yardstick for evaluating the financial position and performance of a firm. The point to note is that the ratio indicates a quantitative relationship, which can be, in turn, used to make a qualitative judgment.

NATURE OF RATIO ANALYSIS

Ratio analysis is a technique of analysis of financial statements. It is the process of establishing various ratios for helping in making certain decisions. However, ratio analysis is not an end itself. It is only a means of better understanding of financial strengths and weaknesses of a firm. Calculation of mere ratios does not serve any purpose, unless several appropriate ratios are analyzed and interpreted. There are a number of ratios which can be calculated from the information given in the financial statements. But the analyst has to select the appropriate data and calculate only a few appropriate ratios from the same keeping in mind the objective of analysis. "The ratio may be used as a symptom like blood pressure, the pulse rate or the body temperature and their interpretation depends upon the caliber and competence of the analyst."[8]

USE OF RATIO ANALYSIS

The use of ratio is not confined to financial managers only. There are different parties interested in ratio analysis for knowing the financial position of a firm for different purposes. The supplier of goods on credit, banks, financial institutions, investors, shareholders and management all make use of ratio analysis as a tool in evaluating the financial position and a performance of a firm for granting credit, providing loans or making investment in the firm. With the use of ratio analysis, one can measure the financial conditional of a firm and can point out whether the condition is strong, good, questionable or poor. The conclusion can also be drawn as to whether the performance of the firm is improving or deteriorating. Thus, ratio has wide applications and is of immense use today.

RATIOS TO STUDY THE CAPITAL STRUCTURE

Different parties are interested in the financial statements of a firm. The short-term creditors, like bankers and suppliers of raw materials, are more concerned with the firm's current debt paying capacity. On the other hand, long term creditors like debenture holders, financial institutions etc. are more concerned with the firm's long term financial strength. Management is interested in knowing the proportion of Net Worth to Net Fixed Assets and Net Fixed Assets to Funded Debt. Although all these three groups are interested in the financial conditions and operating results of an enterprise, the primary intimation that each seek to obtain from these statements differ materially, reflecting the purpose that the statement is to serve. The significance of ratios varies for these three groups. In fact, a firm should have a strong short term as well as long term financial position.[9] Current ratio is calculated to indicate the current financial position of the firm. To judge the long term financial position of the firm, leverage or capital structure ratios are calculated. These ratios indicate the funds provided by owners and creditors. As a general rule, there should be an appropriate mix of debt and owner's equity in financing the firm's assets.[10]

The manner in which the assets have been financed has a number of implications. First, between debt and equity. Debt is more risky from the firm's point of view. The firm has a legal obligation to pay interest to debt holders, irrespective of the profits made or losses incurred by the firm. If the firm fails to pay debt holders in time, they can take legal actions against the firm to get payments and in extreme cases; they can force the firm into liquidation.

Second, employment of debt is advantageous to shareholders in two ways: (a) they can retain control of the firm with a limited stake; (b) their earnings will be magnified, when the firm earns a rate higher than the interest rate on the invested funds. The process of magnifying the shareholders return through the employment of debt is called 'trading on equity'. However, leverage can work in opposite direction as well. If the cost of debt is higher than the firm's overall rate of return, the earnings of the shareholders will be reduced. In addition, there is threat of insolvency. If the firm is actually liquidated for non-payment of debt-holders dues, the worst sufferers will be the shareholders—the residual owners.

Thirdly, a high debt burdened firm will find difficulty in raising funds from creditors and owners in future. Creditors treat the owner's equity as a margin of safety. If the equity base is thin, the creditors risk will be high. Thus, the capital structure ratios are calculated to measure the financial risk and the firm's ability of using debt for the benefit of shareholders.[11]

Capital structure ratios may be calculated from the balance sheet items to determine the proportion of debt in total financing. Many variations of these ratios exist, but all these ratios indicate the same thing—the extent to which the firm has relied on debt funds in financing assets. The different ratios on which the capital structure study is based are as follows: (*a*) Net Fixed Assets to Net Worth; (*b*) Net Worth to Total Assets; (*c*) Total Debt to Total Net Worth; (*d*) Current Ratio.

Net Fixed Assets to Net Worth: This ratio gives an indication of the extent to which equity capital is invested in Net Fixed Assets. In case of net worth, difficulties may arise to provide depreciation, resulting in a reduction of profits. In addition, the more the shareholder's contribution is tied up in fixed assets, the less is the amount available for investment in current assets. In other words, it means that creditors have contributed towards large proportion of the net fixed assets. The higher the ratio, lesser is the protection for creditors. Where net fixed assets exceed net worth, it may be a signal for many industrial concerns which should plan for an additional equity capital.[12]

The Ratio is calculated as : $\frac{\text{Net Fixed Assets} \times 100}{\text{Net Worth}}$

Net Worth to Total Assets: The term total asset comprises all debts, capital stock and reserves and surpluses. The ratio of net worth to total asset is computed by dividing net worth by total assets. It can also be expressed as percentage of the net worth to total assets. No hard and first rule can be set down as to what a proper relationship should be. This ratio acts as supplementary measure to determine security for lenders. A ratio of 2:1 would mean that for every two rupees of total assets, there is a net worth of one rupee. But the book value and actual liquidating value may be greatly at variance and in interpreting this ratio, this fact must be borne in mind. Formula for the computation of this ratio is as follows:

$$\frac{\text{Net Worth} \times 100}{\text{Total Assets}}$$

More the percentage of net worth to total assets better is the result for the outsiders, because they will have a greater claim over the assets in case of liquidation.

Total Debt to Total Net Worth: Due care must be given to the computation and interpretation of this ratio. The definition of debt takes two forms. One includes the current liabilities while the other excludes them. The difference in the meaning of debt is confusing in general. The relationship between borrowed funds and owner's capital is a popular measure of the long-term financial solvency of a firm. This relationship is shown by debt-equity ratio. This ratio reflects the relative claims of creditors and shareholders against the assets of the firm. Alternatively, this ratio indicates the relative proportions of debt and equity in financing the assets of a firm. The relationship between outside claim and owner's capital can be shown on different ways and accordingly there are many variants of the D/E (debt-equity) ratio. One approach is to express the D/E ratio in terms of the relative proportion of long-term debt and shareholder's equity. Thus,

$$\text{D/E Ratio} = \frac{\text{Long-Term Debt}}{\text{Shareholder's Equity}}$$

The debt concerned here is exclusive of current liabilities. The shareholder's equity includes both ordinary as well as preference capital and hence defined as net worth. The D/E ratio computed on this basis may also be called debt to net worth ratio. The D/E ratio is, thus, the ratio of total outside liabilities to total owner's fund.

Interpretation of D/E Ratio: The D/E ratio is an important tool of financial analysis to appraise the financial structure of a firm. It has important implications from the viewpoint of the creditors, owners and the firm itself. The ratio reflects the relative contribution of creditors and owners of business in its financing. A high ratio shows a large share of financing by the creditors relatively to the owners and therefore a larger claim against the assets of the firm. A low ratio implies a smaller claim of creditors. The D/E ratio also indicates the margin of safety to the creditors.

If D/E ratio is high, the owners are putting up relatively less money of their own. It is a danger signal for the creditors. If the project fails financially, the creditors would loose heavily. Moreover, with a small financial stake in the firm, the owners may behave irresponsibly and indulge in speculative activity. If they are heavily involved financially, they will strain every nerve to make the enterprise a success. A high D/E ratio has equally serious implications from the firm's point of view. A high position of debt in the capital structure would lead to inflexibility in the operations of the firm as creditors would exercise pressure and interfere in the management. Secondly, such a firm would be able to borrow only under very restrictive terms and conditions. Further, it would have to face a heavy burden of interest payments, particularly in adverse circumstances when profits decline. Finally, the firm will have to encounter serious difficulties in raising funds in future.

It is no doubt that both high and low D/E ratios are not desirable. What is needed is a ratio, which strikes a proper balance between debt and equity. What is the reasonable relationship between debt and equity? There cannot be any rigid rule. It will depend upon the circumstances, prevailing practices and so on. The general proposition is: outsider's money should be in reasonable proportion to the owner's capital and the owners should have sufficient stake in the fortunes of the enterprise.

CURRENT RATIO

Current ratio may be defined as the relationship between current assets and current liabilities. This ratio, also known as working capital ratio, and is a measure of general liquidity. It is most widely used to make the analysis of a short-term financial position or liquidity of a firm.[13]

It is calculated by dividing current assets by current liabilities.

$$\text{Current Ratio} = \frac{\text{Current Assets}}{\text{Current Liabilities}}$$

The current assets of a firm represents those assets, which can be, in the ordinary course of business, converted into cash within a short period of time, normally not exceeding one year. It includes cash and bank balances, marketable securities, inventory of raw materials, semi-finished and finished good, bills receivable and prepaid expenses etc. The current liabilities are defined as liabilities which are short-term maturing obligations to be met, as originally contemplated, within a year. It consists of trade creditors, bills payable, bank credit, provision for taxation, dividends payable and outstanding expenses.

Interpretation of Current Ratio: The current ratio of a firm measures its short-term solvency, i.e. its ability to meet short-term obligations. As a measure of short-term liquidity, it indicates the rupees of current assets available for each rupee of current liabilities. A relatively high current ratio is an indication that the firm is liquid and has the ability to pay its current obligations in time as and when they become due. On the other hand, a relatively low current ratio represents that the liquidity position of the firm is not good and the firm shall not be able to pay its current liabilities in time without facing difficulties. An increase in the liquidity position of a firm while a decrease in the current ratio indicates that there has been deterioration in the liquidity position of the firm. "Although there is no hard and fast rule, conventionally a current ratio of 2:1 is considered as satisfactory. The logic behind the conventional rule is that even with a drop out of 50% (half) in the value of current assets, a firm can meet its obligations, i.e. a 100% margin of safety is assumed to be sufficient to ward off the worst situation. What is a satisfactory ratio will differ depending on the development of the capital market and the availability of long-term funds to finance current assets, the nature of the industry and so on".[14]

CORRELATION ANALYSIS

The analysis of the trend in capital structure formation is aimed at establishing relationship between sources of funds and uses of funds. In the process we have tried to correlate each individual source with its best possible use. They are internal sources, external long-term fixed assets, current liability (short term sources) with current assets. The co-efficient of correlation are calculated for the total as well as for the classified variables. Significant tests, wherever necessary have also been undertaken to interpret the results of the analysis.

SIZE OF INVESTMENT AND DEBT-EQUITY RATIO

A large asset base calls for more long-term funds. The dichotomy of these funds into debt and equity and their proportions depend upon the earnings, prevailing cost of sources of finance available etc. A greater proportion of incremental funds year after would be sought normally from debt sources rather than from equity. Therefore, the correlation between the size of investment and debt equity ratio of a firm is supposed to be positive and high.[15]

ASSET STRUCTURE AND DEBT-EQUITY RATIO

The association of fixed assets proportion to total assets and with debt equity ratio is also to be done. Higher the ratio of fixed assets to total asset is, more will be the requirement of long-term funds, directly influencing the capital structure. Therefore, there should be a close association between these two.

LIQUIDITY AND DEBT-EQUITY RATIO

Liquidity ratio is directly influenced by the proportion of long-term funds invested in current assets and therefore is supposed to be linearly correlated to the debt-equity ratio.

Limitations of Analysis

The main limitation of our analysis part is that, the study is based on the secondary data collected from the annual financial statements of the sample companies. So the limitations prevailing with secondary data will be found in this study. Despite limitations, financial statements obtained from the Stock Exchange Official Directory, continue to be a major source of data for microanalysis of firm's behaviour. The size of the sample is also restricted. Therefore, the limitations of the small sample apply to this study.

Secondly, the analysis of the study is based on historical funds flow analysis, which has got its own limitations. The accounting year is not the same for all the sample companies as a result of which uniform financial statements could not be obtained. Different companies prepare financial statements according to their own convention and convenience. While preparing the funds flow statements, few adjustments were made in some cases to present the figures as per our requirements.

Conclusion and Promising Research Ideas

India is important to the world economy. We know little about the structure of financing of firms in this country, which is the fourth largest in the world by economy size and among the most important in terms of economic growth rates, and how this affects strategic behavior. Most studies that examine the relationship between capital structure and firm diversification focus on the structure of equity rather than the structure of debt, and on advanced market economies. The issues of how managers choose between debt and equity financing, which factors influence capital structure choices, what factors influence the relative composition of firms' capital structures and whether there are within industry as well as inter-industry variations in capital structure as well as the composition of capital are all issues which have not yielded a consensus so far. By and large, with a few important exceptions the research on how capital structure is related to competitive strategy has been still paid little attention to by strategic management scholars. While capital structure, as measured by the broad leverage ratio is an important construct, it is important to get deeper into analyses of the constituents of capital since each of these will influence firms' strategies and management practice in differing ways. Several follow-up research possibilities still exist.

REFERENCES

1. Das Abhiman, Senapati Manjusha "*Profitability of Indian Corporate Sector: Productivity, Price or Growth*?"
2. Sharma R. K., Gupta S.K., "*Management Accounting, Principles and Practice*", Kalyani Publishers, New Delhi, 1996, pp. 5.1.
3. Sharma R. K., Gupta S.K., "*Management Accounting, Principles and Practice*", Kalyani Publishers, New Delhi, 1996, pp. 5.38 and 5.39.
4. Wixon R, Kell W.G., Bedford N.M., "*Accountants Hand Book*", 1970, p. 39.
5. Kohler E.L., "*A Dictionary for Accountants*", p. 393.
6. Anthony Robert, "*Financial Statement Analysis*", (Homewood, III, Richard D Irwin, inc.) 3rd Edition, 1971, p. 297.
7. Donaldson, M. Charles, "*Basic Business Finance*", (Homewood, Illinois), 3rd Ed. 1966, p. 1541.
8. Sharma P.K., Gupta S.K., "*Management Accounting Principles*", Kalyani Publishers, New Delhi, 1966, p. 4.2.
9. Anthony, Robert, "*Analysis of the Financial Statements*" (New York, DUN & Bradstreet), 4th Ed. 1969, p. 207.
10. Guthmann, G. Harry, "*Analysis of Financial Statements*", (Prentice Hall of India Pvt. Ltd., New Delhi), 1976, p. 157.
11. Pandey I.M., "Capital Structure and Cost of Capital", *Financial Management* (Vikas Publishing House Pvt. Ltd., New Delhi), 3rd Ed., Chapter-18, p. 507.
12. Mayer R.R., "*Capital Expenditure Analysis*" (Prospects Hights, iii, Wave Land) Ed. 3, 1978, Chapter-2, p.109.
13. Sharma R.K., Gupta S.K., "*Management Accounting—Principles and Practice*", Kalyani Publishers, New Delhi, 1996, p. 4.10.
14. Solomn E., "*The Management of Corporate Capital*", (New York, The Free Press) 1959, 2nd Ed., p. 107.
15. Rajeswar Rao K., Sadanandan R., "Impact of Capital Structure Decisions on Operating Preference of State Enterprises of A.P.—A Correlation Analysis", *Finance India*, Vol. IX, No. 1, March, 1995, p. 76.

7 Empirical Analysis of Total Sample Companies

Introduction

In this chapter an empirical analysis relating to the capital structure of the sample companies has been made. At first we will conduct the analysis of the total sample of all the 300 companies on an aggregate basis. Later on we will examine the capital structure of the companies after classifying them into different sizes, ages, regions and sectors. This chapter will highlight the structure of corporate finance in India. The different sources from where the corporate sector has raised the funds and the ways and means by which the so raised funds have been utilized have been analyzed in detail. The analysis of the study is based on the historical funds flow statements of each company. For the total sample, the aggregate of (300 companies) individual sources of funds and their investment in acquiring different assets has also been made.

An attempt has also been made to study the relationship existing between long-term sources of funds and fixed assets and between the current assets and current liabilities. Further, the help of ratio analysis is also taken to supplement the findings. The ratio of net worth and net fixed assets i.e. net block, net worth to total assets, total debts to total equities and between current assets to current liabilities have also been computed for the purpose.

Corporate funds flow statements covering several years of operations in a company, enable the readers to obtain useful information on the financial methods used in the past, dividend policies followed and the contribution of funds derived from the operations to the growth of the company. They also provide reliable clues to future financial requirements.

The funds flow statement is a report of the financial operations of the company. This statement is also more comparable with those of other companies than are the balance sheets and income statement.[1]

To meet the growing needs of decision makers and controllers of modern business and industry, fund management is an invaluable analytical tool for evaluating the employment of funds by a firm and in determining the sources of such funds. Efficient funds management provides the financial managers to assess the growth of the firm, its resulting financial needs and also to determine the best way to finance those needs.[2]

Funds Flow Analysis of Total Sample Companies

The analysis of the funds flow of the total sample of 300 companies of the Indian corporate sector is aimed at examining the following:

1. To analyze trends and structure of sources of financing with a view to point out the diversibilities in the components of sources of funds;
2. To examine the pattern of the components of internal/external sources of funds in order to bring out the significance of each components share in total sources of funds and to identify fluctuations if any in them as well as to point out the reasons for such position;
3. To discuss application of funds in different assets to make out changes if any in their pattern.

The analysis of funds flow statement involves two steps. The first step is the analysis of sources of funds and the second step is the analysis of application of funds. The sources of funds may be further divided into internal sources and external sources. The internal sources of funds comprise the profits retained and transferred to reserves and revaluation reserves whereas the external sources of funds are issue of equity shares, preference shares, secured loans and unsecured loans.

The study of the sources and application of funds in the Indian corporate sector represented by 300 companies is made with the help of annual rate of change and the relative share of components of internal, external sources and application of funds is analyzed by expressing each component as percentage of total sources and application of funds.

The analysis on the trend in various sources of inflow of funds and their utilization is confined to nine years covering 2000 to 2008. The different sources of funds used for financing additional fixed investments and current assets formation and their proportion to the total utilization of sources are also analyzed. The financial theories commonly accepted in the corporate sector have been examined in the course of analyzing the financial behaviour of the total sample. The aggregate figure of individual source and use of such funds help in locating the overall trend for the total sample. The consolidated funds flow statement for the entire sample is presented in Table 7.1 (*See on next page*).

By analyzing the funds flow statement of the total sample companies as shown in Table 7.1, we saw many distinctive features in respect of various items of sources and application of funds during the study period of 2000-2008.

The total share capital which consists of equity share capital and preference share capital has showed a fluctuating trend during the period of study. It increased from ₹ 620.31 crores in 2001 to ₹ 765.93 crores in 2002. But suddenly it decreased to ₹ 269.23 crores in 2003. This has happened due to a sharp decrease in the contribution of both equity and preference shares in the year 2003. Again from 2004 onwards it started showing an increasing trend till 2008 except for the year 2007.

The contribution of equity shares to the total share capital was fluctuating. In 2002, 2003 and 2007 it has shown a decreasing trend but for rest of the years it has shown an increasing trend. The increased growth indicates additional issue of equity shares and a downward trend indicates a caution stand on additional issue of equity shares. Some time, companies think of repurchasing of their own stocks or buying back of the stocks. Stock repurchases are often used as a tax-efficient method to put cash into shareholders' hands, rather than pay dividends. Sometimes, companies do this when they feel that their stock is undervalued on the open market. Other times, companies do this to provide a 'bonus' to incentive compensation plans for employees. Rather than receive cash, recipients receive an asset that might appreciate in value faster than cash saved in a bank account. Another motive for stock repurchase is to protect the company against a takeover threat. When there is a repurchases of stocks, it reduces the balance in equity share capital account. Hence, in 2002, 2003 and in 2007 it might also so happen that companies have gone for repurchasing their equity shares and that's why the balance in these years are less as compared to the previous years.

On the other hand, in case of preference shares a positive contribution implies additional issue of preference shares and a negative contribution is due to the redemption of such preference shares or due to its conversion into equity shares. The study shows that in 2002, 2003, 2005, 2006 and 2008, there is an inflow of funds in the form of preference shares whereas,

Table 7.1 : Consolidated Funds Flow Statement of All Companies

(₹ in Crores)

Sources of Funds	2001	2002	2003	2004	2005	2006	2007	2008
Equity Share Capital	625.38	393.73	82.13	719.12	814.27	1133.34	813.86	1105.87
Preference Share Capital	-5.07	372.2	187.1	-182.32	199.02	191.41	-317.49	49.06
Share Application Money	483.64	12.69	-127.21	-184.22	-26.64	155.61	342.12	409.27
Secured Loans	3297.52	-137.42	1688.62	1842.8	1255.65	2808.48	12680.36	14639.89
Unsecured Loans	-206.92	1601.13	111.24	2537.28	3198.13	11874.93	8597.65	16644.35
Current Liabilities	1040.76	7807.48	2966.56	4996.6	4013.56	9358.66	13807.32	20534.55
Deferred Credit	0	0	0	0	0	0	0	0
Reserves	6615.91	1932.38	4220.58	10759.68	18722.7	27530.32	39879.96	43785.84
Revaluation Reserves	-11.12	433.92	-98.65	882.83	809.56	-113.09	629.36	2784.2
Provisions	587.11	293	898.22	3872.1	295.47	4200.06	1860.31	6142.87
Accumulated Depreciation	3539.61	3933.93	4529.5	5528.78	5001.76	6997.7	6847.17	6502.77
Total Sources of Funds	**15966.82**	**16643.04**	**14458.09**	**30772.65**	**34283.48**	**64137.42**	**85140.62**	**112598.67**
Application of Funds								
Gross Block	6,231.07	8,518.35	7,370.88	11,211.10	11,430.84	20,551.89	25,891.48	35,166.70
Capital Work in Progress	1,707.59	-148.05	-747.92	1,175.62	4,545.20	5,902.64	9,038.29	3,136.08
Investments	4,357.20	1,792.49	2,738.40	6,915.95	5,579.88	8,198.44	16,905.90	25,278.71
Current Assets	2,431.40	2,275.73	1,794.77	8,008.50	7,414.15	16,192.54	15,053.10	22,083.17
Loans and Advances	1,541.11	2,522.76	688.28	1,118.76	2,629.28	9,159.39	12,088.29	20,703.88
Fixed Deposits	-163.66	1,738.65	2,243.97	2,812.44	2,630.70	4,206.54	6,143.54	6,432.45
Miscellaneous Expenses	-137.89	-56.89	369.71	-469.72	53.43	-74.02	20.02	-202.32
Total Application of Funds	**15,966.82**	**16,643.04**	**14,458.09**	**30,772.65**	**34,283.48**	**64,137.42**	**85,140.62**	**112,598.67**

Source: Computed from the database collected from www.moneycontrol.com

in 2001, 2004 and 2007 it was showing a negative contribution because of either the redemption of such shares or its conversion into equity shares.

The share application money has showed a positive contribution of ₹ 483.64 crores, ₹ 12.69 crores, ₹ 155.61 crores, ₹ 342.12 crores, and ₹ 409.27 crores in the years 2001, 2002, 2006, 2007 and 2008 respectively. For rest of the period i.e. in 2003, 2004 and 2005 it has showed a negative contribution of ₹ 121.27 crores, ₹ 184.22 crores and ₹ 26.64 crores respectively.

The amount received towards share application is normally shown as a current liability until such time as the stock is issued, then it would be considered as part of equity. Hence the positive contribution in this account indicates application money received during the year in respect of fresh issue of shares, and a negative contribution implies the transfer of share application money to equity capital because of issue of stocks.

Funds raised through secured loans also indicate a fluctuating trend during this period of study. A negative growth has witnessed in second year i.e. in 2002 indicating the redemption or repayment of the loans or it might be conversion of debentures forming part of the secured loans into equity shares.

Unsecured loans contributed to a great extent. In the year 2001 it has showed a negative contribution indicating either repayment of such loans or conversion of same into shares or secured debentures. But from 2002 onwards it has shown a positive contribution till the end. Except the year 2003 in which the amount raised through unsecured loans was only ₹ 111.24 crores, in all other years a sizable amount has been raised through unsecured loans and particularly from 2006 onwards, the trend has showed a remarkable increase.

Current liabilities which consists of creditors, bills payable etc. contributed a lot to total sources of funds inflow in all the years under study. The analysis shows that from 2001 to 2005 the growth trend of current liabilities was fluctuating but from 2006 onwards it has showed a remarkable increase. The most important fact about the current liabilities is that it has remained one of the biggest sources of finances throughout the period of study.

The analysis shows that the amount of deferred credit is nil throughout our period of study.

Reserves, which consists of retained earnings has showed an increasing trend constantly during all the nine years of study. This has remained the largest source of internal finance almost all the years of the study.

Revaluation reserve is the amount arising from the appreciated value of property; the difference between the former book value of property on the balance sheet and the present (revalued) book value of the property. It is regarded as a source of funds. A positive contribution in the revaluation reserve indicates in the appreciation in the valuation of the property and a negative contribution implies depreciation in the valuation of property during the year. In 2001, 2003 and 2006 it was showing a negative contribution where as in other years it is positive.

Provisions also contributed as one of the internal sources of finance. Though the trend was fluctuating, yet it was impressive particularly after 2006.

As we have discussed earlier, we have taken accumulated depreciation as one of the sources of internal finance in our study. It has been found that next to reserve which is otherwise known as retained earnings, depreciation has remained the second largest source of internal finance throughout the study period. And, reserve combined with depreciation which is otherwise known as funds from operation constitutes the biggest source of funds among all the sources, internal and external.

With regard to application of funds in gross block, the growth is remarkable. It indicated that a lot has been invested in acquiring fixed assets like land and building, plant and machinery etc. In the second phase i.e. from 2005 to 2008, the investment is higher in comparison to the first phase period i.e. 2001 to 2004.

Capital Work in Progress is the amount invested in the tangible fixed assets which are under course of construction and the nature of investment being long term (capital) in nature. A negative balance in this account implies the work in progress being converted into tangible fixed assets. Our analysis shows that for the year 2002 and 2003, the conversion of work in progress to completed fixed assets is more as compared to the amount invested in the tangible fixed assets which are under course of construction and that's why the balance for these two years are showing negative. For rest of the years, the analysis shows that a huge amount is invested every year in constructing tangible fixed assets, which remains under construction and as a result a positive balance is carried over in that account.

Application of funds in investment stood next to fixed assets. In 2001, an amount of ₹ 4357.20 crores has been invested in purchasing financial assets, intangible assets and also in subsidiaries. But this figure has come down to ₹ 1792.49 crores in 2002. From 2002 onwards the trend was increasing till end except for the year 2005. In 2008 the amount of investment was ₹ 25278.71 crores, which signifies that the investments in financial and intangible assets are growing day by day.

Investment in current assets shows a fluctuating trend through out the period. For the first three years, the trend was decreasing. In 2004 it increased sharply and again in 2005 it decreased. Similarly, 2006 witnessed a sharp increase followed by a decrease in 2007 and again a heavy increase in 2008.

Amount given as loans and advances also constitute a major portion of the total application of funds. With respect to fixed deposits, in the first year the figure was negative which indicates that money has been received on maturity of the fixed deposits. But for rest of the years, it was positive and also showed an increasing trend. In the case of miscellaneous assets, except for the year 2003 and 2007, all other years are showing a negative balance. A detailed analysis of each item of various sources of funds and their applications is done separately here after in this chapter.

Analysis of Total Inflow of Funds

The Table 7.2 and its graph show the funds raised by the sample companies during the period of study.

Table 7.2 : Trend Analysis of Total Inflow of Funds

Year	Total Inflow of Funds (₹ In Crores)	Increase/Decrease as compared to the previous year (₹ In Crores)	Percentage of Increase/ Decrease
2001	15966.82	—	—
2002	16643.04	676.22	4.24
2003	14458.09	-2184.95	-13.13
2004	30772.65	16314.56	112.84
2005	34283.48	3510.83	11.41
2006	64137.42	29853.94	87.08
2007	85140.62	21003.2	32.75
2008	112598.67	27458.05	32.25
Total	**374000.79**	**96631.85**	**267.44**
Average	**46750.09**	**13804.55**	**38.21**

Source: Computed from the database collected from www.moneycontrol.com

The data given on the above table is also depicted through the following graph.

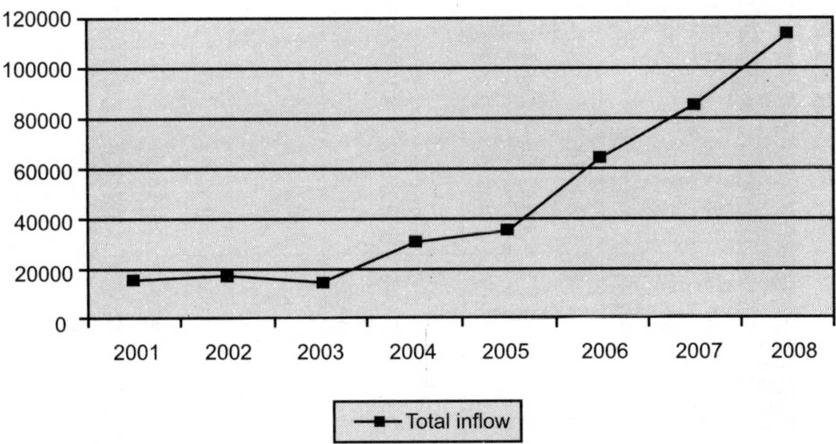

Graph 7.1 : Trend Analysis of Total Inflow of Funds

It is very interesting to note that, in 2002 the rate of growth in the inflow of funds is only 4.24 per cent amounting to ₹ 676.22 crores, which is far below the average growth of the total period, which is 38.21 per cent. In 2003 there was a negative growth of 13.13 per cent indicating that the total inflow of funds decreased to ₹ 14458.09 crores from ₹ 16643.04 crores in 2002.

But in 2004, there was a remarkable growth of 112.84 per cent, which is the highest among all the years. The total inflow of funds has been raised from ₹ 14458.09 crores in 2003 to ₹ 30772.65 crores in 2004, which registers a growth of ₹ 16314.56 crores in a single year.

In 2005 the growth rate was only 11.41 per cent amounting to ₹ 3510.83 crores of excess inflow of funds as compared to 2004. But again in 2006 the growth rate sharply increased to 87.08 per cent amounting to ₹ 29853.94 crores of increase in inflow of funds as compared to 2005. In 2007 and 2008, the rates of increase in the total inflow of funds were 32.75 and 32.25 per cent respectively.

The total funds raised by the sample companies for the study period may be divided into internal sources and external sources. External sources include the funds raised through the issue of equity shares, preference shares, share application money, secured and unsecured loans, current liabilities etc. Internal sources include the funds raised through reserves, revaluation reserves, accumulated depreciation and provisions.

A detailed analysis of both internal sources of finance as well as external sources of finance is presented in table 7.3 and the respective share of these two sources in the total source is shown in table 7.4 and its graph is presented in a composite bar chart.

Table 7.3 : Detailed Analysis of Internal Sources and External Sources of Funds

(₹ in Crores)

Sources of Funds	2001	2002	2003	2004	2005	2006	2007	2008
Equity Share Capital	625.38	393.73	82.13	719.12	814.27	1133.34	813.86	1105.87
Preference Share Capital	-5.07	372.2	187.1	-182.32	199.02	191.41	-317.49	49.06
Share Application Money	483.64	12.69	-127.21	-184.22	-26.64	155.61	342.12	409.27
Secured Loans	3297.52	-137.42	1688.62	1842.8	1255.65	2808.48	12680.36	14639.89
Unsecured Loans	-206.92	1601.13	111.24	2537.28	3198.13	11874.93	8597.65	16644.35
Current Liabilities	1040.76	7807.48	2966.56	4996.6	4013.56	9358.66	13807.32	20534.55
Deferred Credit	0	0	0	0	0	0	0	0
Total—External Sources	**5235.31**	**10049.81**	**4908.44**	**9729.26**	**9453.99**	**25522.43**	**35923.82**	**53382.99**
Percentage to Total Source	32.78	60.38	33.94	31.61	27.57	39.79	42.19	47.40
Reserves	6615.91	1932.38	4220.58	10759.68	18722.7	27530.32	39879.96	43785.84
Revaluation Reserves	-11.12	433.92	-98.65	882.83	809.56	-113.09	629.36	2784.2
Provisions	587.11	293	898.22	3872.1	295.47	4200.06	1860.31	6142.87
Accumulated Depreciation	3539.61	3933.93	4529.5	5528.78	5001.76	6997.7	6847.17	6502.77
Total—Internal Sources	**10731.51**	**6593.23**	**9549.65**	**21043.39**	**24829.49**	**38614.99**	**49216.8**	**59215.68**
Percentage to Total Source	**67.22**	**39.62**	**66.06**	**68.39**	**72.43**	**60.21**	**57.81**	**52.60**
Total Funds Raised	**15966.82**	**16643.04**	**14458.09**	**30772.65**	**34283.48**	**64137.42**	**85140.62**	**112598.67**

Source: Computed from the database collected from www.moneycontrol.com

Table 7.4 : Shares of Internal and External Sources of Funds to Total Funds Raised

Year	Internal Sources (₹ In Crores)	Percentage	External Sources (₹ In Crores)	Percentage	Total Source (₹ In Crores)	Percentage
2001	10731.51	67.22	5235.31	32.78	15966.82	100
2002	6593.23	39.62	10049.81	60.38	16643.04	100
2003	9549.65	66.06	4908.44	33.94	14458.09	100
2004	21043.39	68.39	9729.26	31.61	30772.65	100
2005	24829.49	72.43	9453.99	27.57	34283.48	100
2006	38614.99	60.21	25522.43	39.79	64137.42	100
2007	49216.8	57.81	35923.82	42.19	85140.62	100
2008	59215.68	52.60	53382.99	47.40	112598.67	100
Total	**219794.74**	**484.29**	**154206.05**	**315.71**	**374000.79**	**800**
Average	27474.34	60.54	19275.75	39.46	46750.09	100

Source: Computed from the database collected from www.moneycontrol.com

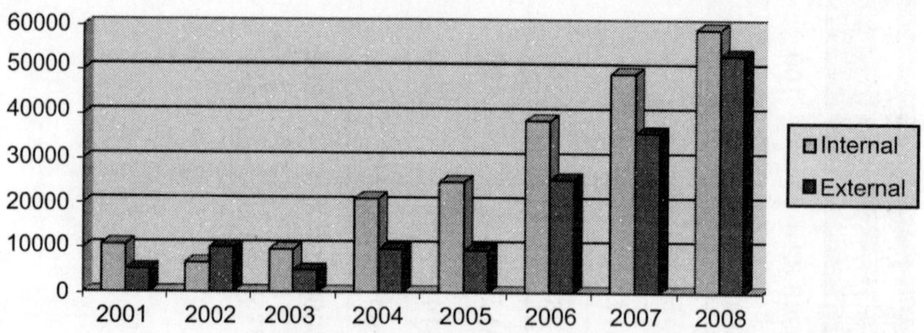

Graph 7.2 : Internal Sources and External Sources of Funds

Analysis of Total Inflow of Funds from Internal Sources

The internal source of inflow of funds indicated a constant growth through out the study period. The only exception to this was in 2001, the total amount of internally generated funds was ₹ 10731.51 crores and the amount generated in 2002 was ₹ 6593.23 crores. This shows that in 2002 the focus towards external funds was more as compared to internal funds. But from 2003 onwards this tendency has been changed and since then it shows a rising trend throughout the study. It has also seen that from 2003 onwards, the amount raised though internal sources have always remained more than the amount raised through external sources for all the years. Here we can draw the conclusion that the preferences of companies towards internal sources are more as compared to external sources.

The analysis shows that in total i.e. from 2001 to 2008, a sum of ₹ 374000.79 crores has been generated, both internally and externally. Out of this, an amount of ₹ 219794.74 crores has been generated through internal sources, which constitutes nearly 58.77 per cent of the total funds. The average inflow of internal funds was also more as compared to external funds. The annual average of internal funds was ₹ 27474.34 crores constituting to 60.54 per cent of the total average against ₹ 19275.75 crores raised through external sources, which constitutes only 39.46 per cent of the total annual average.

Table 7.3 in which a detailed analysis of different sources of internal and external funds has been made shows that, reserves which are otherwise known as retained earnings and depreciation has remained two major sources of internal financing to companies.

Barring to the year of exception 2002, reserve has shown a constant growth throughout the study period and depreciation has shown a fluctuating growth. But a large amount transferred every year as retained earnings and charging of heavy depreciation every year indicates that companies were very much interested to create internal funds for future use instead of relying on external sources which is a complex and costly affair. A comparative year-wise analysis of funds raised through internally has been made in table 7.5.

Table 7.5 : Trend of Internal Sources of Funds

Year	Internal Sources (₹ In Crores)	Increase/ Decrease	Per cent of Change
2001	10731.51	—	—
2002	6593.23	-4138.28	-38.56
2003	9549.65	2956.42	44.84
2004	21043.39	11493.74	120.36
2005	24829.49	3786.1	17.99
2006	38614.99	13785.5	55.52
2007	49216.8	10601.81	27.45
2008	59215.68	9998.88	20.32
Total	**219794.74**	**48484.17**	**81.88**
Average	**27474.34**	**6926.31**	**11.70**

Source: Computed from the database collected from www.moneycontrol.com

The data given on the table 7.5 is also depicted through the following graph:

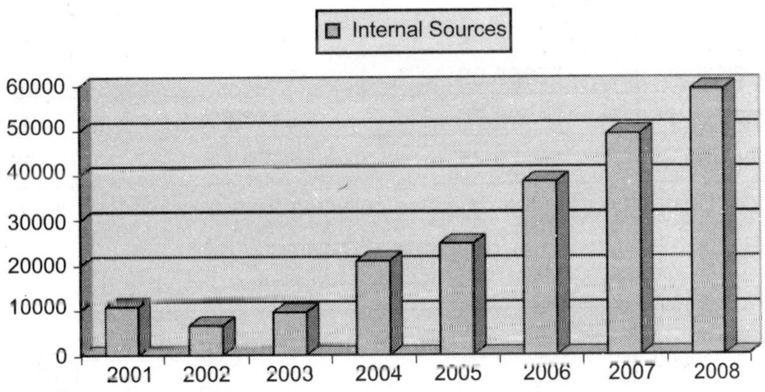

Graph 7.3 : Trend Analysis of Internal Sources of Funds

The above graph clearly indicates that except for the year 2002, which we have assumed as the year of exception, for all other years starting from 2003, there has been a steady growth in the generation of funds internally. Heavy dependence on internal source manifest that the funds from other sources have been quite dear to obtain. Capital formation of companies more or less depends on the availability of such internal savings as it has a positive correlation with incremental fixed assets.

Analysis of Total Inflow of Funds from External Sources

In case of external funds, the growth trend was fluctuating. In 2001 the amount of funds generated was ₹ 5235.31 crores and in 2002 it has been almost doubled i.e. ₹ 10049.81 crores. But this growth trend could not be maintained and sharply it decreased to ₹ 4908.44 crores in 2003. Once again it started showing a growth trend in 2004 and again it showed a negative trend in 2005. The annual average amount of external funds generated during the study period was ₹ 19275.75 crores, which constitutes on an average of 39.46 per cent of the total annual average of funds generated. Table 7.6 and its graph depict the inflow of funds from external sources.

Table 7.6 : Trend of External Sources of Funds

Year	External Sources (In Crores)	Increase/ Decrease	Per cent of Change
2001	5235.31	—	—
2002	10049.81	4814.5	91.96
2003	4908.44	-5141.37	-51.15
2004	9729.26	4820.82	98.21
2005	9453.99	-275.27	-2.82
2006	25522.43	16068.44	169.96
2007	35923.82	10401.39	40.75
2008	53382.99	17459.17	48.60
Total	**154206.05**	**48147.68**	**395.50**
Average	**19275.75**	**6878.24**	**56.50**

Source: Computed from the database collected from www.moneycontrol.com

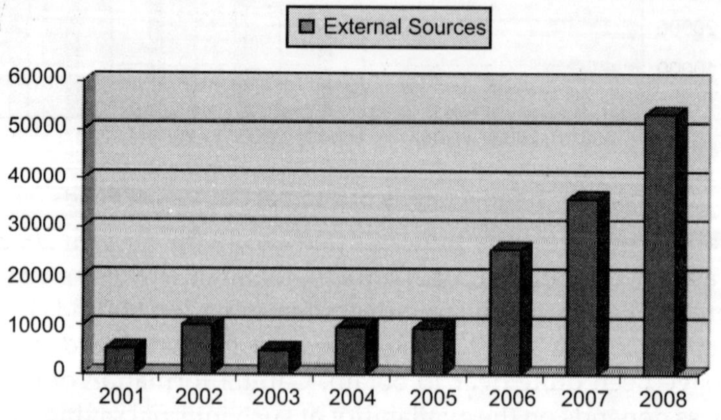

Graph 7.4 : Trend Analysis of External Sources of Funds

The external sources of finance can also be divided into long term sources comprising issue of equity shares, preference shares, share application money, deferred credits, secured loans and unsecured loans. The short term source comprises current liabilities only. A detailed analysis of each component of the long-term and short-term sources of funds is shown in Table 7.7 (*See on next page*) and Graph 7.5 (*See on page 105*).

On the analysis of the table 7.7 and graph 7.5, we find that though the total funds raised from long-term sources indicated a rising trend with exceptions in 2001 to 2002, but the growth trend of all the long-term sources are different from each other.

To start with equity share capital, the amount raised in 2001 was ₹ 625.38 crores, which decreased to 393.73 crores in 2002. It further reduced to 82.13 crores in 2003. The reduction in issue of equity share capital indicates that the companies went for repurchasing of shares, or they might have decided to go for debt capital instead of equity or due to reduction in the scale of operation, the fresh issue of equity shares was less.

In the case of preference shares, it shows negative balances in the years 2001, 2004 and in 2007 indicating a repayment or conversion into equity during these years. In 2002 and 2003 the amount raised through issue of preference shares were ₹ 372.2 crores and ₹ 187.1 crores respectively. Similarly, the amount raised in 2005, 2006 and 2008 were ₹ 199.02 crores, ₹ 191.41 crores and ₹ 49.06 crores respectively. This shows a declining interest of companies towards preference shares.

The amount received in the form of share application money in 2001 was ₹ 483.64 crores and in 2002 it was ₹ 12.69 crores. In 2003, 2004 and 2005 the balance in share application account shows a negative balance. A positive contribution in this account indicates application money received during the year in respect of fresh issue of shares, and a negative contribution implies the transfer of share application money to equity capital because of issue of stocks.

Funds raised through secured loans also indicate a fluctuating trend during this period of study. A negative growth has witnessed in second year i.e. in 2002 indicating the redemption or repayment of the loans or it might be conversion of debentures forming part of the secured loans into equity shares.

Unsecured loans contributed to a great extent. In the year 2001 it has showed a negative contribution indicating either repayment of such loans or conversion of same into shares or secured debentures. But from 2002 onwards it has shown a positive contribution till the end. Except the year 2003 in which the amount raised through unsecured loans was only

Table 7.7 : External Long-term and Short-term Sources of Inflow of Funds (₹ *in Crores*)

Sources of Funds	2001	2002	2003	2004	2005	2006	2007	2008
Equity Share Capital	625.38	393.73	82.13	719.12	814.27	1133.34	813.86	1105.87
Preference Share Capital	-5.07	372.2	187.1	-182.32	199.02	191.41	-317.49	49.06
Share Application Money	483.64	12.69	-127.21	-184.22	-26.64	155.61	342.12	409.27
Secured Loans	3297.52	-137.42	1688.62	1842.8	1255.65	2808.48	12680.36	14639.89
Unsecured Loans	-206.92	1601.13	111.24	2537.28	3198.13	11874.93	8597.65	16644.35
Deferred Credit	0	0	0	0	0	0	0	0
Total of Long-term Sources	**4194.55**	**2242.33**	**1941.88**	**4732.66**	**5440.43**	**16163.77**	**22116.5**	**32848.44**
Increase/Decrease as compared to previous year	—	-1952.22	-300.45	2790.78	707.77	10723.34	5952.73	10731.94
Percent of Change	—	-46.54	-13.39	143.71	14.95	197.10	36.82	48.52
Current Liabilities	1040.76	7807.48	2966.56	4996.6	4013.56	9358.66	13807.32	20534.55
Total of Short-term Sources	**1040.76**	**7807.48**	**2966.56**	**4996.6**	**4013.56**	**9358.66**	**13807.32**	**20534.55**
Increase/Decrease as compared to previous year	—	6766.72	-4840.92	2030.04	-983.04	5345.1	4448.66	6727.23
Per Cent of Change		650.17	-62.00	68.43	-19.67	133.17	47.53	48.72
Total - External Sources	**5235.31**	**10049.81**	**4908.44**	**9729.26**	**9453.99**	**25522.43**	**35923.82**	**53382.99**

Source: Computed from the database collected from www.moneycontrol.com

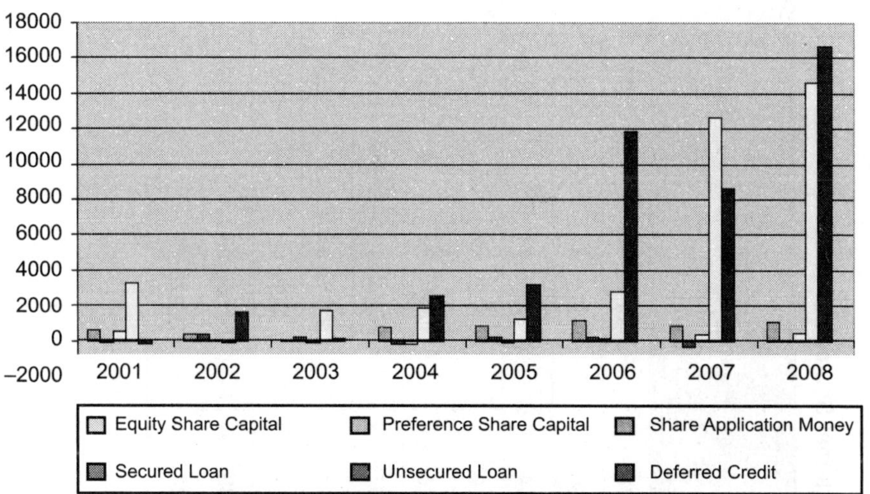

Graph 7.5 : Trend Analysis of Long-term External Sources of Funds

Rs. 111.24 crores, in all other years a sizable amount has been raised through unsecured loans and particularly from 2006 onwards, the trend has showed a remarkable increase.

The amount of increase and decrease and the rate of change in the generation of total long-term funds show a negative trend in 2002 and 2003 as compared with their respective previous years. In other years, though the trend was positive, but it is fluctuating. The percentage of total long-term funds to total external funds shows an increasing trend for all the years except from 2001 to 2002. In 2001 the share of long-term funds to total external funds was 80.12 per cent where as it decreased to 22.31 per cent in 2002. From 2003 onwards it has showed an increasing trend till 2006 but in 2007 and 2008 the rate has been decreased a little bit.

From the above analysis the conclusion has been derived that, issue of share capital had never been a major source of finance for the corporate sector. The dependence on debt capital i.e. secured and unsecured loan is more as compared to equity.

In the total source of funds inflow, short-term finance i.e. current liabilities are an important item of funds inflow. Current liabilities which consists of creditors, bills payable etc. contributed a lot to total sources of funds inflow in all the years under study. The analysis shows that from 2001 to 2005 the growth trend of current liabilities was fluctuating but from 2006 onwards it has showed a remarkable increase. The most important fact about the current liabilities is that it has remained one of the biggest sources of finances through out the period of study. Even in

Table 7.8 : Comparative Analysis of Long-term & Short-term External Sources of Funds

Year	External Long-term Sources (Rs. In Crores)	Percentage to Total External Funds	External Short-term Sources (Rs. In Crores)	Percentage to Total External Funds	Total of External Source (Rs. In Crores)	Total Percentage
2001	4194.55	80.12	1040.76	19.88	5235.31	100
2002	2242.33	22.31	7807.48	77.69	10049.81	100
2003	1941.88	39.56	2966.56	60.44	4908.44	100
2004	4732.66	48.64	4996.6	51.36	9729.26	100
2005	5440.43	57.54	4013.56	42.46	9453.99	100
2006	16163.77	63.33	9358.66	36.67	25522.43	100
2007	22116.5	61.56	13807.32	38.44	35923.82	100
2008	32848.44	61.53	20534.55	38.47	53382.99	100
Total	**89680.56**	**434.61**	**64525.49**	**365.39**	**154206.05**	**800**
Average	**11210.07**	**54.32**	**8065.68**	**45.68**	**19275.75**	**100**

Source: Computed from the database collected from www.moneycontrol.com

2002, 2003 and 2004 the amount raised through short-term finances i.e. through current liabilities exceed the total amounts raised through all the long-term sources.

Table 7.8 shows (*See on page 106*) the detail of external funds raised through long-term as well as short-term sources. Graph 7.6 followed by the table depicts the trend analysis of long-term and short-term external sources of funds.

The data given on the table 7.8 is also depicted through the following graph.

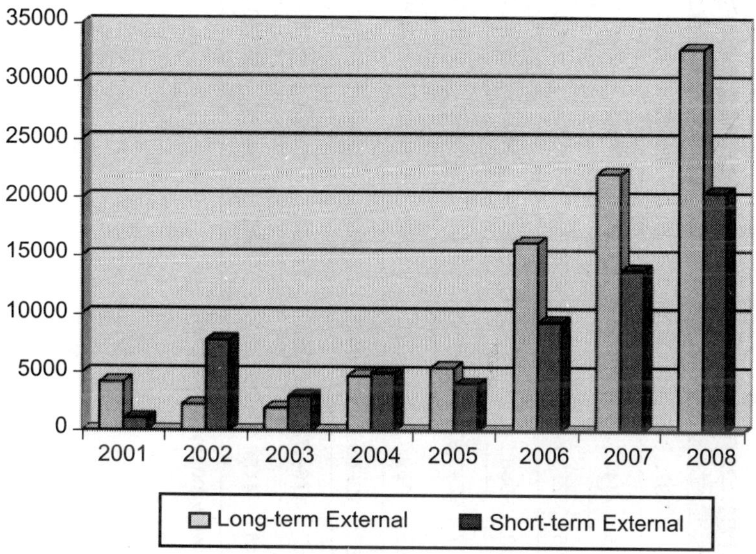

Graph 7.6 : Trend Analysis of Long-term and Short-term External Sources of Funds

Analysis of Total Outflow/Uses of Funds

The law of funds flow analysis states that the total inflow of funds should be equal to the total outflow of funds. Hence the total inflow of funds over the years was utilized in acquiring tangible and intangible fixed assets, financial assets, and miscellaneous assets. Some amount of funds also invested in fixed deposits, loans and advances and application in current assets like trade debtors, inventories, cash and bank deposits etc. The table 7.9 depicts a detailed analysis of different components of uses of funds.

The data given on the above table is also depicted through the following bar chart.

Table 7:9 : Detailed Analysis of Total Application/Uses of Funds

(Rs. in Crores)

Application of Funds	2001	2002	2003	2004	2005	2006	2007	2008	Total	% of Total
Gross Block	6231.1	8518.4	7370.88	11211.1	11431	20552	25891.5	35166.7	126372	33.79
Capital Work in Progress	1707.6	-148.1	-747.92	1175.62	4545.2	5902.6	9038.29	3136.08	24609.5	6.58
Investments	4357.2	1792.5	2738.4	6915.95	5579.9	8198.4	16905.9	25278.7	71767	19.19
Loans and Advances	1541.1	2522.8	688.28	1118.76	2629.3	9159.4	12088.3	20703.9	50451.8	13.49
Fixed Deposits	-163.66	1738.7	2243.97	2812.44	2630.7	4206.5	6143.54	6432.45	26044.6	6.96
Miscellaneous Expenses	-137.89	-56.89	369.71	-469.72	53.43	-74.02	20.02	-202.32	-497.68	-0.13
Gross Fixed Assets	**13535**	**14367**	**12663.3**	**22764.2**	**26869**	**47945**	**70087.5**	**90515.5**	**298747**	**79.88**
Current Assets	**2431.4**	**2275.7**	**1794.77**	**8008.5**	**7414.2**	**16193**	**15053.1**	**22083.2**	**75253.4**	**20.12**
Total Application of Funds	**15967**	**16643**	**14458.1**	**30772.7**	**34283**	**64137**	**85140.6**	**112599**	**374001**	**100**

Source: Computed from the database collected from www.moneycontrol.com

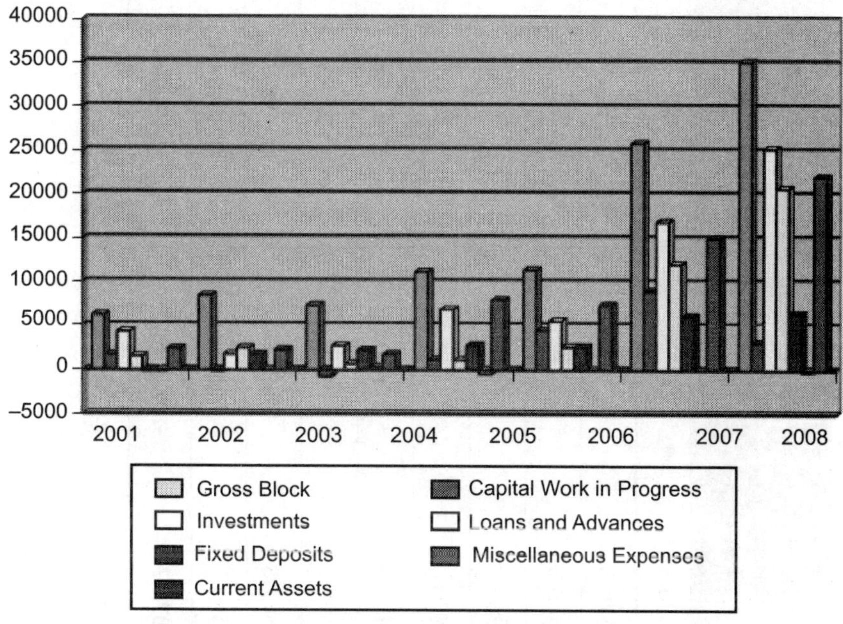

Graph 7.7 : Trend Analysis of Total Application/Uses of Funds

Analysis of Total Uses of Funds in Fixed Assets

Table 7.9 (*See on page 108*) depicts the details of application of funds during the study period for different purposes. Out of the total funds available, a major portion was utilized in acquiring the fixed assets. During the period of study, the total funds utilized for the above purpose amounted to ₹ 298747 crores, which constitutes nearly 80 per cent of the total application of funds. Out of the total investment in fixed assets, a heavy chunk has been diverted in acquiring tangible fixed assets like land and building, plant and machinery etc. which is shown under the head gross block. Out of the total investment of ₹ 298747 crores in fixed assets, an amount of ₹ 126372 crores has been invested in gross block i.e. in gross tangible fixed assets and ₹ 24610 crores in capital work-in-progress during the period of study. Investment in gross block and capital work in progress is taken as the money spent for acquiring tangible fixed assets.

Table 7.10 shows the trend analysis of uses of funds in tangible fixed assets, which constitutes gross block and capital work in progress. The data given on the above table is also depicted through the following graph—7.8 :

Table 7.10 : Analysis of Uses of Funds in Gross Tangible Fixed Assets

Year	Investment in Gross Block (Rs. In Crores)	Investment in Capital Work-in-progress (Rs. In Crores)	Total Investment in Gross Tangible Fixed Assets (Rs. In Crores)	Increase/ Decrease	Percentage of Increase/ Decrease
2001	6231.07	1707.59	7938.66		
2002	8518.35	-148.05	8370.3	431.64	5.43
2003	7370.88	-747.92	6622.96	-1747.3	-20.87
2004	11211.1	1175.62	12386.7	5763.76	87.02
2005	11430.84	4545.2	15976	3589.32	28.97
2006	20551.89	5902.64	26454.5	10478.5	65.58
2007	25891.48	9038.29	34929.8	8475.24	32.03
2008	35166.7	3136.08	38302.8	3373.01	9.65
Total	**126372.31**	**24609.45**	**150982**	**30364.1**	**207.84**
Average	**15796.53**	**3076.18**	**18872.7**	**4337.73**	**29.69**

Source: Computed from the database collected from www.moneycontrol.com

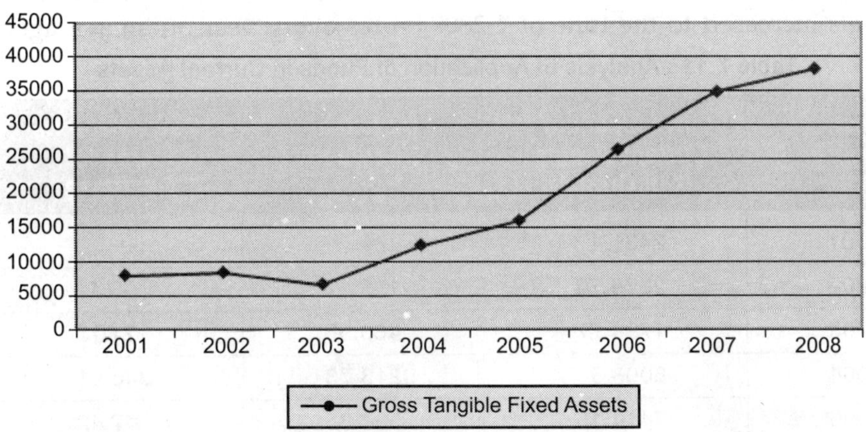

Graph 7.8 : Trend Analysis of Uses of Funds in Gross Tangible Fixed Assets

The trend of investment in gross tangible fixed assets is shown in Table 7.10 and followed by the Graph 7.8. The trend is constantly increasing throughout the study period except for the year 2003 which shows a negative trend. The analysis shows that the average investment in gross tangible fixed assets during the period of study is ₹ 18872 crores but amazingly for the first five years i.e. 2001 to 2005, the total investment is less than the above average figure. But from 2006 onwards, it increased sharply.

The amount of investment in other fixed assets i.e. in investments, loans and advances, fixed deposits and in miscellaneous assets constitutes nearly half of the total investment in fixed assets. A heavy chunk of the money has been applied in investments which amount to ₹ 71767 crores. Amount invested in loans and advances and fixed deposits were ₹ 50451 crores and ₹ 26044 crores respectively.

Analysis of Total Uses of Funds in Current Assets

With respect to current assets, the total amount invested during the whole period was ₹ 75253, constituting around 20 per cent of the total application of funds. Table 7.11 shows the trend analysis of uses of funds in current assets. The analysis shows that the trend of investment in current assets is fluctuating throughout the study period. For the first three years i.e. from 2001 to 2003 the trend of investment in current assets is decreasing. But in 2004 the trend shows a sudden increase of 346 per cent amounting to ₹ 6213 crores. Again in 2005 the trend is negative followed by a positive trend of 118 per cent in 2006. In 2007 also it was negative and in 2008 again it shows a positive growth. The average amount of investment in current assets was ₹ 9406 crores. On the whole, the investment in current assets increased to the tune of ₹ 2807 crores every year on an average.

Table 7.11 : Analysis of Application of Funds in Current Assets

Year	Investment in Current Assets (₹ In Crores)	Increase/ Decrease	Percentage of Increase/ Decrease
2001	2431.4	—	—
2002	2275.73	-155.67	-6.4
2003	1794.77	-480.96	-21.13
2004	8008.5	6213.73	346.21
2005	7414.15	-594.35	-7.42
2006	16192.54	8778.39	118.40
2007	15053.1	-1139.44	-7.03
2008	22083.17	7030.07	46.70
Total	**75253.36**	**19651.77**	**469.32**
Average	**9406.67**	**2807.39**	**67.04**

Source: Computed from the database collected from www.moneycontrol.com

The data given on the table 7.11 is also depicted through the following graph:

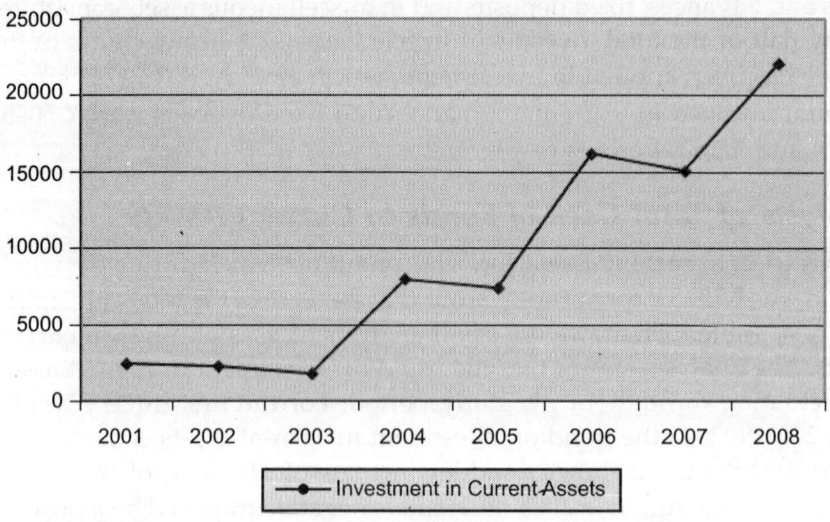

Graph 7.9 : Trend Analysis of Application of Funds in Current Assets

Ratio Analysis of Total Sample Companies

A company's proportion of short and long-term debt is considered when analyzing capital structure. When people refer to capital structure they are most likely referring to a firm's debt-to-equity ratio, which provides insight into how risky a company is. Usually a company more heavily financed by debt poses greater risk, as this firm is relatively highly levered.

Debt-Equity Ratio

The debt-to-equity ratio (D/E) is a financial ratio indicating the relative proportion of shareholder's equity and debt used to finance a company's assets.[3] Closely related to leveraging, the ratio is also known as Risk, Gearing or Leverage. The two components are often taken from the firm's balance sheet or statement of financial position (so-called book value), but the ratio may also be calculated using market values for both, if the company's debt and equity are publicly traded, or using a combination of book value for debt and market value for equity. But for our study purpose, the two components of this variable, viz. debt and equity in this context is taken at book values. Maintenance of a desired capital structure is sought, perhaps more in book value term than in market value proportions.[4] For the reason that when sales grow, assets increase or taxes rise, the impact on the financial structure as recorded in the firms books emerges through changes in the book values of debt and equity.

Debt equity ratio is calculated by dividing borrowed funds by owner's capital. The overall objectives in determining a particular debt equity ratio is to ensure that there is a proper balance between the owned funds and borrowed funds. While deciding about the appropriate level of debt equity ratio, the guiding factor must be the ability of a project to generate enough surpluses so that it is able to serve both the share capital and loans. The other major factor determining the level of debt equity ratio are the nature of industry, size of investment, gestation period, profitability potential, debt servicing capacity, current capital market conditions and other economic situations. A high debt equity ratio shows a relatively larger share of financing by the creditors to the owners and therefore, a larger claim against the assets of the firm. A high debt equity ratio is a danger signal for the creditors, because if the project failed financially, the creditors would lose heavily from the point of view of the company. A high proportion of debt in the capital structure would lead to inflexibility in the operations of the firm as creditors would exercise pressure and interfere in management.

Secondly, such a firm would be able to borrow only under very restrictive terms and conditions. Further it would have to face a heavy burden of interest payments, particularly in adverse circumstances when profits decline.

On the other hand, a low debt equity ratio has just the opposite implications. To the creditors a relatively high stake of the owners implies sufficient safety of margin and substantial protection against shrinkage in assets. For the company also, the servicing of debt is low burdensome and consequently, its capital standing is not adversely affected, its operational flexibility is not in jeopardy and it will be able to raise additional funds. But the shareholders of the firm are deprived of the benefits of trading on equity or leverage.

Debt equity ratio, also known as External-Internal equity, calculated for the purpose of determining the solvency. It measures the relative claims of outsiders and the owners (i.e. shareholders) against the firm's assets. This ratio indicates the relationship between the external equities or the outsider's funds and the external equities or the shareholders' funds.

Thus, Debt Equity Ratio = Outsider's Funds/Shareholder's Funds

The outsider's funds include all debt/liabilities to outsiders, whether long term or short term or whether in the form of secured or unsecured loans, current liabilities or deferred liabilities. The shareholders funds consist of equity share capital, Preference share capital, share application money, shareholders reserve and revaluation reserve. The latter is called net worth and the ratio may be termed as debt to net worth ratio.[5]

The debt equity ratio is calculated to measure the extent to which debt financing has been used in a business. The ratio indicates the proportionate claims of owners and the outsiders against assets of the firm. Interpretation of this ratio depends primarily upon the financial policy of the firm. A ratio of 1:1 may be usually considered to be a satisfactory ratio, although there cannot be any 'rules of thumbs' or standard norm. A high ratio indicates that the claims of outsiders (creditors) are greater than those of owners. The creditors may not consider it as good because it gives a lesser margin of safety for them at the time of liquidation of the firm. In case of a very high ratio, it may not be possible for the firm to get credit without paying a very high rate of interest. A very low ratio is not considered satisfactory for the shareholders because it indicates that the firm has not been able to use outsider's funds to magnify their earnings. The table 7.12 shows the yearly debt equity ratios for all the years under study.

Table 7.12 : Debt - Equity Ratio for the Total Sample

(₹ in Crores)

Year	Long Term Debts	Current Liabilities	Total Debt	Equity or Net Worth	Debt Equity Ratio (Debt/Equity)
2000	41093.86	17,041.65	58135.51	45193.03	1.29
2001	44184.46	18,082.41	62266.87	52901.77	1.18
2002	45648.17	25,889.89	71538.06	56046.69	1.28
2003	47448.03	28,856.45	76304.48	60310.64	1.26
2004	51828.11	33,853.05	85681.16	72305.73	1.18
2005	56281.89	37,866.61	94148.5	92824.64	1.01
2006	70965.3	47,225.27	118190.57	121722.23	0.97
2007	92243.31	61,032.59	153275.9	163070.04	0.94
2008	123527.55	81,567.14	205094.69	211204.28	0.97
Total	**573220.68**	**351,415.06**	**924635.74**	**875579.05**	**10.08**
Average	**63691.18**	**39046.12**	**102737.3**	**97286.56**	**1.12**

Source: Calculated from Consolidated Balance Sheet of Total Sample Companies computed from the database collected from www.moneycontrol.com

The data depicted in the table 7.12 is also presented in the following graph:

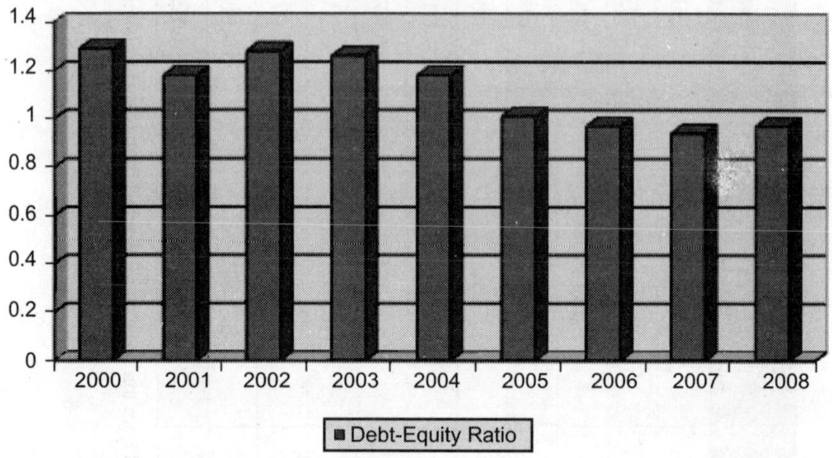

Graph 7.10 : Trend Analysis of Debt - Equity Ratio of Sample Companies

The data presented in the above table and graph is calculated from the consolidated balance sheet of sample companies for the period from 2000 to 2008. The debt-equity ratio as presented in the table indicated a variance from 0.94 to 1.29. The average ratio for the total period of study worked out to 1.12, which is fairly lower than the generally accepted norm of 2:1. The ratio 1.12 revealed that for every rupee worth of equity, sample companies had used ₹ 1.12 worth of debt in its capital structure. This made it clear that the sample companies had followed a conservative policy while deciding in the debt equity mix in the capital structure. Thus the long-term solvency position was satisfactory.

The most important observation of this debt equity ratio analysis is that the ratio has fell down continuously through out the period of study, barring a few exceptions. The analysis shows that in 2000 the debt equity ratio was 1.29, which decreased to 1.18 in 2001. In 2002 though the ratio increased to 1.28, but since than it started falling continuously. It fell down even to 0.94 in 2007, the lowest debt equity ratio of the entire period. The downward trend in debt-to-equity ratio reflects corporate India's reluctance to go for borrowings and increased reliance on internal accruals for growth. The strong profitability of companies during the bull-run has ensured rapid expansion in their net worth. It also indicates that most of the apex plans tend to get funded out of internal cash flows. This also results in lesser funds for investors as companies reinvest profits to fund further growth.

The debt-to-equity ratio measures the extent to which a company is using borrowed money. It is obtained by dividing the total debt (total loan funds) of the company by its shareholders' equity (net worth). A high debt-to-equity ratio generally means that a company has been aggressive in financing its growth with debt. This can result in volatile earnings because of additional interest expenses. If a lot of debt is used to finance increased operations, the company could potentially generate more earnings than it would have without outside financing.

The D/E ratio is an important tool of financial analysis to assess the financial structure of a company. It indicates the relative claims of the creditors and shareholders against the capital employed by the company. A lower debt equity ratio indicates that operational flexibility is not in jeopardy and the companies had the ability to raise additional funds.

No doubt, too much debt can put the business at risk, but too little debt may mean that the company is not realizing the full potential of the business and may actually hurt the overall profitability. This is particularly true for larger companies where shareholders want a higher reward (dividend rate) than lenders (interest rate). But the fact is that, a debt equity ratio of less than at least 1:1 would indicate an unsatisfactory debt situation in an under-developed country like India as the shareholders are deprived of the benefits of trading on equity or leverage. But it is not uncommon to find firms having debt equity ratio of 2:1 or even 3:1 in case of joint stock enterprises in India.

Size of Investment

The total investment represented by the sum of Net Fixed Assets i.e. Net Block and Current Assets has been adopted to represent the size of investment. The only controversy proposed by 'Economic Studies Research Foundation' to the measure of size of investment is that it could be vitiated because of different valuation bases adopted by various firms. But this problem does not arise in case of companies as they normally follow uniform depreciation and other accounting policies recommended by Registrar of Companies Act 1956.

The analysis shows that the size of investment has been constantly increasing throughout the study period (*See Table 7.13*). In the year 2000, the amount of investment in net fixed assets and current assets was ₹ 74980.24 crores and in 2008 it increased to ₹ 233724.69 crores, indicating an increase of more than three times over the entire period of study. In other words, the growth was about three fold in nine years i.e. from 2000 to 2008. The average net fixed assets in this period was ₹ 71321.16 crores and that of current assets was ₹ 53529.08 crores, amounting to an average of ₹ 124850.24

Table 7.13 : Size of Investment (Total Samples)

Year	Net Fixed Assets/Net Block (₹ in Crores)	Current Assets (₹ in Crores)	Total Investment (₹ in Crores)	Growth (₹ in Crores)	Growth Percent
2000	45519.61	29460.63	74980.24	—	—
2001	48211.07	31892.03	80103.1	5122.86	6.83
2002	52795.49	34167.76	86963.25	6860.15	8.56
2003	55636.87	35962.53	91599.4	4636.15	5.33
2004	61319.19	43971.03	105290.22	13690.82	14.94
2005	67748.27	51385.18	119133.45	13843.23	13.15
2006	81302.46	67577.72	148880.18	29746.73	24.97
2007	100346.77	82630.82	182977.59	34097.41	22.90
2008	129010.7	104713.99	233724.69	50747.1	27.73
Total	**641890.43**	**481,761.69**	**1123652.1**	**158744.45**	**124.43**
Average	**71321.16**	**53529.08**	**124850.24**	**19843.056**	**15.55**

Source: Calculated from Consolidated Balance Sheet of Total Sample Companies computed from the database collected from www.moneycontrol.com

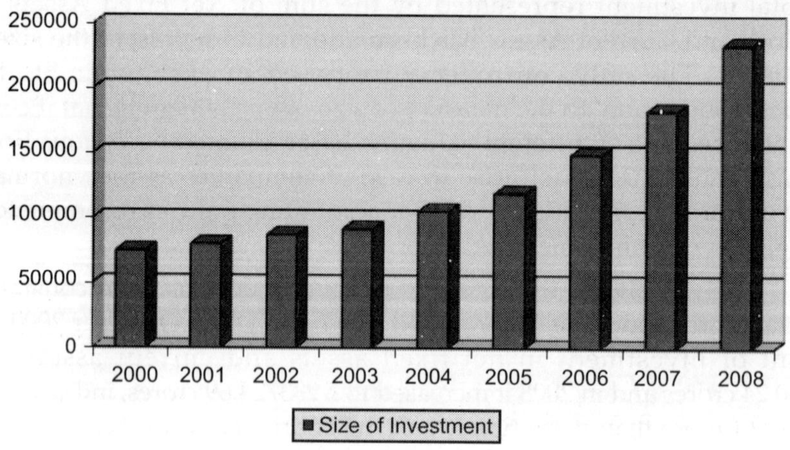

Graph 7.11 : Trend Analysis of Size of Investment in Net Fixed Assets and Current Assets

crores in total. From 2000 to 2005 the yearly total investment was less than the average. But from 2006 onwards the yearly total investment figures crossed the annual average investment and it started rising sharply at a rate of more than 20 per cent every year. The growth per cent of total investment was calculated in comparison to previous year. The annual average rate of growth was 15.55 per cent. Till 2005 the annual growth rate was less than the average and it started growing at a faster rate from 2006 onwards. The highest growth rate is recorded in the year 2008 which was 27.73 per cent.

Ratio of Net Worth to Net Fixed Assets

This ratio establishes relationship between fixed assets and shareholders fund, i.e. share capital plus reserves including the revaluation reserve. The ratio of fixed assets to net worth indicates the extents to which shareholders fund are sunk in fixed assets. Normally it is the shareholders duty to finance the purchase of fixed assets of the company. Therefore coverage of fixed assets by shareholders funds is a good test of long term solvency. Table 7.14 shows the ratio of net worth to net fixed assets.

Table 7.14 : Ratio of Net Worth to Net Fixed Assets

Year	Equity or Net Worth (₹ In Crores)	Net Fixed Assets/Net Block (₹ in Crores)	Ratio (%)
2000	45193.03	45519.61	0.99
2001	52901.77	48211.07	1.09
2002	56046.69	52795.49	1.06
2003	60310.64	55636.87	1.08
2004	72305.73	61319.19	1.18
2005	92824.64	67748.27	1.37
2006	121722.23	81302.46	1.49
2007	163070.04	100346.77	1.62
2008	211204.28	129010.7	1.63
Total	**875579.05**	**641890.43**	**11.54**
Average	**97286.56**	**71321.16**	**1.28**

Source: Calculated from Consolidated Balance Sheet of Total Sample Companies computed from the database collected from www.moneycontrol.com

The data presented in the above table is also depicted through graph 7.12.

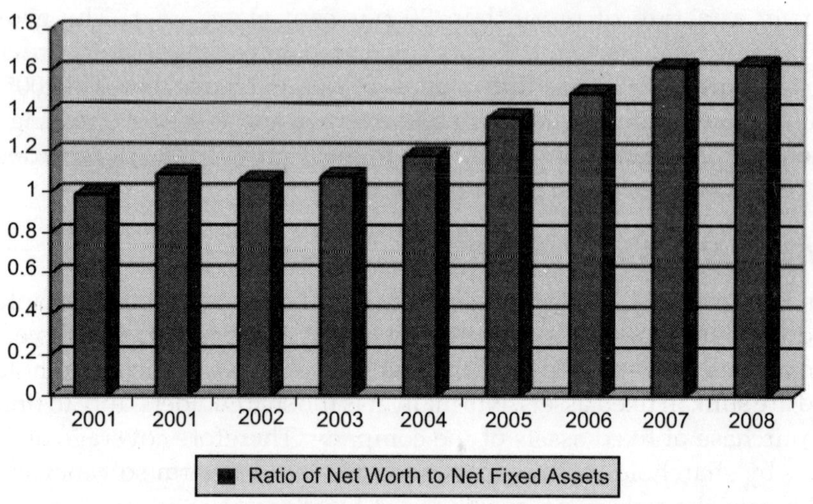

Graph 7.12 : Ratio of Net Worth to Net Fixed Assets

The ratio of net worth to fixed assets indicates the extent to which shareholder's funds are sunk into the fixed assets. Generally, the purchase of fixed assets should be financed by shareholder's equity including reserves, surpluses and retained earnings. If the ratio is more than 100 per cent, it implies that owners funds are more than fixed assets and a part of the working capital is provide by the shareholders. When the ratio is less than 100 per cent, it implies that owners' funds are not sufficient to finance the fixed assets and the firm has to depend upon outsiders to finance the fixed assets.

From the above table it is evident that the net worth to fixed assets ratio for all the years under study was more than 1 (i.e. 100%) only except for the first year i.e. in 2000 in which the ratio was 0.99, which is also very nearer to 100 per cent. A ratio of 1 or above indicates that the money spent on fixed assets was fully financed from the shareholders funds and companies are not dependent on outsiders' funds to finance the fixed assets. There has been a constant growth in the ratio starting from 0.99 in 2000 to 1.63 in 2008 and the average ratio for the whole period stood at 1.28.

Asset Structure

As the fixed assets depend on long-term funds, their proportion in the total assets structure will have a direct bearing on the determination of the proportion of long-term funds in the total finances, i.e. capital structure. The asset structure as one of the variable closely interacting with the capital structure is analyzed with the help of net fixed assets to total assets ratio in Table 7.15.

Table 7.15 : Ratio of Net Fixed Assets to Total Assets

Year	Net Block/ Net Fixed Assets (₹ in Crores)	Total Assets (Rs. in Crores)	Ratio (%)
2000	45519.61	106096.03	0.43
2001	48211.07	118523.24	0.41
2002	52795.49	131232.35	0.40
2003	55636.87	141160.94	0.39
2004	61319.19	166404.81	0.37
2005	67748.27	195686.53	0.34
2006	81302.46	252826.25	0.32
2007	100346.77	331119.7	0.30
2008	129010.7	437215.6	0.29
Total	**641890.43**	**1880265.5**	**3.26**
Average	**71321.16**	**208918.38**	**0.36**

Source: Calculated from Consolidated Balance Sheet of Total Sample Companies computed from the database collected from www.moneycontrol.com

(Total Assets = Net Block + Capital WIP + Investment + Current Assets + Loans and Advances + Fixed Deposits + Miscellaneous Assets)

The data presented in the table 7.15 is also depicted through graph 7.13.

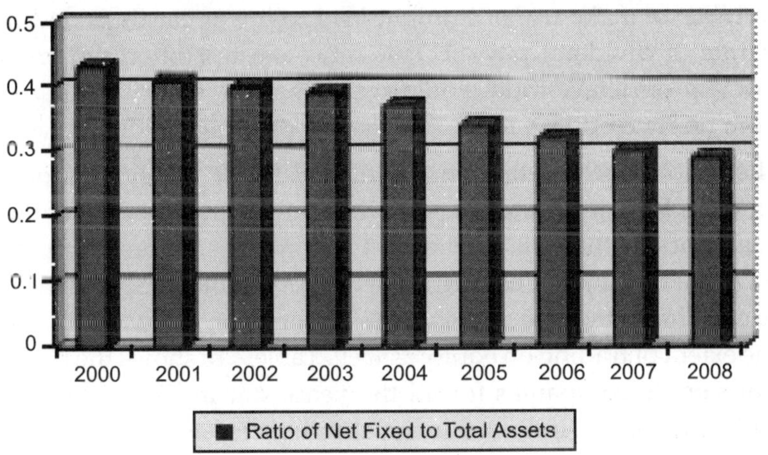

Graph 7.13 : Ratio of Net Fixed Assets to Total Assets

This ratio measure the extent to which fixed assets are financed with owners' equity (capital) (Net Fixed Assets/Total Assets). A high ratio, e.g. .5 or higher, indicates an inefficient use of working capital which reduces the enterprise's ability to carry accounts receivable and maintain inventory and usually means a low cash reserve. This will often limit the ability of the business to respond to increased demand for the products or services.

By analyzing Table 7.15, it was observed that the proportion of net fixed assets in the total assets structure was decreasing constantly through out the period of study. In 2000 the amount utilized for the purpose of net fixed assets was 43 per cent of the amount utilized in total assets, whereas in 2008 the ratio of net fixed assets to total assets has been decreased to 29 per cent. But the average ratio for the entire study period stood at 36 per cent. A decreasing trend in the ratio indicates that corporate are keeping more and more for working capital needs, which will help them to increase the profitability.

Ratio of Net Worth to Total Assets

This is also known as proprietary or equity ratio. This ratio establishes relationship between shareholders funds and total assets of the firm. A higher proprietary ratio denotes that the shareholders have provided the funds to purchase the assets of the concern instead of relying on other sources of funds like bank borrowings, trade creditors and others. However, too high a proprietary ratio say 100 per cent or above means that management has not effectively utilize cheaper sources of finance like trade and long term creditors. As these sources of funds are cheaper, the inability to make use of it might lead to lower earnings and hence a lower rate of dividend payout. This ratio is a test of credit strength as too low a proprietary ratio would mean that the enterprise is relying a lot more on its creditors to supply its working capital.

The ratio of proprietary funds to total funds is very important for determining long-term solvency of a firm. In general, the higher the share of proprietors in the total capital of the company (either in the form of share capital or retained earnings) the less is the likelihood of insolvency in future. This ratio also measures the protection available to creditors and the extent of trading on equity as well. Table 7.16 shows the proprietary ratio of sample companies for all the years starting from 2000 to 2008. The ratios calculated in the table are also depicted through a bar chart in Graph 7.14.

Table 7.16 : Ratio of Net Worth to Total Assets

Year	Net Worth (₹ in Crores)	Total Assets (₹ in Crores)	Ratio
2000	45193.03	106096	0.42
2001	52901.77	118523.2	0.44
2002	56046.69	131232.4	0.43
2003	60310.64	141160.9	0.43
2004	72305.73	166404.8	0.43
2005	92824.64	195686.5	0.47
2006	121722.2	252826.3	0.48
2007	163070	331119.7	0.49
2008	211204.3	437215.6	0.48
Total	**875579.1**	**1880265**	**4.07**
Average	**97286.56**	**208918.4**	**0.45**

Source: Calculated from Consolidated Balance Sheet of Total Sample Companies computed from the database collected from www.moneycontrol.com

The data presented in the above table is also depicted through graph 7.14.

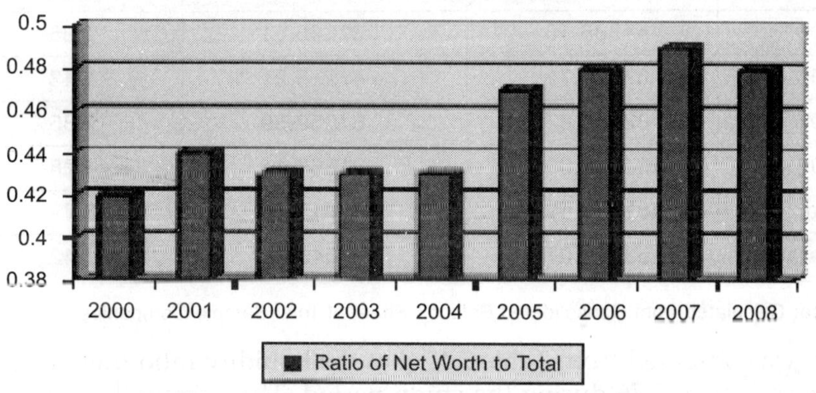

Graph 7.14 : Ratio of Net Worth to Total Assets

Table 7.16 presents the ratio of net worth to total assets of the firm. This proprietary ratio of sample companies for the period from 2000 to 2008 varied in between 42 per cent to 49 per cent. And the annual average of this ratio was calculated at 45 per cent for 2000-2008. Thus, out of every rupee invested in the total assets of sample companies the shareholders contribution was ₹ 0.45 whereas creditors contributed ₹ 0.55. This margin was satisfactory as there was sufficient cushion against fall in price of assets.

Liquidity

The principles and conventions of finance suggest that a portion of funds should be invested in current assets so as to ease the firm for short term risks and to ensure liquidity by reducing the burden of current liabilities. While the liquidity is governed by cash flows, the discretionary components of cash out flows such as interest charges, dividends will influence the debt-equity mix. The liquidity ratio is measured by calculating a ratio of current assets to current liabilities. The liquidity ratio of the sample companies is shown in Table 7.17.

Table 7.17 : Ratio of Current Assets to Current Liabilities

Year	Current Assets (₹ in Crores)	Current Liabilities (₹ in Crores)	Ratio (%)
2000	29460.63	17041.65	1.73
2001	31892.03	18082.41	1.76
2002	34167.76	25889.89	1.32
2003	35962.53	28856.45	1.24
2004	43971.03	33853.05	1.30
2005	51385.18	37866.61	1.36
2006	67577.72	47225.27	1.43
2007	82630.82	61032.59	1.35
2008	104713.99	81567.14	1.28
Total	**481761.69**	**351415.06**	**12.77**
Average	**53529.07**	**39046.11**	**1.42**

Source: Calculated from Consolidated Balance Sheet of Total Sample Companies

It was observed from Table 7.17 that the liquidity ratio fluctuated in between 1.28 to 1.76 during the study period. The average ratio for the sample companies was 1.44. For the first two years i.e. in 2000 and 2001 the ratio was 1.73 and 1.76 respectively, which was much above the average ratio for the entire period. But in 2002 the ratio decreased to 1.32 and for the rest of the years also the observed variation was very less.

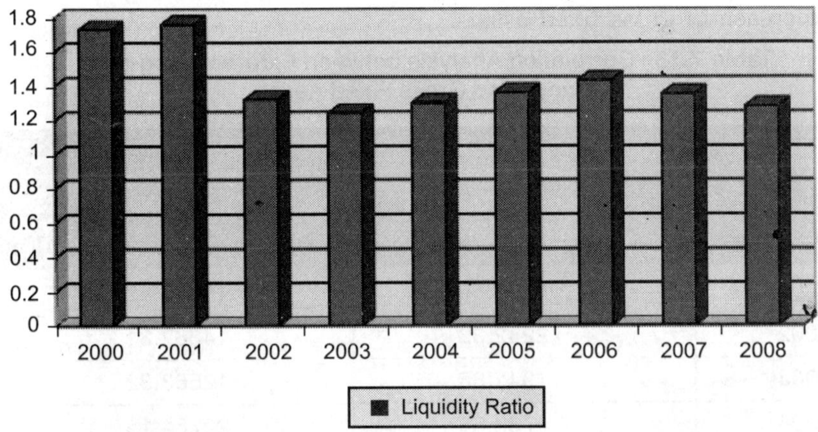

Graph 7.15 : Trend of Liquidity Ratio of Sample Companies

From the study it was observed that the current assets had maintained its position with the current liabilities. For every rupee of current liability, the average current assets available were ₹ 1.42. It showed that current assets were more than sufficient to meet current liabilities. Though the ratio is much below the normal standard which is 2:1, yet the liquidity position was very much satisfactory. As per the theory, the higher the current ratio, the more capable the company is of paying its obligations. A ratio under one suggests that the company would be unable to pay off its obligations if they came due at that point. Thus, in our study the sample companies indicated a good short-term solvency position, i.e. ability to meet short-term obligations.

Correlation Analysis

Now it is proposed to examine the correlation between each individual sources and uses of funds. We will also correlate each of the selected variables and debt-equity ratio, i.e. capital structure and draw inferences about the impact of the latter on the former and vice versa.

External Long Term Funds and Gross Fixed Assets

In general, investment in fixed assets is not a regular phenomenon. It is well established that fixed assets should be financed only out of long-term funds. The correlation between external long term funds and fixed assets indicates as-to what extent fixed assets are financed out of long-term funds. A low degree of coefficient of correlation between these two indicates that the firm has adopted the impudent policy of using short-term funds for acquiring fixed assets. On the other hand, a very high degree would indicate that long-term funds are being used for short-term purposes, i.e. for financing working capital. Table 7.18 shows the calculation of coefficient of correlation between increase in external long-term funds and increase in gross fixed assets.

Table 7.18 : Correlation Analysis between External Long-term Funds and Gross Fixed Asset

Year	Amount Raised from External Long-term Sources (₹ In Crores) (X)	Investments made Gross Fixed Assets in (₹ In Crores) (Y)
2001	4194.55	13535.42
2002	2242.33	14367.31
2003	1941.88	12663.32
2004	4732.66	22764.15
2005	5440.43	26869.33
2006	16163.77	47944.88
2007	22116.5	70087.52
2008	32848.44	90515.5

Coefficient of Correlation between X and Y = 0.99

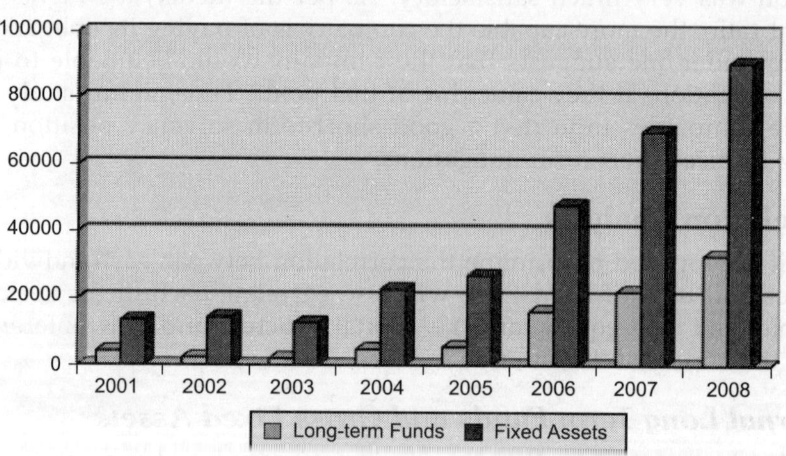

Graph 7.16 : Correlation between External Long-term Funds and Gross Fixed Assets

The analysis shows that the coefficient of correlation between the long term external sources of finance and gross fixed assets is +0.99, which is statistically very much significant. A high degree of positive correlation between these two indicates that the additional investment in fixed assets was duly supported by the additional long-term funds. It also indicates that the investment in fixed assets was very much influenced by the availability of funds from long term external sources.

Current Assets and Current Liabilities

Table 7.19 shows the relationship between current assets and current liabilities. The correlation between current assets and current liabilities was found to be +0.88, which is statistically significant. This high degree of positive correlation implies that increase in current assets was very much influenced by increase in current liabilities and vice versa. As the correlation between the two is positively significant, it may be concluded that overall rise in the current assets was associated with overall rise in the current liabilities.

Table 7.19 : Correlation Analysis between Current Assets and Current Liabilities

Year	Amount Raised from Current Liabilities (₹ In Crores) (X)	Investments made in Current Assets (₹ In Crores) (Y)
2001	1040.76	2431.4
2002	7807.48	2275.73
2003	2966.56	1794.77
2004	4996.6	8008.5
2005	4013.56	7414.15
2006	9358.66	16192.54
2007	13807.32	15053.1
2008	20534.55	22083.17

Coefficient of Correlation between X and Y = 0.88

Source: Calculated from Consolidated Balance Sheet of Total Sample Companies computed from the database collected from www.moneycontrol.com

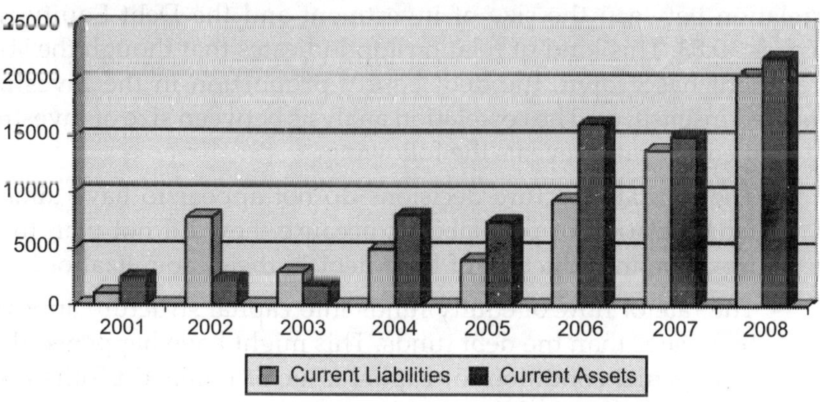

Graph 7.17 : Correlation between Current Assets and Current Liabilities

Size of Investment and Debt Equity Ratio

A larger asset base calls for more long-term funds. The dichotomy of these funds into debt and equity and their proportion depend upon the earnings, prevailing cost of sources of finance available etc. A greater proportion of incremental funds year after year would be short normally from debt sources rather than from equity. Therefore, the correlation between the size of investment and debt equity ratio of a firm is supposed to be positive. Table 7.20 shows the correlation between size of investment and debt equity ratio.

Table 7.20 : Correlation between Size of Investment and Debt Equity Ratio

Year	Size of Investment (₹ in Crores) (X)	Debt Equity Ratio (Y)
2000	74980.24	1.29
2001	80103.1	1.18
2002	86963.25	1.28
2003	91599.4	1.26
2004	105290.22	1.18
2005	119133.45	1.01
2006	148880.18	0.97
2007	182977.59	0.94
2008	233724.69	0.97

Coefficient of Correlation between X and Y = –0.83814

Source: Calculated from Consolidated Balance Sheet of Total Sample Companies computed from the database collected from www.moneycontrol.com

The analysis shows that there is a fairly high degree of negative correlation between the size of investment and the Debt-Equity ratio, which is –0.83. This kind of relationship indicates that though the size of investment has grown, the debt equity proportion in the investment remained insensitive. The correlation analysis between size of investment and debt equity ratio reveals the following:

- The capital structure decisions do not appear to have aimed at maximization of profitability, because they did not plan to gain from the introduction of high debt in their capitalization;
- The rate of flow of equity funds into capital structure appears to be greater than the debt funds. This might have happened due to a congenial condition for capital issue of retained profits raising the reserve fund of shareholders.

Asset Structure and Debt-Equity Ratio

The association of fixed proportion of total assets with debt equity ratio is examined in Table 7.21. Higher the rate of fixed assets to total assets, more will be the requirement of long-term funds, directly influencing the capital structure. Therefore, there should be a close association between the two.

Table 7.21 : Correlation between Asset Structure and Debt - Equity Ratio

Year	Asset Structure (X)	Debt Equity Ratio (Y)
2000	0.43	1.29
2001	0.41	1.18
2002	0.4	1.28
2003	0.39	1.26
2004	0.37	1.18
2005	0.34	1.01
2006	0.32	0.97
2007	0.3	0.94
2008	0.29	0.97

Coefficient of Correlation between X and Y = 0.93988

Source: Calculated from Consolidated Balance Sheet of Total Sample Companies computed from the database collected from www.moneycontrol.com

Table 7.21 shows the association of fixed assets proportion to total assets with debt-equity ratio. It was found to be +0.94 which implies a high degree of positive correlation between the two. It indicates that there is a direct positive correlation between the debt proportion in the total capital and the investment in fixed assets. The analysis shows that as the debt portion in the debt equity mix started decreasing gradually, simultaneously the fixed assets proportion in the total assets also started decreasing. Looking into the degree of correlation between the two, we can say that the sample companies utilized a major portion of financing in fixed assets.

Liquidity and Debt Equity Ratio

Liquidity ratio is directly influenced by the proportion of long-term funds invested in current assets and therefore, is supposed to be linearly related to the debt equity ratio. Such a correlation is shown in Table 7.22.

Table 7.22 : Correlation between Liquidity and Debt-Equity Ratio

Year	Liquidity Ratio (X)	Debt Equity Ratio (Y)
2000	1.73	1.29
2001	1.76	1.18
2002	1.32	1.28
2003	1.24	1.26
2004	1.3	1.18
2005	1.36	1.01
2006	1.43	0.97
2007	1.35	0.94
2008	1.28	0.97

Coefficient of Correlation between X and Y =0.28164

Source: Calculated from Consolidated Balance Sheet of Total Sample Companies computed from the database collected from www.moneycontrol.com

Table 7.22 shows that the correlation between liquidity ratio and debt equity ratio is +0.28. This indicates a low degree of positive association between the two. It implies that only a small portion of the long-term fund is invested in current assets. In other words, major portion of the long-term funds are invested in fixed assets and the current assets are mostly financed by current liabilities.

Summary and Concluding Remarks

This chapter contained an analysis relating to the capital structure of the total sample companies (300). It also highlighted different sources of funds along with their applications in the various assets. For this, the funds flow statements of the total sample companies are calculated. The trend analysis of different sources of funds and their investment in acquiring different assets are also shown. An attempt has also been made to find out the coefficient of correlation between sources and uses of funds. Further, ratio analysis is also taken to supplement the study.

The analysis of funds flow statement involved two steps, viz., analysis of sources of funds and analysis of uses of funds. The aim of such analysis is to point out the diversities in the components of sources and uses of funds, their pattern of growth, and share of each component to total funds and to identify fluctuations if any. Wherever necessary, such analysis was expressed in percentage.

The analysis of funds flow statement of sample companies is confined to nine years covering 2000 to 2008. After analyzing the funds flow statement, it revealed that funds from operation i.e. reserves plus accumulated depreciation, showed a constantly increasing trend. Contributions from equity share as well as preference share capital were fluctuating through out the period. Funds raised through debt capital i.e. secured and unsecured loans were also fluctuating. But the amount raised through debt was much more than the amount raised through share capital during the period of study. Current liabilities also contributed a lot towards the total funds raised during this period.

With regard to application of funds, investment in gross block (fixed assets before depreciation) indicated a rising trend of growth. Funds invested in all other assets like investments, loans and advances, fixed deposits and current assets showed both increasing and decreasing pattern of growth.

Trend analysis of total inflow of funds revealed a rising trend through out the period of study except for the year 2003 in which the total inflow was ₹ 14458.09 crores, whereas in 2002 the inflow was ₹ 16643.04 crores. Barring to this, the inflow of all the years has shown an increasing trend.

Total funds raised by the sample companies during the study period were again divided into internal sources and external sources. Internal sources of funds included reserves, revaluation reserve, provisions and accumulated depreciation whereas external sources included equity and preference share capital, share application money, secured and unsecured loan, current liabilities and deferred credit.

The annual average of funds raised from internal sources was ₹ 27474.34 crores and that of external sources was ₹ 19275.75 crores. The average of internal sources and external sources to total sources calculated at 60.53 per cent and 39.47 per cent respectively.

The analysis shows that companies prefer more for the internal sources of funds as compared to external. The reason could be that the internal sources of funding have the advantage of being less expensive and taking less time to secure. That's why the internal sources of inflow of funds indicated an increasing growth except for the year 2002. On the other hand, the trend of external sources showed both increasing and decreasing sign.

With regard to uses of funds, it was observed that a major portion was utilized in acquiring fixed assets. The average investment in fixed assets came to ₹ 18872.72 crores every year, which is about 40.37 per cent of the average amount of funds raised every year. Investment in current assets stood next to fixed assets acquisition. The average annual investment in current assets was ₹ 9406.67 crores which consists of 20.12 per cent of the yearly average inflow of funds. The respective share of application of funds in investments, loans and advances, and fixed deposits are 19.19, 13.49 and 6.96 per cent of the total application of funds.

After funds flow statement analysis, we started analyzing some of the key financial ratios as ratio analysis can help us to check whether the business is doing better this year than it was last year. At first the debt-equity ratio is analyzed which was calculated from the total inflow of funds of the sample companies. The main objective of analyzing the debt equity ratio was to ensure a proper balance between the owned funds and borrowed funds. The factors, which determine the level of debt-equity ratio, are the nature of industry, size of investment, gestation period, profitability potential, debt servicing capacity, current capital market condition and other economic situation.

A high debt-equity ratio shows a relatively larger share of financing by the creditors to the owners and therefore a larger claim against the assets. On the other hand a low debt equity ratio implies high stake of owners and a sufficient safety margins.

Debt-equity ratio was calculated to serve the purpose of determining the solvency. It measures the relative claims of outsiders and owners against the assets of the company. Thus debt equity ratio is equal to outsiders' funds divided by shareholders funds. For our study purpose, outsider's funds included all debt and liabilities to outsiders both long term and short term. Shareholders fund included equity shares, preference shares, share application money, reserves and revaluation reserves. The latter is called the net worth.

A ratio of 1:1 is considered to be a satisfactory ratio, although there cannot be any rule of thumb or standard norm. A very low ratio is not considered satisfactory for the shareholders because it indicates that the firm has not been able to use outsider's funds to magnify their earnings.

The debt equity ratio of sample companies indicated a large variance from 0.94 to 1.29. The average ratio of debt to equity for the total period of study was 1.12 which was fairly lower than the generally accepted norm of 2:1 in a developing country like India. This makes it clear that sample companies had followed a conservative policy while deciding the debt-equity mix in the capital structure.

By analyzing the size of investment in fixed and current assets of the sample company, it was observed that the growth in the size of investment was about three-fold in nine years i.e. from 2000 to 2008. Net worth to fixed assets ratio fluctuated in between 0.99 to 1.63 during the period of study, the average being 1.28. It was found that the net worth to fixed assets ratio for all the years under study was more than one (i.e. 100%) only except for the first year i.e. in 2000 in which the ratio was 0.99, which is also very nearer to 100 per cent. A ratio of one or above indicates that the money spent on fixed assets was fully financed from the shareholders funds and companies are not dependent on outsiders' funds to finance the fixed assets. It was also observed that the proposition of net fixed assets in the total assets structure remained almost constant with an average of 0.36. The ratio varied in between 0.29 to 0.43.

e proprietary ratio or ratio of net worth to total assets varied in between 42 per cent to 49 per cent, the average being 45 per cent. Thus out of every rupee invested in the total assets of sample companies, the shareholders contribution was Rs. 0.45. The margin was satisfactory.

The principle and convention of finance suggests that a portion of funds should be invested in current assets so as to ease the firm for short term risks and to ensure liquidity by reducing the burden of current liabilities. Here in case of sample companies, liquidity ratio fluctuated in between 1.24 to 1.76 during the study period. The average ratio for the total period was found to be 1.42. Thus, current assets were more than sufficient to meet current liabilities and the liquidity position was satisfactory. Though the absolute standard was 2:1, in this case the liquidity ratio was in the halfway, indicating a good solvency position, i.e. ability to meet short-term obligations.

The correlation between size of investment and debt-equity ratio was –0.83, indicated a fairly high degree of negative correlation between the two. The relationship between the two implied that though the size of investment had grown, the debt-equity proportion remained insensitive.

The association of fixed assets proportions to total assets with debt equity ratio was found to be +0.94 which implies a high degree of positive correlation between the two. It indicates that there is a direct positive correlation between the debt proportion in the total capital and the investment in fixed assets. The correlation between liquidity ratio and debt equity ratio showed a low degree of positive correlation which is +0.28.

In conclusion, it can only be said that the process of capital structure planning is not a one time job, but needs reviews, revision and monitoring through time, in different situations. Financial executives are to pay adequate attention to the multidimensional implications of the capital structure decision. In order to achieve optimal capital structure, time to time judgments in decision making play a crucial part and influences the capital structure planning process.

REFERENCES

1. Beraneck W., '*Working Capital Management*', (Belment, Wordsworth), 1968, 4th Ed., p. 301.
2. Gangadhar V., Yadagiri M., 'Sources and Application of Funds', *Finance India*, Vol. IX, March 1995, p. 53.
3. Peterson, Pamela (1999) '*Analysis of Financial Statements*' New York: Wiley. p. 92. ISBN 1883249597.
4. Brenan M.J., 'A New Look at the Weighted Average Cost of Capital', *Journal of Business Finance, Spring* 1973, Vol. 21, No. 1, March 1966, p. 73.
5. Sharma R.K., Gupta S.K., Management Accounting, Principles and Practice, Kalyani Publishers, New Delhi, 1996.

8 Variable-wise Analysis of Total Sample Companies

Introduction

In the preceding chapter, we examined the pattern of capital structure of the total sample companies. But, it gives only an aggregate picture of the corporate sector as a whole. Moreover, the pattern of capital structure, sources and utilization of funds of the total sample companies analyzed, which comprises the companies of different industrial activities, sizes, ages and regions. The ability to raise funds and the capital structure (debt equity mix) is, more or less, expected to differ for companies pertaining to different industries, regions, size-group as well as age groups.

The capital structure and funds flow is expected to differ, if the industrial activity differs. Likewise, the size variable may be important if the companies take time to establish themselves and capture the market. New companies find difficulties in raising both debt and equity capital. Therefore, companies of different ages might be expected to have different degrees of capital mix and quantity of funds raised. The study implicitly assumes inter-group differences and inter-group similarities in the trend and pattern of funds flow and capital mix. Thus, if the conclusions drawn on the basis of group-wise analysis held at the group level, they may also be expected to hold at the individual level.

In attempting to study differences in funds flow and capital mix across firms, a variable-wise analysis of funds flow and capital structure of the sample companies has been undertaken. Accordingly, the sample companies were classified on the basis of region, industry or sector, size-group and age-group. The details regarding classification of the sample companies have been dealt within Chapter — 6. In this chapter, an attempt has been made to analyze and interpret the trend and pattern of sources and uses of funds and the capital structure of each group of sample companies vis-à-vis the overall trend and pattern.

The required data is obtained by aggregating the data of sample companies belonging to a particular group. The trend analysis of different sources of funds and their application have been made. The help of ratio analysis is taken between debt-equity, current assets, current liability etc. and their correlation.

Region-wise Variable Analysis

The purpose of this section is to study the funds flow and capital structure of sample companies divided into different regions. The region of a company more or less influences its quantum of inflow of funds both debt and equity. The nature of capital structure and the behaviour of quantum of sources and uses of funds of the companies of each region not only differ from one another, but also they exert different degrees of impact on the over all trend of the total sample. The total sample companies are classified into four regional groups, namely eastern, western, southern and northern companies. The number of companies in eastern region was 34, western region 135, northern region 46 and southern region 85. The funds flow statements of region-wise companies are shown in appendices.

Total Inflow of Funds from Different Sources (Region-wise Analysis)

The total funds inflow from different sources and their application by sample companies divided into above four regions are shown in Table 8A.1.

Table 8A.1 : Analysis of Total Inflow of Funds from Different Sources (Region-wise)

Year	Eastern Region (₹ in Crores) (34 Companies)	Western Region (₹ in Crores) (135 Companies)	Northern Region (₹ in Crores) (46 Companies)	Southern Region (₹ in Crores) (85 Companies)
2001	153.3	7458.16	2110.02	6245.36
2002	457.69	8886.11	2039.02	5260.2
2003	644.15	4288.81	2205.32	7319.81
2004	817.87	16905.81	4474.71	8574.26
2005	1753.65	15869.34	2804.98	13855.52
2006	3757.11	33310.78	8293.41	18776.13
2007	4321.49	41304.38	11467.06	28047.68
2008	2756.82	49620.36	12787.79	47433.7
Total	**14662.08**	**177643.75**	**46182.31**	**135512.66**
Average	**1832.76**	**22205.46**	**5772.78**	**16939.08**

Source: Computed from the database collected from www.moneycontrol.com

Table 8A.2 : Inflow of Funds from Internal Sources (Region-wise Analysis)

(Rs. in Crores)

EASTERN REGION

Internal Sources of Funds	2001	2002	2003	2004	2005	2006	2007	2008
Reserves	14.88	-388.07	3.9	475.81	680.1	1362.48	2281.32	1632.23
Revaluation Reserves	-12.06	-79	-12.71	-14.73	-65.66	-7.37	-9.52	-39.77
Provisions	62.9	-55.86	58.34	77.39	151.85	315.78	364.83	121.99
Accumulated Depreciation	283.03	288.8	262.22	175.94	295.65	309.36	452.14	243.41
Total	**348.75**	**-234.13**	**311.75**	**714.41**	**1061.94**	**1980.25**	**3088.77**	**1957.86**

WESTERN REGION

Internal Sources of Funds	2001	2002	2003	2004	2005	2006	2007	2008
Reserves	2304.78	-531.34	581.09	7495.55	9291.76	15187.13	19882.88	18686.58
Revaluation Reserves	19.64	642.09	-239.74	-16.3	-101.59	33.17	41.31	2661.49
Provisions	436.52	1.03	263.17	1666.23	605.84	1484.9	1344.87	1739.76
Accumulated Depreciation	1791.35	1959.96	2159.58	3001.6	2558.47	3781.91	3953.99	2660.16
Total	**4552.29**	**2071.74**	**2764.1**	**12147.08**	**12354.5**	**20487.11**	**25223.05**	**25747.99**

NORTHERN REGION

Internal Sources of Funds	2001	2002	2003	2004	2005	2006	2007	2008
Reserves	815.35	512.55	898.16	1004.29	465.36	2671.16	2697.23	3929.54
Revaluation Reserves	1.68	-49.29	-11.19	-12.61	69.99	-3.94	801.83	-78.81
Provisions	76.16	201.84	295.83	371.46	-73.72	195.62	594	486.19
Accumulated Depreciation	473.18	526.63	590.14	927.65	323.56	743.7	1294.73	1057.9
Total	**1366.37**	**1191.73**	**1772.94**	**2290.79**	**785.19**	**3606.54**	**5387.79**	**5394.82**

(Contd....)

SOUTHERN REGION

Internal Sources of Funds	2001	2002	2003	2004	2005	2006	2007	2008
Reserves	3480.9	2339.24	2737.43	1784.03	8285.48	8309.55	15018.53	19537.49
Revaluation Reserves	-20.38	-79.88	164.99	926.47	906.82	-134.95	-204.26	241.29
Provisions	11.53	145.99	280.88	1757.02	-388.5	2203.76	-443.39	3794.93
Accumulated Depreciation	992.05	1158.54	1517.56	1423.59	1824.08	2162.73	1146.31	2541.3
Total	**4464.1**	**3563.89**	**4700.86**	**5891.11**	**10627.9**	**12541.09**	**15517.19**	**26115.01**

Source: Computed from the database collected from www.moneycontrol.com

From the analysis of Table 8A.1 it was found that the western region which comprises of 135 companies has raised the highest amount of funds among all the four regions during the period of study. The average amount of funds raised by the sample companies of eastern region was ₹ 1832.76 crores, western region ₹ 22205.46 crores, northern region ₹ 5772.78 crores and southern region ₹ 16939.08 crores. If the study period is divided into two phases, first phase from 2001 to 2004, and the second phase from 2005 to 2008, the analysis shows that the funds raised by the sample companies in second phase is much more as compared to first phase in the case of all regions. The highest amount of funds raised by western, northern and southern region was in 2008 whereas in case of eastern region it was in 2007.

Inflow of Funds from Internal Sources (Region-wise Analysis)

As discussed earlier, internal source comprises of reserves, revaluation reserves, provisions and accumulated depreciation. Table 8A.2 (*See on page 137*) depicts the amount of funds raised by each region from internal sources during the period of study.

Table 8.3 : Analysis of Total and Average Inflow of Internal Funds (Region-wise)

(₹ *in Crores*)

Year	Eastern Region	Western Region	Northern Region	Southern Region
2001	348.75	4552.29	1366.37	4464.1
2002	-234.13	2071.74	1191.73	3563.89
2003	311.75	2764.1	1772.94	4700.86
2004	714.41	12147.08	2290.79	5891.11
2005	1061.94	12354.48	785.19	10627.88
2006	1980.25	20487.11	3606.54	12541.09
2007	3088.77	25223.05	5387.79	15517.19
2008	1957.86	25747.99	5394.82	26115.01
Total	**9229.6**	**105347.84**	**21796.17**	**83421.13**
Average	**1153.7**	**13168.48**	**2724.52**	**10427.64**

Source: Computed from the database collected from www.moneycontrol.com

By analyzing the table 8A.2 and 8A.3, we saw that western region companies has raised highest amount of funds from internal sources. The eastern region companies raised funds internally ₹ 9229.6 crores in total during the study period with an average of ₹ 1153.7 crores yearly. The analysis shows that only from 2006 onwards it started raising funds more than the average. And in 2002 it was a negative figure which indicates that companies might have suffered loss due to certain reasons in that year. In case of western region companies, the total amount of funds raised internally was ₹ 105347.84 crores with an average of ₹ 13168 annually, which is the highest among all the four regions. Similarly, the total internal funds raised by northern and southern companies during the period of study were ₹ 21796.17 crores and 83421.13 crores respectively.

Inflow of Funds from Share Capital (Region-wise Analysis)

Table 8A.4 shows the detailed analysis of funds raised by all the regions through issue of equity and preference share capital. (*See on next page*)

By analyzing table 8A.4 it was observed that in case of eastern region companies, the total funds raised through share capital during the period of study shows a negative figure i.e. ₹ (4.97) crores. It indicates that during the study period, most of the companies of this region either redeemed the preference shares or converted the preference shares into equity as for all the years the funds raised through preference shares shows negative balances. In 2002 and 2007 the equity shares also shows a negative figure implying that the companies might have gone for repurchasing or buying back of their shares. Thus, it can be concluded that during our study period most of the eastern region companies raised their required funds either from internal sources or from debt.

The analysis shows that funds raised by western region companies from share capital are highest among all the regions. In 2007 the amount raised through issue of equity shares was ₹ 537.05 crores, which was the highest among all the regions in any particular year. These companies also raised funds through issue of preference shares in 2001, 2002, 2003, 2005 and in 2006. In the year 2004, 2007 and 2008 the preference shares are either redeemed or converted into equity shares.

The total amount raised by northern region companies through share capital during the period of study was ₹ 1250.44 crores, whereas by southern region companies was ₹ 2521.65 crores. It should be noted that southern region companies have raised ₹ 2344.93 crores through equity shares which was the highest among all the four regions.

Inflow of Funds from Long-term Debts/Loans (Region-wise)

Table 8A.5 shows the detailed analysis of funds raised by sample companies of all the four regions through long-term debts and loans.

Table 8A.4 : Inflow of Funds from Share Capital (Region-wise)

(₹ in Crores)

EASTERN REGION

Funds Flow from Share Capital	2001	2002	2003	2004	2005	2006	2007	2008	TOTAL
Equity Share Capital	47.86	-1.12	0.23	360.55	19.53	52.64	-334.13	98.24	243.8
Preference Share Capital	-17.36	-3.88	-0.01	-34.02	-37.11	-8.38	-177.31	-5.68	-283.75
Share Application Money	159.9	85.54	114.63	-327.23	4.96	12.05	54.02	-68.89	34.98
Total	**190.4**	**80.54**	**114.85**	**-0.7**	**-12.62**	**56.31**	**-457.42**	**23.67**	**-4.97**

WESTERN REGION

Funds Flow from Share Capital	2001	2002	2003	2004	2005	2006	2007	2008	TOTAL
Equity Share Capital	111.81	328.42	2.24	188.38	289.71	347.9	537.05	316	2121.51
Preference Share Capital	86.58	389.53	193.86	-244.69	160.52	169.95	-24.68	-61.29	669.78
Share Application Money	299.2	-13.24	-270.2	108.36	-83.49	160.17	197.98	289.72	688.47
Total	**497.59**	**704.71**	**-74.13**	**52.05**	**366.74**	**678.02**	**710.35**	**544.43**	**3479.76**

NORTHERN REGION

Funds Flow from Share Capital	2001	2002	2003	2004	2005	2006	2007	2008	TOTAL
Equity Share Capital	241.57	122.14	9.83	20.96	31.57	197.21	161.24	192.95	977.47
Preference Share Capital	-0.2	-3.38	-1.68	89.4	-9.58	18.61	-57.51	17.26	52.92
Share Application Money	25.87	-63.81	3.44	4.46	34.69	-1.93	8.96	208.37	220.05
Total	**267.24**	**54.95**	**11.59**	**114.82**	**56.68**	**213.89**	**112.69**	**418.58**	**1250.44**

(Contd. ...)

SOUTHERN REGION

Funds Flow from Share Capital	2001	2002	2003	2004	2005	2006	2007	2008	TOTAL
Equity Share Capital	224.16	-55.73	69.83	149.23	473.47	535.6	449.69	498.68	2344.93
Preference Share Capital	-74.09	-10.07	-5.07	6.99	85.19	11.23	-57.99	98.77	54.96
Share Application Money	-1.33	4.2	24.95	30.19	17.2	-14.68	81.16	-19.93	121.76
Total	**148.74**	**-61.6**	**89.71**	**186.41**	**575.86**	**532.15**	**472.86**	**577.52**	**2521.65**

Inflow of Funds from Share Capital (Region-wise)

Source: Computed from the database collected from www.moneycontrol.com

Table 8A.5 : Inflow of Funds from Long-term Debt/Loan (Region-wise Analysis)

(₹ in Crores)

EASTERN REGION

Funds Flow from Debt/Loan	2001	2002	2003	2004	2005	2006	2007	2008	Total
Secured Loans	-2.28	-205.5	176.37	-2.83	237.55	811.3	1160.68	558.03	2733.34
Unsecured Loans	-338.98	166.59	57.08	-68.32	-61.65	393.9	446.75	-187.3	408.04
Deferred Credit	0	0	0	0	0	0	0	0	0
Total	**-341.26**	**-38.89**	**233.45**	**-71.15**	**175.9**	**1205.2**	**1607.43**	**370.7**	**3141.38**

WESTERN REGION

Funds Flow from Debt/Loan	2001	2002	2003	2004	2005	2006	2007	2008	TOTAL
Secured Loans	1871.19	377.66	42.14	965.06	357.09	287.2	6323.39	6030.6	16254.4
Unsecured Loans	335.73	1423.9	486.84	1347.23	1150.2	6848.9	3022.27	8046.1	22661.1
Deferred Credit	0	0	0	0	0	0	0	0	0
Total	**2206.92**	**1801.5**	**528.98**	**2312.29**	**1507.2**	**7136.1**	**9345.66**	**14077**	**38915.4**

NORTHERN REGION

Funds Flow from Debt/Loan	2001	2002	2003	2004	2005	2006	2007	2008	TOTAL
Secured Loans	303.24	202.53	173.22	607.64	1057.2	763.79	2883.57	2564.3	8555.43
Unsecured Loans	-115.66	-130.1	-105.6	85.69	810.52	2856.6	313.67	671.08	4386.13
Deferred Credit	0	0	0	0	0	0	0	0	0
Total	**187.58**	**72.4**	**67.58**	**693.33**	**1867.7**	**3620.4**	**3197.24**	**3235.4**	**12941.6**

(Contd...)

SOUTHERN REGION

Funds Flow from Debt/Loan	2001	2002	2003	2004	2005	2006	2007	2008	TOTAL
Secured Loans	1125.37	-512.1	1296.9	272.93	-396.1	946.19	2312.72	5487	10532.8
Unsecured Loans	-88.01	140.81	-327	1172.68	1299.1	1775.5	4814.96	8114.5	16902.6
Deferred Credit	0	0	0	0	0	0	0	0	0
Total	**1037.36**	**-371.3**	**969.85**	**1445.61**	**902.97**	**2721.7**	**7127.68**	**13601**	**27435.3**

Source: Computed from the database collected from www.moneycontrol.com

Table 8A.5 shows the total amount of funds raised by companies of different regions through secured loans, unsecured loans and deferred credits. The common observation for the companies of all the four regions was that they have raised more funds through debt capital as compared to equity, may be due to the reason of easy and availability of cheap debt capital. Not a single company of any region has raised any fund through differed credit.

Total funds raised by eastern region companies through secured loans during the period of study were ₹ 2733.34 crores. The years 2001, 2002 and 2004 shows negative figures which indicate the repayment or redemption of the secured loans. Funds raised through unsecured loans by eastern region companies in total stood ₹ 408.04 crores.

Funds raised by western region companies through secured loan as well as unsecured loan stood highest among all the regions. Funds raised through secured loans were ₹ 16254.4 crores whereas funds raised through unsecured loans was ₹ 22661.1 crores. The most important observation in the case of western region companies was that not in a single year either the secured loan or the unsecured loan shows the negative figure, which was common with all other regions. This may be because of western region comprises of more number of companies and it might also be possible that the western region companies were accessible to easy and cheap debt capital.

The amount of funds raised by northern region companies through secured loan was ₹ 8555.43 crores while amount raised through unsecured loan was ₹ 4386.13 crores.

In the case of southern region companies, the amount of funds raised through secured loan was ₹ 10532.8 crores and through unsecured loan was ₹ 16902.6 crores.

Inflow of Funds from Current Liabilities (Region-wise Analysis)

The funds raised from current liabilities by the sample companies of each region are shown in Table 8A.6.

The table indicated an annual average inflow of funds of ₹ 287 crores by the eastern region companies, ₹ 3737.59 crores by the western region, ₹ 1274.26 crores by the northern region and ₹ 2766.81 crores by the southern region companies through current liabilities. In case of eastern region the highest amount raised was in 2005 amounting to ₹ 528.43 crores whereas all other regions were raised highest amounts through current liabilities in 2008. For western region it was ₹ 9251.23 crores, northern region it was ₹ 3739.02 crores and for southern region it was ₹ 7139.71 crores. The total funds raised by eastern, western, northern and southern region companies through current liabilities during the period of study amounted to ₹ 2296.07 crores, ₹ 29900.73 crores, ₹ 10194.14 crores and ₹ 22134.55 crores respectively.

Table 8A.6 : Funds Raised From Current Liabilities (Region-wise Analysis)

(₹ in Crores)

Year	Eastern Region	Western Region	Northern Region	Southern Region
2001	-44.59	201.36	288.83	595.16
2002	650.17	4308.14	719.94	2129.23
2003	-15.9	1069.86	353.21	1559.39
2004	175.31	2394.39	1375.77	1051.13
2005	528.43	1640.88	95.44	1748.81
2006	515.35	5009.55	852.59	2981.17
2007	82.71	6025.32	2769.34	4929.95
2008	404.59	9251.23	3739.02	7139.71
Total	**2296.07**	**29900.73**	**10194.14**	**22134.55**
Average	**287.00**	**3737.59**	**1274.26**	**2766.81**

Source: Computed from the database collected from www.moneycontrol.com

Outflow of Funds for Acquiring Fixed Assets (Region-wise Analysis)

The application of funds in acquiring fixed assets by the sample companies grouped under region-wise is shown in Table 8A.7.

Here the funds utilized for acquiring fixed assets includes the funds invested in gross block as well as in capital work in progress. By analyzing the table 8A.7, we saw that an annual average of ₹ 938.16 crores were invested in acquiring fixed assets by the eastern region companies. The same in case of western region was ₹ 9327.66 crores, northern region ₹ 2768.21 crores and southern region ₹ 5838.67 crores. The highest amount invested by eastern region was ₹ 2123.96 crores in the year 2006, in case of western region it was ₹ 18230.05 crores in 2008, in case of northern region it was ₹ 7366.98 crores in 2007 and in case of southern region it was ₹ 15454.4 crores in 2008.

Table 8.7 : Application of Funds in Fixed Assets by Companies (Region-wise)

(₹ in Crores)

Year	Eastern Region	Western Region	Northern Region	Southern Region
2001	321.38	4263.83	1062.84	2290.61
2002	392.87	5260.26	1098.43	1618.74
2003	88.53	2961.02	969.55	2603.86
2004	384.67	5961.38	2418.27	3622.4
2005	1025	6584.41	2155.27	6211.36
2006	2123.96	14354.35	3943.45	6032.77
2007	1681.49	17006.02	7366.98	8875.28
2008	1487.44	18230.05	3130.89	15454.4
Total	**7505.34**	**74621.32**	**22145.68**	**46709.42**
Average	**938.16**	**9327.66**	**2768.21**	**5838.67**

Source: Computed from the database collected from www.moneycontrol.com

Application of Funds in Additional Current Assets (Region-wise)

The application of funds in acquiring additional current assets by the sample companies of each region are shown in table 8A.8.

Table 8A.8 : Application of Funds in Current Assets by Companies (Region-wise)

(₹ in Crores)

Year	Eastern Region	Western Region	Northern Region	Southern Region
2001	-186.27	1,088.08	397.14	1,132.45
2002	-69.86	1,185.49	709.58	450.52
2003	17.79	1,047.99	-190.50	919.49
2004	196.62	4,373.02	1,634.23	1,804.63
2005	664.43	3,674.21	-14.38	3,089.89
2006	93.78	8,651.99	757.37	6,689.40
2007	718.17	6,102.48	1,412.18	6,820.27
2008	494.69	8,949.32	2,851.56	9,787.60
Total	**1,929.35**	**35,072.58**	**7,557.18**	**30,694.25**
Average	**241.16**	**4384.07**	**944.64**	**3836.78**

Source: Computed from the database collected from www.moneycontrol.com

By analyzing the table 8A.8 it was observed that an annual average of ₹ 241.16 crores were invested additionally every year in current assets by the eastern region companies whereas that in case of western region it was ₹ 4384.07 crores, ₹ 944.64 crores in case of northern region and ₹ 3836.78 crores by the southern region companies. The total amount invested by the companies of eastern, western, northern and southern region in current assets were ₹ 1929.35 crores, 35072.58 crores, ₹ 7557.18 crores and ₹ 30694.25 crores respectively. Western region stood highest in terms of average as well as total amount of investment in current assets during the study period.

Debt – Equity Ratio of Sample Companies (Region-wise)

Table 8A.9 shows the detailed debt-equity ratio analysis of the sample companies of all the four regions.

Table 8A.9 : Analysis of Debt-Equity Ratio of Companies (Region - wise)

Year	Eastern Region	Western Region	Northern Region	Southern Region
2000	1.22	1.38	0.99	1.3
2001	1.09	1.32	0.92	1.11
2002	1.32	1.52	0.95	1.07
2003	1.33	1.57	0.91	1.04
2004	1.23	1.35	1.01	1.02
2005	1.23	1.11	1.13	0.81
2006	1.22	1.02	1.22	0.77
2007	1.16	0.94	1.31	0.78
2008	1.06	0.97	1.37	0.84
Total	**10.86**	**11.18**	**9.81**	**8.74**
Average	**1.21**	**1.24**	**1.09**	**0.97**

Source: Computed from the database collected from www.moneycontrol.com

Here we would like to make it clear that the debt-equity ratios presented in the above table are calculated from the consolidated balance sheets of the respective regions. For our study purpose, debt includes secured loans, unsecured loans, current liabilities and deferred credits, i.e. all types of debts. Similarly equity or net worth consists of equity share capital, preference share capital, share application money, reserves and revaluation reserves. The debt-equity ratio for the above purpose is calculated by dividing debt by equity.

The debt-equity ratio as presented in the table reflected a variance of 1.06 to 1.33 in case of eastern region companies, 0.94 to 1.57 in case of western region companies, 0.92 to 1.37 in case of northern region companies and 0.77 to 1.30 in case of southern region companies. The annual average ratio for the total period was 1.21, 1.24, 1.09 and 0.97 respectively for eastern, western, northern and southern region companies. The average so worked out for all the regions were fairly lower than the generally accepted norm of 2:1.

The ratios revealed that for every rupee worth of equity, the eastern region companies had ₹ 1.21, western region companies had ₹ 1.24, northern region companies had ₹ 1.09 and southern region companies had Rs.0.97 worth of debt in their capital structure.

This made it clear that companies of all the regions had followed a conservative policy while deciding the debt-equity mix in the capital structure. Moreover, the gradual fall in the debt-equity ratio of all the regions indicates that the companies gradually dropped their debt by repaying a major portion of long-term as well as short-term liabilities. Side by side they had also increased their net worth by issue of shares and formation of reserves.

Size of Investment of Sample Companies (Region–wise Analysis)

The size of investment, which includes the sum of net fixed assets i.e. net block and current assets in terms of the rate of growth, is shown in Table 8A.10.

The analysis of the size of investments as presented in Table 8A.10 shows that, in case of eastern region companies the size of investment in first phase i.e. in 2001 to 2005, was comparatively low than the second phase i.e. from 2006 to 2008. Yearly investments in first phase were less than the annual average which was ₹ 8925.76 crores. Only after 2006 onwards, the total investment in fixed as well as current assets became more than the average investment. The annual average of size of investment for the whole period worked out to be ₹ 60983.47 crores for western region companies, ₹ 16470.68 crores for northern region companies and ₹ 38470.31 crores for southern region companies. Western region shows the highest with respect to average as well as total size of investments among all the regions.

Table 8A.10 : Analysis of Size of Investments (Region-wise)

(₹ in Crores)

Year	Eastern Region			Western Region		
	Total Investment	Growth	Growth Rate	Total Investment	Growth	Growth Rate
2000	7366.57	—	—	36086.19	—	—
2001	7202.09	-164.48	-2.23	38,366.73	2,280.54	6.31
2002	7253.63	51.54	0.71	42,491.89	4,125.16	10.75
2003	7503.35	249.72	3.44	45,197.58	2,705.69	6.36
2004	7830.5	327.15	4.36	52,023.89	6,826.31	15.10
2005	8513.9	683.4	8.72	57,754.81	5,730.92	11.01
2006	10082.35	1568.45	18.42	73,603.93	15,849.12	27.44
2007	11778.17	1695.82	16.81	88,837.51	15,233.58	20.69
2008	12801.28	1023.11	8.68	114,488.74	25,651.23	28.87
Total	**80331.84**	**5434.71**	**58.94**	**548,851.27**	**78,402.55**	**126.57**
Average	**8925.76**	**679.33**	**7.36**	**60983.47**	**9800.31**	**15.82**

(Contd....)

(Table 8A.10 Contd.....)

Year	Northern Region			Southern Region		
	Total Investment	Growth	Growth Rate	Total Investment	Growth	Growth Rate
2000	9551.47	—	—	21976.01	—	—
2001	10,457.65	906.18	9.48	24,076.63	2,100.62	9.55
2002	11,888.19	1,430.54	13.67	25,329.54	1,252.91	5.20
2003	12,024.46	136.27	1.14	26,874.01	1,544.47	6.09
2004	14,920.03	2,895.57	24.08	30,515.80	3,641.79	13.55
2005	16,017.37	1,097.34	7.35	36,847.37	6,331.57	20.74
2006	18,635.01	2,617.64	16.34	46,558.89	9,711.52	26.35
2007	24,132.62	5,497.61	29.50	58,229.29	11,670.40	25.06
2008	30,609.35	6,476.73	26.83	75,825.32	17,596.03	30.21
Total	**148,236.15**	**21,057.88**	**128.43**	**346,232.86**	**53,849.31**	**136.80**
Average	**16470.68**	**2632.23**	**16.05**	**38470.31**	**6731.16**	**17.10**

Size of Investment of Sample Companies (Region-wise)

Source: Computed from the database collected from www.moneycontrol.com

Asset Structure of Sample Companies (Region-wise Analysis)

Table 8A.11 : Asset Structure of Sample Companies (Region-wise)
Asset Structure (Ratio of Net Fixed Assets to Total Assets)

Year	Eastern Region	Western Region	Northern Region	Southern Region
2000	0.44	0.44	0.33	0.43
2001	0.45	0.42	0.33	0.39
2002	0.46	0.42	0.34	0.37
2003	0.46	0.43	0.33	0.34
2004	0.45	0.39	0.33	0.32
2005	0.40	0.35	0.34	0.31
2006	0.40	0.32	0.32	0.29
2007	0.37	0.30	0.34	0.26
2008	0.36	0.32	0.33	0.23
Total	**3.84**	**3.44**	**3.05**	**2.97**
Average	**0.41**	**0.38**	**0.33**	**0.33**

Source: Computed from the database collected from www.moneycontrol.com

Table 8A.11 depicts the assets structure of sample companies of each region. The table reflects the ratio of net fixed assets to total assets. The ratios were calculated from the consolidated balance sheets of respective region.

By analyzing Table 8A.11, it was observed that the proportion of net fixed assets to total assets for the eastern region companies varied in between 0.36 to 0.46. In case of western region it was 0.30 to 0.43, northern region 0.32 to 0.34 and in case of southern region it was in between 0.23 to 0.43. The average ratio of eastern, western, northern and southern region companies was 0.41, 0.38, 0.33 and 0.33 respectively.

Current Ratio of Sample Companies (Region-wise Analysis)

The current ratios otherwise known as liquidity ratio of sample companies of different regions are presented in Table 8A.12.

By looking the Table 8A.12 which reflects the liquidity ratio of different regions for the study period, it was observed that it varied from 0.89 to 1.41 with an annual average of 1.07 in case of eastern region companies, 1.23 to 1.77 with an annual average of 1.42 in case of western region companies, 0.96 to 1.87 with an annual average of 1.42 in case of northern region companies and 1.25 to 1.85 with an annual average of 1.48 in case of southern region companies. As the theory suggests that this ratio should be 2:1, this was not seen in case of any region. Rather the ratios are far below the required norm indicating that, the margin of safety to short-term creditors was not good in any region.

Table 8A.12 : Analysis of Current Ratio of Sample Companies (Region-wise)

(Ratio of Current Assets to Current Liabilities)

Year	Eastern Region	Western Region	Northern Region	Southern Region
2000	1.41	1.68	1.87	1.84
2001	1.33	1.77	1.82	1.85
2002	0.94	1.25	1.65	1.38
2003	0.95	1.23	1.45	1.25
2004	0.96	1.32	1.38	1.29
2005	1.01	1.40	1.35	1.36
2006	0.89	1.47	1.29	1.54
2007	1.07	1.38	1.04	1.50
2008	1.08	1.28	0.96	1.46
Total	**9.64**	**12.78**	**12.81**	**13.37**
Average	**1.07**	**1.42**	**1.42**	**1.48**

Source: Computed from the database collected from www.moneycontrol.com

Correlation between Size of Investment and Debt Equity Ratio (Region-wise)

Table 8A.13 shows the coefficient of correlation between size of investment and debt-equity ratio of all the four regions.

A large asset base calls for more long-term funds. A greater proportion of incremental funds are normally sought from debt sources. So the correlation between size of investment and debt-equity ratio is supposed to be positive. If the correlation is negative, it would indicate that equity sources played an important role in the incremental size of investment.

From table 8A.13, it was observed that the correlation between size of investment and debt-equity ratio for eastern, western and southern region were negative. This indicates that the investments are influenced much by equity funds than by the debt funds. But in case of northern region, the coefficient of correlation shows a positive figure which is 0.94371. This kind of high degree positive correlation indicates that a greater proportion of debt funds are used for acquiring fixed as well as current assets.

Table 8A.13 : Correlation between Size of Investment and Debt-Equity Ratio

(Region-wise Analysis)

Year	Eastern Region		Western Region		Northern Region		Southern Region	
	Size of Investment (X)	D/E Ratio (Y)	Size of Investment (X)	D/E Ratio (Y)	Size of Investment (X)	D/E Ratio (Y)	Size of Investment (X)	D/E Ratio (Y)
2000	7366.57	1.22	36086.19	1.38	9551.47	0.99	21976.01	1.3
2001	7202.09	1.09	38366.73	1.32	10457.65	0.92	24076.63	1.11
2002	7253.63	1.32	42491.89	1.52	11888.19	0.95	25329.54	1:07
2003	7503.35	1.33	45197.58	1.57	12024.46	0.91	26874.01	1.04
2004	7830.5	1.23	52023.89	1.35	14920.03	1.01	30515.8	1.02
2005	8513.9	1.23	57754.81	1.11	16017.37	1.13	36847.37	0.81
2006	10082.35	1.22	73603.93	1.02	18635.01	1.22	46558.89	0.77
2007	11778.17	1.16	88837.51	0.94	24132.62	1.31	58229.29	0.78
2008	12801.28	1.06	114488.74	0.97	30609.35	1.37	75825.32	0.84
Coefficient of Correlation	**-0.58349**		**-0.82911**		**0.94371**		**-0.74606**	

Source: Computed from the database collected from www.moneycontrol.com

Correlation between Asset Structure and D/E Ratio (Region-wise)

Table 8A.14 (*See on next page*) shows the coefficient of correlation between the asset structure and debt-equity ratio of all the four regions. It shows the association of fixed assets proportions to total assets proportions to total assets with D/E ratio. Higher the rate of fixed assets to total assets, more will be the requirement for long-term funds, from debt or equity, directly influencing the capital structure. A positive correlation between asset structure and debt-equity ratio indicates that investment in fixed assets were directly influenced by the debt funds. Similarly, a negative correlation indicates that the fixed assets proportion was negatively associated with debt resources i.e. it has a positive dependence on equity funds.

The analysis of table 8.14 shows that eastern, western and southern region companies had high degree of positive correlation between the asset structure and D/E ratio. This indicated that the proportions of fixed assets greatly depended on long term debt funds. In the case of northern region, the coefficient of correlation between the asset structure and debt-equity ratio is -0.01077 which is a very low degree of negative correlation. This indicates that the fixed assets depended negatively on debt funds and positively on equity funds, particularly in case of northern region companies.

Correlation between Liquidity Ratio and D/E Ratio (Region-wise)

The correlation between liquidity ratio and D/E ratio of various regions are shown in table 8A.15. (*See on page 157*)

The liquidity ratio is directly influenced by the proportion of long-term funds invested in current assets. But in the sample study, except for the southern region, all other regions indicated a negative association between the two variables. It implies that the current assets of the companies of those regions were negatively influenced by long-term debts. It might be from short-term sources or from equity sources. The positive correlation shown by southern region indicated that a portion of the long-term debt funds have been invested by the companies of this region in current assets.

Age-wise Variable Analysis

The age of the company, more or less, influences the quantum of inflow of funds of the company concerned. This section studies the impact of age-variable on the overall trend of inflow and outflow of funds. The ability of

Table 8A.14 : Correlation between Asset Structure and Debt-Equity Ratio

(Region-wise Analysis)

Year	Eastern Region		Western Region		Northern Region		Southern Region	
	Asset Structure (X)	D/E Ratio (Y)	Asset Structure (X)	D/E Ratio (Y)	Asset Structure (X)	D/E Ratio (Y)	Asset Structure (X)	D/E Ratio (Y)
2000	0.44	1.22	0.44	1.38	0.33	0.99	0.43	1.3
2001	0.45	1.09	0.42	1.32	0.33	0.92	0.39	1.11
2002	0.46	1.32	0.42	1.52	0.34	0.95	0.37	1.07
2003	0.46	1.33	0.43	1.57	0.33	0.91	0.34	1.04
2004	0.45	1.23	0.39	1.35	0.33	1.01	0.32	1.02
2005	0.4	1.23	0.35	1.11	0.34	1.13	0.31	0.81
2006	0.4	1.22	0.32	1.02	0.32	1.22	0.29	0.77
2007	0.37	1.16	0.3	0.94	0.34	1.31	0.26	0.78
2008	0.36	1.06	0.32	0.97	0.33	1.37	0.23	0.84
Coefficient of Correlation	**0.60498**		**0.94099**		**-0.01077**		**0.90083**	

Source: Computed from the database collected from www.moneycontrol.com

Table 8A.15: Correlation between Liquidity Ratio and Debt-Equity Ratio

(Region-wise Analysis)

Year	Eastern Region		Western Region		Northern Region		Southern Region	
	Liquidity Ratio (X)	D/E Ratio (Y)	Liquidity Ratio (X)	D/E Ratio (Y)	Liquidity Ratio (X)	D/E Ratio (Y)	Liquidity Ratio (X)	D/E Ratio (Y)
2000	1.41	1.22	1.68	1.38	1.87	0.99	1.84	1.3
2001	1.33	1.09	1.77	1.32	1.82	0.92	1.85	1.11
2002	0.94	1.32	1.25	1.52	1.65	0.95	1.38	1.11
2003	0.95	1.33	1.23	1.57	1.45	0.91	1.25	1.04
2004	0.93	1.23	1.32	1.35	1.38	1.01	1.29	1.02
2005	1.01	1.23	1.4	1.11	1.35	1.13	1.36	0.81
2006	0.89	1.22	1.47	1.02	1.29	1.22	1.54	0.77
2007	1.07	1.16	1.38	0.94	1.04	1.31	1.5	0.78
2008	1.08	1.06	1.28	0.97	0.96	1.37	1.46	0.84
Coefficient of Correlation	**–0.47685**		**–0.0428**		**–0.86381**		**0.42113**	

Source: Computed from the database collected from www.moneycontrol.com

a company to generate internal funds and attract funds from outside is mostly influenced by age of the company. Hence in this chapter variable-wise analysis of funds flow and capital structure were done by aggregating the funds flow statements and balance sheets of companies belonging to specified variable. So this section studies the impact of age variable on the overall trends of inflow of funds and their investment. Further, an attempt has been made to study the capital structure and its components for companies grouped under different ages, viz., very old, old, and new companies.

The companies registered before independence i.e. 1947 were grouped under the category 'very old' companies. There were 44 companies in this group. Companies registered after 1947 but before 1980 were grouped under the head 'old' companies. There were 95 companies under this head. Companies came into existence after 1980 were grouped under the head 'new' and there were 161 companies under this category.

Total Inflow of Funds from Different Sources (Age-wise Analysis)

Table 8B.1 (*See on next page*) shows the yearly details of total funds generated by the sample companies, categorized as per the age variable. On analyzing the table, it was observed that in case of very old companies, the average inflow of funds was ₹ 8297.97 crores. The total yearly amounts varied from the lowest ₹ 2508.52 crores in 2003 to the highest ₹ 17908.89 crores in 2008.

In case of old companies, the flow of funds varied in between ₹ 2274.77 crores in 2001 to ₹ 36996.29 crores in 2008, the annual average being ₹ 14040.57 crores. There was a constant increase in the total inflow of funds by the old companies.

In case of new companies, the lowest amount of inflow was ₹ 6294.78 crores in 2003 and the highest was ₹ 57693.49 crores in 2008, the annual average being ₹ 24411.55, which is highest among all the three groups. In case of new companies, the upward trend started from 2004 onwards and continued till end. In 2004 the rate of growth was 169.71 per cent, the highest in any particular year for all the three categories.

Inflow of Funds from Internal Sources (Age-wise Analysis)

Table 8B.2 (*See on next 160*) shows the total amount of funds raised by all the three categories from internal sources.

Table 8B.1 : Analysis of Total Inflow of Funds from Different Sources by Sample Companies (Age-wise)

(₹ in Crores)

Year	Very Old Companies (44)			Old Companies (95)			New Companies (161)		
	Total Inflow of Funds	Growth	Rate of Growth	Total Inflow of Funds	Growth	Rate of Growth	Total Inflow of Funds	Growth	Rate of Growth
2001	3189.89			2274.77			10502.18		
2002	2807.34	–382.55	–11.99	2970.38	695.61	30.57	10865.3	363.12	3.45
2003	2508.52	–298.82	–10.64	5654.79	2684.41	90.37	6294.78	–4570.52	–42.06
2004	6399.77	3891.25	155.12	7395.01	1740.22	30.77	16977.87	10683.09	169.71
2005	4810.73	–1539.04	–24.82	11696.89	4301.88	58.17	17775.87	798	4.70
2006	12674.46	7863.73	163.46	19295.43	7598.54	64.96	32167.54	14391.67	80.96
2007	16084.21	3409.75	26.90	26041	6745.57	34.95	43015.4	10847.86	33.72
2008	17908.89	1824.68	11.34	36996.29	10955.29	42.06	57693.49	14678.09	34.12
Total	66383.81			112324.6			195292.4		
Average	**8297.97**			**14040.57**			**24411.55**		

Source: Computed from the database collected from www.moneycontrol.com

Table 8B.2 : Inflow of Funds from Internal Sources (Age-wise Analysis)

(₹ in Crores)

VERY OLD COMPANIES

Internal Sources of Funds	2001	2002	2003	2004	2005	2006	2007	2008	Total	Average
Reserves	1739.47	-67.28	1497.92	1541	2960.06	7010.1	8313.38	8069.18	31063.8	3882.97
Revaluation Reserves	-39.34	-201.36	-14.28	950.72	15.04	-7.04	-11.1	-177.89	514.75	64.34
Provisions	38.1	65.46	-59.17	1309.2	165	1001.8	657.65	1163.77	4341.78	542.72
Accumulated Depreciation	876.7	810.39	1035.92	999.96	829.73	1609.9	320.59	343	6826.23	853.27
Total	**2614.93**	**607.21**	**2460.39**	**4800.9**	**3969.83**	**9614.7**	**9280.52**	**9398.06**	**42746.6**	**5343.3**

OLD COMPANIES

Internal Sources of Funds	2001	2002	2003	2004	2005	2006	2007	2008	Total	Average
Reserves	694.83	-1261.4	1471.31	2668.2	5516.62	6530.9	12511.8	20257.6	48389.8	6048.72
Revaluation Reserves	-98.09	-77.56	128.35	-38.17	865.39	-100.64	-139.35	478.93	1018.86	127.35
Provisions	186.56	117.7	535.61	459.14	213.44	1272.4	592.63	1491.89	4869.34	608.66
Accumulated Depreciation	816.74	1358.98	1427.77	1357.1	1851.29	2547.3	2746.71	2396.11	14502	1812.74
Total	**1600.04**	**137.68**	**3563.04**	**4446.2**	**8446.74**	**10250**	**15711.7**	**24624.5**	**68779.9**	**8597.47**

(Contd....)

NEW COMPANIES

Internal Sources of Funds	2001	2002	2003	2004	2005	2006	2007	2008	Total	Average
Reserves	4181.61	3261.1	1251.35	6550.5	10246	13989	19054.8	15459.1	73993.8	9249.22
Revaluation Reserves	126.31	712.84	–212.72	–29.72	–70.37	-5.41	779.81	2483.16	3783.4	472.92
Provisions	362.45	109.84	421.78	2103.7	–82.97	1925.9	610.03	3487.21	8938.02	1117.25
Accumulated Depreciation	1846.17	1764.56	2065.81	3171.7	2320.74	2840.5	3779.87	3763.66	21553	2694.13
Total	**6516.54**	**5848.34**	**3526.22**	**11796**	**12412.9**	**18750**	**24224.5**	**25193.1**	**108268**	**13533.52**

Source: Computed from the database collected from www.moneycontrol.com

On analyzing the table 8B.2, it was observed that in case of very old companies the flow of funds from internal sources was ₹ 5343.3 crores on an average during the period. The total amount raised from internal sources during the period was ₹ 42746.6 crores. In case of old companies, the total internal funds generated during the period was ₹ 68779.9 crores with an annual average of ₹ 8597.47 crores. Similarly, with respect to new companies, the total funds raised internally amounted to ₹ 108268 crores with an annual average of ₹ 13533.52 crores. In all the three categories, amount generated from reserves which consists of retained earnings, was highest among the internal sources of funds. Funds generated from accumulated depreciation remained the second biggest source of internal funds in all the cases.

Inflow of Funds from Share Capital (Age-wise Analysis)

The funds raised by different age group companies from issue of shares are shown in Table 8B.3. It is observed from the table that, an average of ₹ 135.96 crores were raised by the very old companies by issue of equity shares, preference shares as well as through share application money. In case of old companies, the average amount raised was ₹ 253.14 crores and that of for new companies it was ₹ 516.73 crores.

The analysis shows that very old companies were redeemed the preference shares on an average of ₹ 7.87 crores per year. In total they have redeemed preference shares worth of ₹ 62.96 crores during the period of study. In case of old and new companies, the frequency of issue of preference shares was more as compared to redemption.

Inflow of Funds from Long-term Debts/Loans (Age-wise Analysis)

Funds raised from long-term debts or loans by the age-wise grouped companies are shown in Table 8B.4. (*See on page 165*)

It was observed from the table 8.4 that, on an average every year the very old companies generated ₹ 1350.9 crores of funds through long-term debts and loans. In case of old companies, this yearly average is ₹ 2802.62 crores whereas in case of new companies the average is ₹ 6150.67 crores, being the highest among three groups. During the whole period, the total funds generated by very old companies through secured loans amounted to ₹ 2499.64 crores and through unsecured loans was ₹ 8307.64 crores. For all the categories, funds generated through deferred credit were nil.

Table 8.3 : Inflow of Funds from Share Capital (Age-wise Analysis)

(₹ in Crores)

VERY OLD COMPANIES (44)

Funds Flow from Share Capital	2001	2002	2003	2004	2005	2006	2007	2008	Total	Average
Equity Share Capital	62.49	36.55	78.45	52.19	116.2	320.51	374.96	47.74	1089.09	136.13
Preference Share Capital	-11.84	6.9	5.59	-49.21	69.17	13.61	-61.72	-35.46	-62.96	-7.87
Share Application Money	-20.54	213.3	-207.74	67.65	-55.45	17.87	5.73	40.82	61.64	7.70
Total	**30.11**	**256.75**	**-123.7**	**70.63**	**129.92**	**351.99**	**318.97**	**53.1**	**1087.77**	**135.96**

OLD COMPANIES (95)

Funds Flow from Share Capital	2001	2002	2003	2004	2005	2006	2007	2008	Total	Average
Equity Share Capital	44.61	163.91	71.11	429.85	96.64	147.82	-179.81	303.23	1077.36	134.67
Preference Share Capital	-53.59	433.41	-32.31	-124.47	167.81	116.18	-223.08	13.42	297.37	37.17
Share Application Money	455.14	-209.64	115.14	-301.27	26.11	227.79	167.27	169.86	650.4	81.3
Total	**446.16**	**387.68**	**153.94**	**4.11**	**290.56**	**491.79**	**-235.62**	**486.51**	**2025.13**	**253.14**

(Contd....)

NEW COMPANIES (161)

Funds Flow from Share Capital	2001	2002	2003	2004	2005	2006	2007	2008	Total	Average
Equity Share Capital	518.3	193.25	-67.43	237.08	601.44	665.02	618.7	754.9	3521.26	440.15
Preference Share Capital	60.36	-68.11	213.82	-8.64	-37.96	61.62	-32.69	71.1	259.5	32.43
Share Application Money	49.04	9.03	-34.61	49.4	2.7	-90.05	169.12	198.59	353.22	44.15
Total	**627.7**	**134.17**	**111.78**	**277.84**	**566.18**	**636.59**	**755.13**	**1024.59**	**4133.98**	**516.73**

Source: Computed from the database collected from www.moneycontrol.com

Table 8B.4 Inflow of Funds from Long-term Debts/Loans (Age-wise Analysis)

(₹ in Crores)

VERY OLD COMPANIES (44)

Funds Flow from Long-term Debt/Loan	2001	2002	2003	2004	2005	2006	2007	2008	Total	Average
Secured Loans	534.89	-275.83	-228.31	127.3	-275.42	-739.32	2795.96	560.37	2499.64	312.45
Unsecured Loans	-22.38	-68.48	-258.72	989.52	364.58	1359.7	304.66	5638.73	8307.64	1038.45
Deferred Credit	0.00	0.00	0.00	0.00	0.00	0.00	0.00	0.00	0.00	0
Total	**512.51**	**-344.31**	**-487.03**	**1116.8**	**89.16**	**620.41**	**3100.62**	**6199.1**	**10807.3**	**1350.9**

OLD COMPANIES (95)

Funds Flow from Long-term Debt/Loan	2001	2002	2003	2004	2005	2006	2007	2008	Total	Average
Secured Loans	648.17	-271.23	1196.85	480.78	-119.37	1072	5038.59	4138.46	12184.2	1523.03
Unsecured Loans	-527.39	-151.47	-398.29	1240	1764.68	4836.5	2001.87	1470.8	10236.7	1279.59
Deferred Credit	0.00	0.00	0.00	0.00	0.00	0.00	0.00	0.00	0.00	0
Total	**120.78**	**-422.7**	**798.56**	**1720.8**	**1645.31**	**5908.5**	**7040.46**	**5609.26**	**22421**	**2802.62**

NEW COMPANIES (161)

Funds Flow from Long-term Debt/Loan	2001	2002	2003	2004	2005	2006	2007	2008	Total	Average
Secured Loans	2114.46	409.64	720.08	1234.7	1650.44	2475.8	4845.81	9941.06	23392	2924.00
Unsecured Loans	342.85	1821.08	768.25	307.74	1068.87	5678.7	6291.12	9534.82	25813.4	3226.67
Deferred Credit	0.00	0.00	0.00	0.00	0.00	0.00	0.0	0.00	0.0	0
Total	**2457.31**	**2230.72**	**1488.33**	**1542.5**	**2719.31**	**8154.5**	**11136.9**	**19475.9**	**49205.5**	**6150.67**

Source: Computed from the database collected from www.moneycontrol.com

Similarly, old companies generated ₹ 12184.2 crores of funds through secured loans and ₹ 10236.7 crores through unsecured loans. In case of new companies, funds generated through secured loans were ₹ 23392 crores and through unsecured loans were ₹ 25813.4 crores, both being the highest among the three groups.

Inflow of Funds from Current Liabilities (Age-wise Analysis)

Funds raised through current liabilities by the age grouped companies during the study period were shown in Table 8B.5. On analyzing the table, it was marked that the average inflow of funds from this source by the very old companies were ₹ 1467.77 crores, old companies were ₹ 2387.32 crores and new companies were ₹ 4210.59 crores.

Table 8B.5 : Inflow of Funds Raised from Current Liabilities (Age-wise Analysis)

(₹ in Crores)

Year	Very Old Companies (44)	Old Companies (95)	New Companies (161)
2001	32.34	107.79	900.63
2002	2287.69	2867.72	2652.07
2003	658.86	1139.25	1168.45
2004	411.4	1223.86	3361.34
2005	621.82	1314.28	2077.46
2006	2087.36	2645.26	4626.04
2007	3384.1	3524.42	6898.8
2008	2258.63	6275.98	11999.94
Total	**11742.2**	**19098.56**	**33684.73**
Average	**1467.77**	**2387.32**	**4210.59**

Source: Computed from the database collected from www.moneycontrol.com

The amount raised through current liabilities by very old companies varied from ₹ 32.34 crores in 2001 to ₹ 3384.1 crores in 2007. In case of old companies it varied in between ₹ 107.79 crores in 2001 to 6275.98 crores in 2008 and in case of new companies it was ₹ 900.63 crores in 2001 and ₹ 11999.94 crores in 2008.

Outflow of Funds for Acquiring Fixed Assets (Age-wise Analysis)

The application of funds in fixed assets by the age-group companies during the period is shown in Table 8B.6 (*See on next page*). On analyzing the table, it was observed that an average of ₹ 3030.15 crores were invested in acquiring additional fixed assets by the very old companies. The same in case of old companies were ₹ 5234.29 crores and in case of new companies, it recorded ₹ 10608.26 crores.

In case of very old companies, the highest investment in fixed assets was recorded in 2007 which came to ₹ 6518.52 crores and the lowest investment recorded in 2002, which was ₹ 673.71 crores. In case of old companies, the highest investment was ₹ 10303.65 crores in 2008 and the lowest was ₹ 1612.89 crores. Similarly, in case of new companies, the highest investment was recorded in the year 2008 amounting to ₹ 25075.81 crores whereas the lowest was ₹ 3169.02 crores in 2003.

Application of Additional Funds in Current Assets (Age-wise)

Outflow of funds in acquiring current assets by the age group companies is shown in Table 8B.7 (*See on page 169*).

On analysis, it was observed that the average investment in additional current assets in case of very old companies were ₹ 1842.45 crores whereas in case of old companies the average was ₹ 2380.25 crores and in case of new companies the average was ₹ 5183.95 crores, being the highest in the group.

In case of very old companies a highest investment was recorded in 2008 which was ₹ 5055.49 crores and a negative investment (inflow by sale of such assets) was there in the year 2003 which reflected ₹ 120.39 crores. In case of old companies, highest investment was in 2008 amounted to ₹ 5585.21 crores and a negative investment to the tune of ₹ 250.92 crores in 2001. With regard to new companies, the highest was in 2008, which amounted to ₹ 11442.47 crores and the lowest investment in current assets was ₹ 1415.19 in 2002.

Debt-Equity Ratio Analysis of Sample Companies (Age-wise)

The Debt-Equity ratios of age grouped companies of the entire study period are presented in Table 8B.8. On analyzing the table it was observed that an average of 1.04 ratio of debt to equity was there in case of very old companies. That in case of old companies was 1.13 and for new companies it was around 1.00. All the averages were below the accepted norm 2:1. In case of very old companies, the ratio varied in between 0.84 to 1.44. The average 1.04 reveals that for every rupee worth of equity, the companies had used 1.04 worth of debt in their capital structure. In

Table 8B.6 : Application of Funds in Fixed Assets (Age-wise Analysis)

(₹ in Crores)

VERY OLD COMPANIES (44)

Funds used for Fixed Assets	2001	2002	2003	2004	2005	2006	2007	2008	Total	Average
Gross Block	1,040.01	1,190.03	1,476.14	2,811.47	1,714.99	4,219.48	5,630.07	2,311.41	20,393.60	2549.2
Capital Work in Progress	313.75	–516.32	–59.90	193.37	862.76	1,553.62	888.45	611.91	3,847.64	480.95
Total	**1,353.76**	**673.71**	**1,416.24**	**3,004.84**	**2,577.75**	**5,773.10**	**6,518.52**	**2,923.32**	**24241.24**	**3030.15**

OLD COMPANIES (95)

Funds used for Fixed Assets	2001	2002	2003	2004	2005	2006	2007	2008	Total	Average
Gross Block	1,206.41	2,552.92	1,742.28	1,911.39	5,185.81	8,070.73	6,300.33	9,376.56	36,346.43	4543.30
Capital Work in Progress	406.48	–663.36	295.42	759.95	1,875.07	-1,022.83	2,950.11	927.09	5,527.93	690.99
Total	**1,612.89**	**1,889.56**	**2,037.70**	**2,671.34**	**7,060.88**	**7,047.90**	**9,250.44**	**10,303.65**	**41874.36**	**5234.29**

NEW COMPANIES (161)

Funds used for Fixed Assets	2001	2002	2003	2004	2005	2006	2007	2008	Total	Average
Gross Block	3,984.65	4,775.40	4,152.46	6,488.24	4,530.04	8,261.68	13,961.08	23,478.73	69,632.28	8704.03
Capital Work in Progress	987.36	1,031.63	–983.44	222.30	1,807.37	5,371.85	5,199.73	1,597.08	15,233.88	1904.23
Total	**4,972.01**	**5,807.03**	**3,169.02**	**6,710.54**	**6,337.41**	**13,633.53**	**19,160.81**	**25,075.81**	**84866.16**	**10608.26**

Source: Computed from the database collected from www.moneycontrol.com

case of old companies the ratio varied in between 0.92 to 1.39 and for new companies it was 0.89 to 1.21.

Table 8B.7 : Analysis of Funds utilized in Current Assets (Age-wise)

(₹ in Crores)

Year	Very Old Companies (44)	Old Companies (95)	New Companies (161)
2001	391.20	–250.92	2,291.12
2002	291.07	569.47	1,415.19
2003	–120.39	144.61	1,770.55
2004	1,481.32	2,038.87	4,488.31
2005	1,154.39	2,555.35	3,704.41
2006	3,211.45	4,001.17	8,979.92
2007	3,275.14	4,398.26	7,379.70
2008	5,055.49	5,585.21	11,442.47
Total	**14,739.67**	**19,042.02**	**41,471.67**
Average	**1842.45**	**2380.25**	**5183.95**

Source: Computed from the database collected from www.moneycontrol.com

In all the three categories, the average ratios are more or less equal and were fairly below the standard norm of 2:1. This indicated that the companies followed conservative policy in raising debts, which shows a satisfactory long-term solvency position. A low debt-to-equity ratio, which indicates conservative financing and low risk, results in fewer possibilities of large losses or large gains in earnings.

In general, a high debt-to-equity ratio indicates that a company may not be able to generate enough cash to satisfy its debt obligations. However, low debt-to-equity ratios may also indicate that a company is not taking advantage of the increased profits that financial leverage may bring.

Capital-intensive industries tend to have higher debt-to-equity ratios than low-capital industries because capital-intensive industries must purchase more property, plants, and equipment to operate. This is why comparison of debt-to-equity ratios is generally most meaningful among companies within the same industry, and the definition of a 'high' or 'low' ratio should be made within this context.

Size of Investment of Sample Companies (Age-wise Analysis)

The size of investment of age-wise grouped companies is shown in table 8B.9 (*See on page 171*). This indicates the growth of net fixed assets and current assets.

Table 8B.8 : Debt-Equity Ratio of Sample Companies (Age-wise)

(₹ in Crores)

Very Old Companies	2000	2001	2002	2003	2004	2005	2006	2007	2008	Total
Secured Loans	8943.35	9478.24	9202.41	8974.1	9101.4	8825.98	8086.66	10882.62	11442.99	84937.75
Unsecured Loans	2473.01	2450.63	2382.15	2123.43	3112.95	3477.53	4837.26	5141.92	10780.65	36779.53
Current Liabilities	4815.93	4848.27	7135.96	7794.82	8206.22	8828.04	10915.4	14299.5	16558.13	83402.27
TOTAL DEBT	16232.29	16777.1	18720.52	18892.35	20420.57	21131.55	23839.32	30324.04	38781.77	205119.55
NET WORTH or EQUITY	11265.25	12995.5	12983.61	14343.55	16905.93	20010.94	27365.95	35987.2	43931.57	195789.49
Debt-Equity Ratio (Debt/Equity)	1.44	1.29	1.44	1.31	1.20	1.05	0.87	0.84	0.88	1.04
Old Companies	**2000**	**2001**	**2002**	**2003**	**2004**	**2005**	**2006**	**2007**	**2008**	**Total**
Secured Loans	11765.49	12413.7	12142.43	13339.28	13820.06	13700.69	14772.68	19811.27	23949.73	135715.29
Unsecured Loans	3799.25	3271.86	3120.39	2722.1	3962.12	5726.8	10563.3	12565.17	14035.97	59766.96
Current Liabilities	7201.15	7308.94	10176.66	11315.91	12539.77	13854.05	16499.31	20023.73	26299.71	125219.23
TOTAL DEBT	22765.89	22994.5	25439.48	27377.29	30321.95	33281.54	41835.29	52400.17	64285.41	320701.48
NET WORTH or EQUITY	18165.78	19208.7	18257.36	20010.95	22645.05	29317.63	36239.68	48376.47	69599.52	281821.12
Debt-Equity Ratio (Debt/Equity)	1.25	1.19	1.39	1.36	1.33	1.13	1.15	1.08	0.92	1.13
New Companies	**2000**	**2001**	**2002**	**2003**	**2004**	**2005**	**2006**	**2007**	**2008**	**Total**
Secured Loans	10378.75	12493.2	12902.85	13622.93	14857.65	16508.09	18983.9	23829.71	33770.77	157347.86
Unsecured Loans	3734.01	4076.86	5897.94	6666.19	6973.93	8042.8	13721.5	20012.62	29547.44	98673.29
Current Liabilities	5024.57	5925.2	8577.27	9745.72	13107.06	15184.52	19810.56	26709.36	38709.3	142793.56
TOTAL DEBT	19137.33	22495.3	27378.06	30034.84	34938.64	39735.41	52515.96	70551.69	102027.51	398814.71
NET WORTH or EQUITY	15761.99	20697.6	24805.7	25956.12	32754.75	43496.07	58116.6	78706.37	97673.18	397968.38
Debt-Equity Ratio (Debt/Equity)	1.21	1.08	1.10	1.15	1.06	0.91	0.90	0.89	1.04	1.00

Source: Computed from the database collected from www.moneycontrol.com

Table 8B.9 : Size of Investment (Net Fixed Assets + Current Assets)
Age-wise analysis of Sample Companies

(₹ in Crores)

Very Old Companies	2000	2001	2002	2003	2004	2005	2006	2007	2008
Net Block	12283.44	12447	12826.39	13266.6	15078.1	15963.38	18572.92	23882.4	25850.81
Current Assets	7977.14	8368.3	8659.41	8539.02	10020.3	11174.73	14386.18	17661.32	22716.81
Total	**20260.58**	**20815**	**21485.8**	**21805.6**	**25098.5**	**27138.11**	**32959.1**	**41543.72**	**48567.62**
Growth		554.51	670.71	319.83	3292.83	2039.65	5820.99	8584.62	7023.9
Growth Per cent		2.74	3.22	1.49	15.11	8.13	21.45	26.05	16.91
Average Growth Rate					11.88%				
Old Companies	2000	2001	2002	2003	2004	2005	2006	2007	2008
Net Block	17691.94	18082	19275.55	19590.1	20144.4	23478.87	29002.35	32555.97	39536.42
Current Assets	12010.03	11759	12328.58	12473.2	14512.1	17067.41	21068.58	25466.84	31052.05
Total	**29701.97**	**29841**	**31604.13**	**32063.3**	**34656.4**	**40546.28**	**50070.93**	**58022.81**	**70588.47**
Growth		138.75	1763.41	459.12	2593.16	5889.87	9524.65	7951.88	12565.66
Growth Per cent		0.47	5.91	1.45	8.09	17.00	23.50	15.88	21.66
Average Growth Rate					11.74%				
New Companies	2000	2001	2002	2003	2004	2005	2006	2007	2008
Net Block	15544.23	17683	20693.55	22780.2	26096.7	28306.02	33727.19	43908.4	63623.47
Current Assets	9473.46	11765	13179.77	14950.3	19438.6	23143.04	32122.96	39502.66	50945.13
Total	**25017.69**	**29447**	**33873.32**	**37730.5**	**45535.4**	**51449.06**	**65850.15**	**83411.06**	**114568.6**
Growth		4429.6	4426.03	3857.2	7804.83	5913.71	14401.09	17560.91	31157.54
Growth Per cent		17.71	15.03	11.39	20.69	12.99	28.00	26.67	37.35
Average Growth Rate					21.22%				

Source: Computed from the database collected from www.moneycontrol.com

Table 8B.9 indicates that there has been a growth in the size of investment in net fixed assets as well as current assets during the period of study. In case of very old and old companies, the growth rate was more than two times whereas in case of new companies, the growth rate was more than four times. An average growth rate of 11.88 per cent was marked every year in case of very old companies. The same was 11.74 per cent in case of the old companies and 21.22 per cent in case of new companies. Hence a high growth rate in the sum of net fixed assets and current assets were marked in case of new companies.

Analysis of Asset Structure of Sample Companies (Age-wise)

The asset structure of different age group companies is shown in Table 8.10. This table reflects the ratio of net fixed assets to total assets of the companies.

Table 8B.10 : Asset Structure of Companies (Age-wise Analysis)
Net Fixed Assets to Total Assets of Companies (Age-wise Analysis)

Year	Very Old Companies (44)	Old Companies (95)	New Companies (161)
2000	0.43	0.42	0.43
2001	0.4	0.41	0.39
2002	0.39	0.42	0.38
2003	0.38	0.39	0.39
2004	0.37	0.36	0.36
2005	0.36	0.36	0.32
2006	0.33	0.35	0.29
2007	0.33	0.3	0.28
2008	0.29	0.28	0.3
Total	**3.28**	**3.29**	**3.14**
Average	**0.36**	**0.36**	**0.35**

Source: Computed from the database collected from www.moneycontrol.com

It was observed from the table that an average of 36 per cent net fixed assets were there in the total assets in case of both very old and old companies, while that in case of new companies it was 35 per cent. It reflects that companies of all the age groups invested more or less equal proportion of total funds in net fixed assets.

Current Ratio of Sample Companies (Age-wise Analysis)

Table 8B.11 shows the current ratio, otherwise known as liquidity ratio of age grouped companies, for the period of study.

Table 8B.11 : Liquidity Ratio of Companies (Age-wise Analysis)
Ratio of Current Assets to Current Liabilities (Age-wise Analysis)

Year	Very Old Companies (44)	Old Companies (95)	New Companies (161)
2000	1.65	1.66	1.88
2001	1.72	1.6	1.98
2002	1.21	1.21	1.53
2003	1.09	1.1	1.53
2004	1.22	1.15	1.48
2005	1.26	1.23	1.52
2006	1.31	1.27	1.62
2007	1.23	1.27	1.47
2008	1.37	1.18	1.31
Total	**12.06**	**11.67**	**14.32**
Average	**1.34**	**1.30**	**1.60**

Source: Computed from the database collected from www.moneycontrol.com

The liquidity ratio as depicted in table 8B.11 indicates the proportion of current assets to current liabilities. It reflects the short-term solvency of the company, i.e. ability to meet short-term obligations. It measures the current assets to meet current liability. The absolute standard of this ratio is 2:1.

From the table it is observed that an average of ₹ 1.34 worth of current assets were there for covering every rupee of current liability obligations in case of very old companies. In case of old companies, the average ratio was 1.30 and in case of new companies it was 1.60. Thus, in all the three categories, the ratio was below the standard norm of 2:1, but in case of new companies the average was better as compared to the others.

Correlation between Size of Investment and D/E Ratio (Age-wise)

The correlation between size of investment and D/E ratio of sample companies grouped according to age is shown in Table 8.12.

Table 8B.12 : Correlation between Size of Investment and Debt–Equity Ratio (Age-size Analysis)

Year	Very Old Companies		Old Companies		New Companies	
	Size of Investment (X)	D/E Ratio (Y)	Size of Investment (X)	D/E Ratio (Y)	Size of Investment (X)	D/E Ratio (Y)
2000	20260.58	1.44	29701.97	1.25	25017.69	1.21
2001	20815.09	1.29	29840.72	1.19	29447.29	1.08
2002	21485.8	1.44	31604.13	1.39	33873.32	1.1
2003	21805.63	1.31	32063.25	1.36	37730.52	1.15
2004	25098.46	1.2	34656.41	1.33	45535.35	1.06
2005	27138.11	1.05	40546.28	1.13	51449.06	0.91
2006	32959.1	0.87	50070.93	1.15	65850.15	0.9
2007	41543.72	0.84	58022.81	1.08	83411.06	0.89
2008	48567.62	0.88	70588.47	0.92	114568.6	1.04
Coefficient of Correlation	**–0.87527**		**–0.86772**		**–0.55028**	

Source: Computed from the database collected from www.moneycontrol.com

From the table it is observed that the co-efficient of correlation between the size of investment and debt-equity ratio in all the categories are negative. In case of very old companies it was -0.87527 and in case of old companies it was -0.86772. This indicates a very high degree of negative correlation between the two variables which reveals that the larger asset base called not much from the debt but from the equity. A greater proportion of such incremental assets were sought from funds raised from equity sources rather than from debt. In case of new companies, the correlation was calculated at -0.55028. This indicated a moderate degree of negative correlation between assets base and D/E ratio. This implies that the growths in the size of investment were influenced moderately on the equity source than on the debt source.

Correlation between Asset Structure and D/E Ratio (Age-wise)

The correlation between asset structure and D/E ratio of sample companies grouped under age category is shown in Table 8B.13 (*See on next page*). In all the three groups, the degree of correlation is high as well as positive. This indicates that in case of all the companies, the asset structure was influenced greatly by the long term funds raised through debts and loans rather than the equity capital. Higher the proportion of fixed assets to total assets, the more was the requirement from long-term funds.

Correlation between Liquidity Ratio and D/E Ratio (Age-wise)

The correlation between liquidity ratio and D/E ratio of companies under different age group is shown in Table 8B.14 (*See on page 177*).

On analyzing the table, it was observed that in case of very old companies, the correlation was +0.24852. This indicated a low degree of positive correlation between current assets to current liability ratio with debt-equity ratio. It proves that the current assets to current liability position was positively influenced by long-term funds, but not that much.

In case of old companies the coefficient of correlation is calculated at– 0.04209. This indicated a low degree of negative correlation between current ratio to debt-equity ratio. It implies that in case of old companies, the current asset to current liability position is negatively influenced by long-term funds and more dependent on short term equity sources.

In case of new companies the correlation was +0.55918. This indicated a moderate degree of positive correlation. In this case the current assets to liability position had a positive association with long-term debt sources. In other words, we can say that the new companies have financed some of their current assets from long-term loans or debt funds and current liabilities are also paid out from long-term debt funds.

Table 8.13 : Correlation between Asset Structure and Debt-Equity Ratio (Age-wise Analysis)

Year	Very Old Companies		Old Companies		New Companies	
	Asset Structure (X)	D/E Ratio (Y)	Asset Structure (X)	D/E Ratio (Y)	Asset Structure (X)	D/E Ratio (Y)
2000	0.43	1.44	0.42	1.25	0.43	1.21
2001	0.4	1.29	0.41	1.19	0.39	1.08
2002	0.39	1.44	0.42	1.39	0.38	1.1
2003	0.38	1.31	0.39	1.36	0.39	1.15
2004	0.37	1.2	0.36	1.33	0.36	1.06
2005	0.36	1.05	0.36	1.13	0.32	0.91
2006	0.33	0.87	0.35	1.15	0.29	0.9
2007	0.33	0.84	0.3	1.08	0.28	0.89
2008	0.29	0.88	0.28	0.92	0.3	0.89
Coefficient of Correlation	0.90827		0.80177		0.97575	

Table 8B.14 : Correlation between Liquidity Ratio and Debt-equity Ratio (Age-wise Analysis)

Year	Very Old Companies		Old Companies		New Companies	
	Liquidity Ratio (X)	D/E Ratio (Y)	Liquidity Ratio (X)	D/E Ratio (Y)	Liquidity Ratio (X)	D/E Ratio (Y)
2000	1.35	1.44	1.66	1.25	1.88	1.21
2001	1.72	1.29	1.6	1.19	1.98	1.08
2002	1.21	1.44	1.21	1.39	1.53	1.1
2003	1.39	1.31	1.1	1.36	1.53	1.15
2004	1.22	1.2	1.15	1.33	1.48	1.06
2005	1.26	1.05	1.23	1.13	1.52	0.91
2006	1.31	0.87	1.27	1.15	1.62	0.9
2007	1.23	0.84	1.27	1.08	1.47	0.89
2008	1.37	0.88	1.18	0.92	1.31	0.89
Coefficient of Correlation	**0.24852**		**-0.04209**		**0.55918**	

Source: Computed from the database collected from www.moneycontrol.com

Size-wise Variable Analysis

This section aims at studying the impact of size variable on the overall trend of flow of funds, its components and capital structure during the period of study. The total sample under study is classified under three size wise variables. These are small, medium and large size companies. As on 31st March 2008, the companies having total assets below ₹ 100 crores are grouped under 'small sized companies'. There were 75 of such companies in the total sample which are grouped under this category, which constitute 25 per cent of the total sample. The companies having the total assets value ₹ 100 crores and above but less than ₹ 500 crores are grouped under 'medium sized companies'. There was 98 such type of companies constituting 32.67 per cent of the total sample. Companies having their total assets value worth ₹ 500 crores and above as on 31st March, 2008 are grouped as 'large sized companies', which include 127 companies, about 42.33 per cent of the total sample.

Total Inflow of Funds from Different Sources (Size-wise Analysis)

The funds raised and invested by sample companies grouped under 'size' variable are shown in Table 8C.1.

Table 8C.1 : Total Inflow of Funds from Different Sources (Size-wise Analysis)

(₹ in Crores)

Year	Small Size Companies (75)	Medium Size Companies (98)	Large Size Companies (127)
2001	210.4	1368.13	14388.31
2002	-58.21	667.93	16033.3
2003	160.74	1742.93	12554.42
2004	119.06	2043.33	28610.26
2005	550.14	1559.87	32173.48
2006	487.87	3869.36	59780.2
2007	816.38	7102.97	77221.27
2008	679.19	6273.37	105646.11
Total	**2965.57**	**24627.89**	**346407.35**
Average	**370.69**	**3078.48**	**43300.91**
Average per Company	**4.94**	**31.41**	**340.95**

Source: Computed from the database collected from www.moneycontrol.com

From the table 8C.1, it was observed that an average of ₹ 370.69 crores of funds was raised by small sized company with a mean inflow of ₹ 4.94 crores annually by each company under this group. The average inflow of funds in case of 'medium sized companies' was ₹ 3078.48 crores with a mean inflow of ₹ 31.41 crores by each company annually under this group. In case of 'large sized companies', the annual average inflow of funds were ₹ 43300.91 crores and the mean inflow for each company per annum was ₹ 340 .95 crores. So it revealed that large sized companies had drawn large funds in volume both individually and as a group. In case of small sized companies, there was a negative inflow of ₹ 58.21 crores in 2002. It indicates that the funds utilized for different purposes were more in that particular year as compared to the funds generated.

Total Inflow of Funds from Internal Sources (Size-wise Analysis)

Funds raised through various internal sources by the sample companies grouped under the head 'size' during the study period is shown in Table 8C.2 (*See on next page*).

On analysis of the table, it was observed that an annual average of ₹ 133.40 crores was raised by the small sized companies from internal sources. In case of medium sized companies and large sized companies, the inflow of funds from internal sources were ₹ 1468.90 crores ₹ 25872.03 crores respectively. The mean average inflow from such sources was ₹ 1.78 crores in case of a small company, ₹ 14.98 crores in a medium sized company and ₹ 203.71 crores in case of large company.

The average amount of funds raised from reserves by small, medium and large sized companies were ₹ 56.66 crores, ₹ 722.77 crores and ₹ 18401.48 crores respectively. The contribution of depreciation as an internal source of funds was ₹ 68.60 crores in case of small sized companies, ₹ 526.84 crores in case of medium sized companies, and ₹ 4764.70 crores in case of large sized companies.

Total Inflow of Funds from Share Capital (Size-wise Analysis)

Funds raised by different sample companies, grouped under size, from issue of shares both equity and preference, are shown in Table 8C.3 (*See on page 182*).

It was observed from the table that an average of ₹ 43.96 crores were raised by the small sized companies from issue of both preference and equity shares during the period. The same was ₹ 129.15 crores in case of medium sized companies and ₹ 732.72 crores in case of large sized companies. The equity issue as bonus issues causes no inflow of funds.

Table 8C.2 : Inflow of Funds from Internal Sources (Size-wise Analysis)

(₹ in Crores)

SMALL SIZE COMPANIES (75)

Internal Sources of Funds	2001	2002	2003	2004	2005	2006	2007	2008	Total	Average
Reserves	–146.51	–279.25	–160.4	–109.8	349.68	246.1	169.01	384.51	453.34	56.66
Revaluation Reserves	15.58	15.51	–5.21	–10.65	–0.71	–2.4	–15.39	–47.51	–50.78	–6.34
Provisions	–7.81	1.71	9.49	3.09	24.64	41.97	15.96	26.76	115.81	14.48
Accumulated Depreciation	106.1	94.84	125.76	112.98	114.37	69.49	104.53	–179.2	548.87	68.60
Total	**–32.64**	**–167.19**	**–30.36**	**–4.38**	**487.98**	**355.16**	**274.11**	**184.56**	**1067.24**	**133.40**

MEDIUM SIZE COMPANIES (98)

Internal Sources of Funds	2001	2002	2003	2004	2005	2006	2007	2008	Total	Average
Reserves	–224.27	–271.07	9.63	413.17	356.52	1448.05	2239.64	1810.54	5782.21	722.77
Revaluation Reserves	4.94	–99.2	–17.59	4.12	142.78	165.55	48.11	–48.32	200.39	25.05
Provisions	–14.2	27.05	112.92	205.48	143.04	156.11	454.51	469.01	1553.92	194.24
Accumulated Depreciation	517.94	478.67	647.51	455.73	388.61	534.21	913.11	278.96	4214.74	526.84
Total	**284.41**	**135.45**	**752.47**	**1078.5**	**1030.95**	**2303.92**	**3655.37**	**2510.19**	**11751.26**	**1468.90**

(Contd...)

LARGE SIZE COMPANIES (127)

Internal Sources of Funds	2001	2002	2003	2004	2005	2006	2007	2008	Total	Average
Reserves	6986.69	2482.7	4371.35	10456.31	18016.5	25836.17	37471.31	41590.79	147211.8	18401.48
Revaluation Reserves	-3[illegible].64	517.61	-75.85	889.36	667.49	-276.24	596.64	2880.03	5167.4	645.92
Provisions	609.12	264.24	775.81	3663.53	127.79	4001.98	1389.84	5647.1	16479.41	2059.93
Accumulated Depreciation	2915.57	3360.42	3756.23	4960.07	4498.78	6394	5829.53	6403.01	38117.61	4764.70
Total	**10479.7**	**6624.97**	**8827.54**	**19969.27**	**23310.56**	**35955.91**	**45287.32**	**56520.93**	**206976.2**	**25872.03**

Source: Computed from the database collected from www.moneycontrol.com

Table 8C.3: Inflow of Funds from Share Capital (Size-wise Analysis)

(₹ in Crores)

SMALL SIZED COMPANIES (75)

Internal Sources of Funds	2001	2002	2003	2004	2005	2006	2007	2008	Total	Average
Equity Share Capital	20.24	13.08	27.3	21.96	32.14	27.39	48.01	42.51	232.63	29.08
Preference Share Capital	–4.6	1.62	0.01	8.89	29.53	–2	4.87	2.78	41.1	5.14
Share Application Money	1.85	9.17	–16.61	12.4	6.9	33.51	13.89	16.84	77.95	9.74
Total	**17.49**	**23.87**	**10.7**	**43.25**	**68.57**	**58.9**	**66.77**	**62.13**	**351.68**	**43.96**

MEDIUM SIZED COMPANIES (98)

Funds Flow from Share Capital	2001	2002	2003	2004	2005	2006	2007	2008	Total	Average
Equity Share Capital	42.02	52.36	34.45	10.97	115.67	133.95	307.4	154.21	851.03	106.37
Preference Share Capital	5.9	0.39	35.25	–32.95	72.12	111.32	–63.36	8.34	137.01	17.12
Share Application Money	1.1	59.87	6.69	–10.25	-37.07	28.24	–15.03	11.79	45.34	5.66
Total	**49.02**	**112.62**	**76.39**	**–32.23**	**150.72**	**273.51**	**229.01**	**174.34**	**1033.38**	**129.15**

LARGE SIZED COMPANIES (127)

Funds Flow from Share Capital	2001	2002	2003	2004	2005	2006	2007	2008	Total	Average
Equity Share Capital	563.14	328.27	20.38	686.19	666.47	972.01	458.44	909.15	4604.05	575.50
Preference Share Capital	–6.37	370.19	151.84	–158.26	97.37	82.09	–259	37.94	315.8	39.48
Share Application Money	480.69	–56.35	–117.29	–186.37	3.53	93.86	343.26	380.64	941.97	117.74
Total	**1037.46**	**642.11**	**54.93**	**341.56**	**767.37**	**1147.96**	**542.7**	**1327.73**	**5861.82**	**732.72**

Source: Computed from the database collected from www.moneycontrol.com

In case of small sized companies, an average of ₹ 29.08 crores was raised from equity issue and ₹ 17.12 crores from preference issue. The years 2001 and 2006 indicated a negative flow of preference issue depicting a conversion or redemption. In case of medium sized companies, average amount of funds raised from equity issue was ₹ 106.37 crores and from preference issue ₹ 17.12 crores. In 2004 and 2007 there were negative flows of preference issue indicating a conversion or redemption. In case of large sized companies, equity issue showed an average of ₹ 575.50 crores and the preference issue ₹ 39.48 crores, during the period. In case of preference issue, the inflow was negative in 2001 and 2007 which might be because of conversion into equity shares or redemption.

Total Inflow of Funds from Long-term Loans (Size-wise Analysis)

The funds raised through long-term loans and debts by the various size group companies are shown in Table 8C.4 (*See on next page*).

The sources of long-term loans were secured loans, unsecured loans and deferred credit. However, no amount had been raised through deferred credit. The table depicts the average funds raised by the small sized companies from long term loans amounting to ₹ 89.66 crores, which consists of ₹ 65.35 crores through secured loans and ₹ 24.31 crores through unsecured loans.

In case of small sized companies, in the years 2005 and 2006 the secured loans shows a negative inflow indicating that repayments has been made. Similarly, in 2002, 2004 and in 2007 unsecured loans shows negative figures. In case of medium sized companies, an average of ₹ 850.31 crores were raised from long term loans out of which ₹ 744.07 crores was from secured loans and ₹ 106.24 crores was from unsecured loans. In case of large sized companies, the total average was ₹ 9364.22 crores, which consists of ₹ 3950.06 crores from secured loans and ₹ 5414.16 crores from unsecured loans.

Total Inflow of Funds from Current Liabilities (Size-wise Analysis)

The funds raised through current liabilities by the various size group companies are shown in Table 8C.5 (*See on page 185*).

Table 8.4 : Inflow of Funds from Long-term Debts/Loans (Size-wise Analysis)

(₹ in Crores)

SMALL SIZED COMPANIES (75)

Funds Flow from Debt/Loan	2001	2002	2003	2004	2005	2006	2007	2008	Total	Average
Secured Loans	159.65	42.44	93.76	105.02	–158.02	–55.15	96.04	239.07	522.81	65.35
Unsecured Loans	21.31	–35.82	18.38	–14.21	38.31	33.91	–17.35	149.99	194.52	24.31
Deferred Credit	0.00	0.00	0.00	0.00	0.00	0.00	0.00	0.00	0.00	0
Total	**180.96**	**6.62**	**112.14**	**90.81**	**–119.71**	**–21.24**	**78.69**	**389.06**	**717.33**	**89.66**

MEDIUM SIZED COMPANIES (98)

Funds Flow from Debt/Loan	2001	2002	2003	2004	2005	2006	2007	2008	Total	Average
Secured Loans	739.34	14.5	392.65	73.74	347.16	771.04	1766.61	1847.53	5952.57	744.07
Unsecured Loans	106.11	–177.51	17.04	353.09	–30.65	264.67	156.36	160.85	849.96	106.24
Deferred Credit	0.00	0.00	0.00	0.00	0.00	0.00	0.00	0.00	0.00	0
Total	**845.45**	**–163.01**	**409.69**	**426.83**	**316.51**	**1035.71**	**1922.97**	**2008.38**	**6802.53**	**850.31**

LARGE SIZED COMPANIES (127)

Funds Flow from Debt/Loan	2001	2002	2003	2004	2005	2006	2007	2008	Total	Average
Secured Loans	2398.53	–194.36	1202.21	1664.04	1066.51	2092.59	10817.71	12553.29	31600.52	3950.06
Unsecured Loans	–334.34	1814.46	75.82	2198.4	3190.47	11576.35	8458.65	16333.51	43313.32	5414.16
Deferred Credit	0.00	0.00	0.00	0.00	0.00	0.00	0.00	0.00	0.00	0
Total	**2064.19**	**1620.1**	**1278.03**	**3862.44**	**4256.98**	**13668.94**	**19276.36**	**28886.8**	**74913.84**	**9364.22**

Source: Computed from the database collected from www.moneycontrol.com

Table 8.5 : Inflow of Funds from Current Liabilities (Size-wise Analysis)

(₹ in Crores)

Year	Small Sized Companies (75)	Medium Sized Companies (98)	Large Sized Companies (127)
2001	44.59	189.25	806.92
2002	78.49	582.87	7146.12
2003	68.26	504.38	2393.92
2004	–10.62	570.23	4436.99
2005	113.3	61.69	3838.57
2006	95.05	256.22	9007.39
2007	396.81	1295.62	12114.89
2008	43.44	1580.46	18910.65
Total	**829.32**	**5040.72**	**58655.45**
Average	103.66	630.09	7331.93
Average Per Company	**1.38**	**6.43**	**57.73**

Source: Computed from the database collected from www.moneycontrol.com

On analyzing the table, it was observed that an average of ₹ 103.66 crores was raised from current liabilities by the small sized companies with a mean yearly average of ₹ 1.38 crores per company. The average inflow in case of medium sized companies was ₹ 630.09 crores with a mean average of ₹ 6.43 crores each year per company. The large sized companies had drawn an average of ₹ 7331.93 crores into the business during the study period. The mean amount raised by the companies of this group was calculated at ₹ 57.73 crores every year, being the highest among all the three categories.

Outflow of Funds for Acquiring Fixed Assets (Size-wise Analysis)

The funds applied in acquiring additional fixed assets by the various size companies during the study period are shown in the Table 8C.6. From the analysis it was observed that an average of ₹ 114.84 crores were invested in incremental fixed assets by the small sized companies. The mean investment by each company came to an average of ₹ 1.53 crores in case of small size companies. The average investment in case of medium sized companies was ₹ 1552.55 crores with a mean investment of ₹ 15.84 crores

Table 8.6 : Application of Funds in Acquiring Additional Fixed Assets – Size-wise Analysis

(₹ in Crores)

SMALL SIZED COMPANIES (75)

Funds used for Fixed Assets	2001	2002	2003	2004	2005	2006	2007	2008	Average
Gross Block	184.72	54.93	70.86	50.41	171.45	123.65	155.77	12.39	103.02
Capital Work in Progress	–55.27	5.05	–9.96	21.94	1.55	2.94	62.14	66.22	11.82
Total	**129.45**	**59.98**	**60.90**	**72.35**	**173.00**	**126.59**	**217.91**	**78.61**	**114.84**

Average Investment Per Company = Rs.1.53 Crores

MEDIUM SIZED COMPANIES (98)

Funds used for Fixed Assets	2001	2002	2003	2004	2005	2006	2007	2008	Average
Gross Block	1,009.85	447.21	850.57	789.69	767.27	2,065.33	2,701.92	2,321.50	1369.16
Capital Work in Progress	178.34	–55.41	120.56	–214.52	174.74	110.24	764.55	388.67	183.39
Total	**1,188.19**	**391.80**	**971.13**	**575.17**	**942.01**	**2,175.57**	**3,466.47**	**2,710.17**	**1552.55**

Average Investment Per Company = Rs. 15.84 Crores

LARGE SIZED COMPANIES (127)

Funds used for Fixed Assets	2001	2002	2003	2004	2005	2006	2007	2008	Average
Gross Block	5,036.50	8,016.21	6,449.45	10,371.00	10,492.12	18,362.91	23,033.79	32,832.81	14324.35
Capital Work in Progress	1,584.52	–97.69	–858.52	1,368.20	4,368.91	5,789.46	8,211.60	2,681.19	2880.95
Total	**6,621.02**	**7,918.52**	**5,590.93**	**11,739.20**	**14,861.03**	**24,152.37**	**31,245.39**	**35,514.00**	**17205.30**

Average Investment Per Company = ₹ 135.47 Crores

Source: Computed from the database collected from www.moneycontrol.com

by a company. In case of the large sized companies, the application of funds in fixed assets was ₹ 17205.30 crores in average with a mean investment of ₹ 135.47 crores by each company.

In case of small sized companies, the highest investment in fixed assets was observed in 2007 amounting to ₹ 217.91 crores and the lowest of ₹ 59.98 crores in 2002. In case of medium sized companies, the highest investment was ₹ 3466.47 crores in 2007 and the lowest was ₹ 391.80 crores in 2002. In case of large sized companies, the highest was ₹ 35514 crores in 2008 and the lowest was ₹ 5590.93 crores in 2003.

Application of Additional Funds in Current Assets (Size-wise Analysis)

The investment of funds in current assets by the different sized sample companies during the study period is shown in Table 8C.7.

Table 8C.7 : Analysis Funds utilized in Current Assets (Size-wise Analysis)

(₹ in Crores)

Year	Small Sized Companies (75)	Medium Sized Companies (98)	Large Sized Companies (127)
2001	51.06	63.59	2316.75
2002	–134.44	–81.26	2491.43
2003	48.04	378.07	1368.66
2004	81.71	764.92	7161.87
2005	270.24	184.84	6959.07
2006	230.74	1094.89	14866.91
2007	301.35	2007.57	12744.18
2008	385.8	1975.92	19721.45
Total	**1,234.50**	**6,388.54**	**67,630.32**
Average	**154.31**	**798.56**	**8453.79**
Average Per Company	**2.05**	**8.14**	**66.56**

Source: Computed from the database collected from www.moneycontrol.com

On observation of the table, it revealed that an average of ₹ 154.31 crores was invested in additional current assets by the small sized companies. The mean average investment by each company per year was calculated to be ₹ 2.05 crores. The average investment in case of medium sized companies was ₹ 798.56 crores with a mean average investment of

₹ 8.14 crores per company every year. In case of large sized companies, the average investment was ₹ 8453.79 crores and the mean investment was calculated to be ₹ 66.56 crores per company per year.

Debt-Equity Ratio of Sample Companies (Size-wise Analysis)

The debt-equity ratio of the sample companies grouped size-wise is shown in Table 8C.8.

Table 8C.8 : Debt-Equity Ratio of Sample Companies (Size-wise Analysis)

Year	Small Sized Companies (75)	Medium Sized Companies (98)	Large Sized Companies (127)
2000	2.07	1.88	1.17
2001	2.51	2.12	1.03
2002	3.38	2.31	1.13
2003	4.48	2.45	1.11
2004	5.24	2.46	1.04
2005	3	2.27	0.89
2006	2.35	1.9	0.88
2007	2.32	1.76	0.86
2008	2.06	1.77	0.9
Total	**27.41**	**18.92**	**9.01**
Average	**3.04**	**2.10**	**1.00**

Source: Computed from the database collected from www.moneycontrol.com

On analyzing the table, it was observed that the average D/E ratio in case of small sized companies was 3.04, in case of medium sized companies it was 2.10 and in case of large sized companies it was calculated at 1.00. In case of small sized companies, the D/E ratio varied in between 2.07 to 5.24 and the average was much higher than the standard norm of 2:1. It indicates that in case of small sized companies, the component of debt was more in the capital structure as compared to the equity. Theoretically, a high debt/equity ratio generally means that a company has been aggressive in financing its growth with debt. This can result in volatile earnings as a result of the additional interest expense. If a lot of debt is used to finance increased operations (high debt to equity), the company could potentially generate more earnings than it would have without this outside financing. If this were to increase earnings by a greater amount than the debt cost (interest), then the shareholders benefit as more earnings are being spread among the same amount of shareholders. However, the cost of this debt financing may outweigh the return that the company generates on the debt through investment and business activities and become too much for the company to handle. This can lead to bankruptcy, which would leave shareholders with nothing.

In case of medium sized companies, the D/E ratio varied in between 1.76 to 2.46 leading to an average of 2.10, which is slightly above the standard norm of 2:1. But in case of large sized companies, the ratio varied in between 0.86 to 1.17 with an average of 1.00. This shows that the large sized companies followed a strict conservative policy while deciding the debt equity mix. A low ratio of 1.00 means that the company is exposing itself to a large amount of equity. This is certainly better than a high ratio of two or more since this would expose the company to risk such as interest rate increases and creditor nervousness.

But larger exposure to equity or issuing of more and more stocks will definitely dilute the values of outstanding equity shares and existing investors receive a smaller ownership portion with each additional share issued. One way to improve their situation would be to issue more debt and use the cash to buyback some of its outstanding shares.

Analysis of Size of Investment of Sample Companies (Size-wise)

The size of investment by the sample companies grouped according to their size during the study period is shown in Table 8C.9 (*See on next page*).

From the table it was observed that the average investment position in small sized company was ₹ 3255.46 crores. Such a position in case of medium sized companies revealed ₹ 16456.14 crores and large sized companies ₹ 105138.62 crores. The average rate of growth in the investment in fixed assets in the case of small sized companies was 5.6 per cent, for medium sized companies it was 9.58 per cent and for large sized companies it was 16.92 per cent. Thus the growth rate is higher in case of large sized companies and the size of investment has increased more than three times that it had in the beginning.

Analysis of Asset Structure of Sample Companies (Size-wise)

The asset structure of the various size group sample companies of the study period is shown in Table 8C.10 (*See on page 191*).

Table 8C.9 : Size of Investment (Net Fixed Assets + Current Assets) Size-wise Analysis

(₹ in Crores)

Small Sized Companies	2000	2001	2002	2003	2004	2005	2006	2007	2008
Net Block	1474.19	1552.81	1512.9	1458	1395.43	1452.51	1506.67	1557.91	1749.5
Current Assets	1412.6	1463.66	1329.22	1377.26	1458.97	1729.21	1959.95	2261.3	2647.1
Total	**2886.79**	**3016.47**	**2842.12**	**2835.26**	**2854.4**	**3181.72**	**3466.62**	**3819.21**	**4396.6**
Growth		129.68	–174.35	–6.86	19.14	327.32	284.9	352.59	577.39
Growth Per cent		4.49	–5.77	–0.24	0.68	11.47	8.95	10.171	15.12
Average Growth Per Company Per Year = 3255.46Average Growth Rate Per Year = 5.6%									
Medium Sized Companies	**2000**	**2001**	**2002**	**2003**	**2004**	**2005**	**2006**	**2007**	**2008**
Net Block	7271.9	7763.81	7732.35	7935.41	8269.37	8648.03	10179.15	11967.96	14010.5
Current Assets	5364.31	5427.9	5346.64	5724.71	6489.63	6674.47	7769.36	9776.93	11752.85
Total	**12636.2**	**13191.7**	**13078.99**	**13660.12**	**14759**	**15322.5**	**17948.51**	**21744.89**	**25763.35**
Growth		555.5	–112.72	581.13	1098.88	563.5	2626.01	3796.38	4018.46
Growth Per cent		**4.40**	**–0.85**	**4.44**	**8.04**	**3.82**	**17.14**	**21.15**	**18.48**
Average Growth Per Company Per Year = 16456.14Average Growth Rate Per Year = 9.58%									
Large Sized Companies	**2000**	**2001**	**2002**	**2003**	**2004**	**2005**	**2006**	**2007**	**2008**
Net Block	36773.5	38894.5	43550.24	46243.46	51654.39	57647.73	69616.64	86820.9	113250.7
Current Assets	22683.7	25000.5	27491.9	28860.56	36022.43	42981.5	57848.41	70592.59	90314.04
Total	59457.2	63894.9	71042.14	75104.02	87676.82	100629.2	127465.1	157413.5	203564.7
Growth		4437.68	7147.22	4061.88	12572.8	12952.41	26835.82	29948.44	46151.25
Growth Per cent		7.46	11.19	5.72	16.75	14.77	26.67	23.50	29.32
Average Growth Per Company Per Year = 105138.62Average Growth Rate Per Year = 16.92%									

Source: Computed from the database collected from www.moneycontrol.com

Table 8C.10 : Analysis of Asset Structure (Ratio of Net Fixed Assets to Total Assets) of Sample Companies (Size-wise Analysis)

Year	Small Sized Companies (75)	Medium Sized Companies (98)	Large Sized Companies (127)
2000	0.4	0.43	0.42
2001	0.41	0.43	0.4
2002	0.42	0.43	0.39
2003	0.4	0.41	0.38
2004	0.38	0.4	0.36
2005	0.35	0.39	0.33
2006	0.33	0.4	0.31
2007	0.3	0.38	0.29
2008	0.29	0.37	0.28
Total	**3.28**	**3.64**	**3.16**
Average	**0.36**	**0.40**	**0.35**

Source: Computed from the database collected from www.moneycontrol.com

On analyzing the table, it was observed that an average of 36 per cent of net fixed assets were there in the total assets structure in case of small sized companies. The same was 40 per cent in case of medium sized companies and 35 per cent in case of large sized companies. Though medium sized companies had a higher proportion of net fixed assets to total assets as compared to other sized companies, but it is not remarkable.

Analysis of Current Ratio of Sample Companies (Size-wise)

The liquidity ratio of size grouped sample companies for the study period is shown in Table 8C.11.

From the table 8C.11 it was observed that in case of small sized companies, the average liquidity ratio was 1.61, in case of medium sized companies it recorded a ratio of 1.33 and in case of large sized companies the average ratio was 1.42.

This ratio indicated the short term solvency position. In the study, it was revealed that in none of the years the ratio has reached the standard norm of 2:1 by any of the sample groups. Whereas, in case of small sized companies, the situation is little bit satisfactory as compared to the other two groups.

Table 8C.11 : Liquidity Ratio of Sample Companies
Current Assets to Current Liabilities (Size-wise Analysis)

Year	Small Sized Companies (75)	Medium Sized Companies (98)	Large Sized Companies (127)
2000	1.84	1.52	1.77
2001	1.8	1.46	1.84
2002	1.49	1.24	1.32
2003	1.43	1.19	1.24
2004	1.54	1.21	1.3
2005	1.63	1.23	1.36
2006	1.69	1.36	1.43
2007	1.45	1.4	1.34
2008	1.65	1.37	1.26
Total	**14.52**	**11.98**	**12.86**
Average	**1.61**	**1.33**	**1.42**

Source: Computed from the database collected from www.moneycontrol.com

Correlation between Size of Investment and D/E Ratio (Size-wise)

The correlation between size of investment and D/E ratio of sample companies grouped under different sizes is shown in Table 8C.12 (*See on next page*).

On analysis, it was observed that the correlation between size of investment and D/E ratio in case of small sized company was –0.57129, in case of medium sized companies it was –0.66987 and in case of large sized companies, it was –0.77986. Thus, in the case of all the three group of companies there exists a fairly high degree of negative correlation between the size of investments and the debt-equity ratios. It indicated that a greater proportion of investments were influenced more by the long-term equity sources than the debt source.

Correlation between Asset Structure and D/E Ratio (Size-wise)

The correlation between asset structure and debt equity ratio of the different sized companies is shown in Table 8C.13 (*See on page 194*).

Table 8C.12 : Correlation between Size of Investment and Debt-Equity Ratio (Size-wise Analysis)

Year	Small Sized Companies		Medium Sized Companies		Large Sized Companies	
	Size of Investment (₹ in Crores) (X)	D/E Ratio (Y)	Size of Investment (₹ in Crores) (X)	D/E Ratio (Y)	Size of Investment (₹ in Crores) (X)	D/E Ratio (Y)
2000	2886 79	2.07	12636.21	1.88	59457.24	1.17
2001	3016 47	2.51	13191.71	2.12	63894.92	1.03
2002	2842 12	3.38	13078.99	2.31	71042.14	1.13
2003	2835.26	4.48	13660.12	2.45	75104.02	1.11
2004	2854 4	5.24	14759	2.46	87676.82	1.04
2005	3181.72	3	15322.5	2.27	100629.23	0.89
2006	3466.62	2.35	17948.51	1.9	127465.05	0.88
2007	3819.21	2.32	21744.89	1.76	157413.49	0.86
2008	4396.6	2.06	25763.35	1.77	203564.74	0.9
Coefficient of Correlation	–0.57129		–0.66987		–0.77986	

Source: Computed from the database collected from www.moneycontrol.com

Table 8C.13 : Correlation between Asset Structure and Debt-Equity Ratio (Size-wise Analysis)

Year	Small Sized Companies		Medium Sized Companies		Large Sized Companies	
	Asset Structure (X)	D/E Ratio (Y)	Asset Structure (X)	D/E Ratio (Y)	Asset Structure (X)	D/E Ratio (Y)
2000	0.4	2.07	0.43	1.88	0.42	1.17
2001	0.41	2.51	0.43	2.12	0.4	1.03
2002	0.42	3.38	0.43	2.31	0.39	1.13
2003	0.4	4.48	0.41	2.45	0.38	1.11
2004	0.38	5.24	0.4	2.46	0.36	1.04
2005	0.35	3	0.39	2.27	0.33	0.89
2006	0.33	2.35	0.4	1.9	0.31	0.88
2007	0.3	2.32	0.38	1.76	0.29	0.86
2008	0.29	2.06	0.37	1.77	0.28	0.9
Coefficient of Correlation	**0.42978**		**0.36926**		**0.91474**	

Source: Computed from the database collected from www.moneycontrol.com

On analyzing the table, it was revealed that in case of small sized companies, the correlation was 0.42978, medium sized companies 0.36926 and large companies 0.91474. It indicated that in case of small and medium sized companies, there was a moderate degree of positive correlation between the fixed assets proportion to total assets with debt equity ratio. Whereas, in case of large sized companies the correlation between the asset structure and D/E ratio was highly positive. This implies that, in case of small and medium sized companies, there was a moderate level of influence of the long-term debt funds in the acquisition of net fixed assets but the influence of debt funds was much more in case of large sized companies and the influence of equity funds in acquisition of fixed assets was negligible.

Correlation between Liquidity Ratio and D/E Ratio (Size-wise)

The correlation between liquidity and D/E ratio of sample companies grouped according to their size is shown in Table 8C.14 (*See on next page*).

Table 8C.14 shows that the correlation between the current ratio and debt equity ratio of small sized companies was –0.56777, in case of medium sized companies –0.78487 and in case of large sized companies, it was 0.31412. Thus, in case of small and medium sized companies where the degree of correlation is moderate to highly negative indicates that, the long term debt funds invested had a negative influence on liquidity. The share of equity funds were seen to be highly influencing the current position of the company than the debt sources.

But in case of large sized companies, there was a low degree of positive correlation between the liquidity and debt equity ratio. It indicated that the liquidity position of large sized companies was positively influenced by the long-term debt sources rather than equity, which was not seen in case of small and medium sized companies.

Industry/Sector-wise Analysis

It is necessary to study the impact of different industrial groups on the overall trend of inflow and application of funds and the capital structure, because of the fact that the sources of financing of industries of different nature differ from one another. Further, the classification of industries gives an overall idea on the coverage of the sample. For the purpose of the industry-wise variable study, the total sample is classified into four broad groups of industries namely, agro-based manufacturing industries, mineral based manufacturing industries, service industries and plantation industries. The group of companies which obtain their raw materials from agriculture like textiles, sugar, edible oil, paper, food processing

Table 8C.14 : Correlation between Liquidity Ratio and Debt-Equity Ratio (Size-wise Analysis)

Year	Small Sized Companies		Medium Sized Companies		Large Sized Companies	
	Liquidity Ratio (X)	D/E Ratio (Y)	Liquidity Ratio (X)	D/E Ratio (Y)	Liquidity (X)	D/E Ratio (Y)
2000	1.84	2.07	1.52	1.88	1.77	1.17
2001	1.8	2.51	1.46	2.12	1.84	1.03
2002	1.49	3.38	1.24	2.31	1.32	1.13
2003	1.43	4.48	1.19	2.45	1.24	1.11
2004	1.54	5.24	1.21	2.46	1.3	1.04
2005	1.63	3	1.23	2.27	1.36	0.89
2006	1.69	2.35	1.36	1.9	1.43	0.88
2007	1.45	2.32	1.4	1.76	1.34	0.86
2008	1.65	2.06	1.37	1.77	1.26	0.9
Coefficient of Correlation	–0.56777		–0.78487		0.31412	

are grouped under the head agro-based companies. The companies which obtain their raw materials from mining or mineral based products like chemicals, cement, fertilizer, pharmaceuticals, electric equipment, plastics, construction and housing, mining, fabricated metal etc. are grouped under the head mineral-based companies. The group of companies, which are engaged in plantation of tea, coffee and rubber, are categorized as plantation companies. The companies which do not manufacture but are involved in rendering services like transport, computers software, hotel etc. are called service companies. An attempt has been made to study the impact of each industry variable on the overall flow of funds and the capital structure.

Total Inflow of Funds from Different Sources (Industry-wise Analysis)

The total inflow of funds by the companies grouped under different industries is shown in Table 8D.1.

Table 8D.1 : Total Inflow of Funds from Different Sources (Industry-wise Analysis)

(₹ in Crores)

Year	Agro Based Companies (90)	Mineral Based Companies (135)	Service Companies (45)	Plantation Companies (30)
2001	3491.83	5116.8	7268	195.27
2002	1978.77	5802.87	8719.7	123.1
2003	2845.61	8196.51	3242.42	214.06
2004	4949.5	13411.3	12170.93	290.79
2005	4520.25	17001.29	11906.64	452.79
2006	15194.38	27963.29	19870.71	1109.05
2007	10508.30	36770.24	26608.05	2064.02
2008	14029.26	52389.38	45005.18	1174.84
Total	**66607.99**	**166660.68**	**134882.53**	**5623.92**
Average	8325.99	20832.58	16860.31	702.99
Average per Company per Year	92.51	154.31	374.67	23.43

Source: Computed from the database collected from www.moneycontrol.com

By studying the Table 8D.1 it was found that mineral based companies which consist of 135 companies had raised the highest amount of funds during the entire study period in comparison to other three industrial groups. Amount raised and applied by the companies under different industrial groups is worked out to be ₹ 8325.99 crores, ₹ 20832.58 crores, ₹ 16860.31 crores and ₹ 702.99 crores in average annually by the agro based, mineral based, service and plantation companies respectively. On total average, mineral based companies stood highest whereas, the average per company per year is highest for service companies followed by mineral based, agro based and plantation companies. The highest amount raised by the agro based companies was ₹ 19598.39 crores in the year 2007. The same in case of mineral based companies was ₹ 52389.38 crores in 2008, in case of service companies it was ₹ 45005.18 crores in 2008 and in case of plantation companies, it was ₹ 5623.92 crores in 2008. Only mineral based companies had maintained a constantly rising trend in the inflow of funds. In the case of other category of companies, the trend was fluctuating.

Total Inflow of Funds from Internal Sources (Industry-wise Analysis)

The funds generated by different companies grouped industry-wise from their internal source are shown in Table 8D.2 (*See on next page*). By analyzing the table we saw that funds generated from internal sources comprises funds from reserves otherwise known as retained earnings, revaluation reserves, provisions and depreciation. The agro based companies had generated an average of ₹ 3424.40 crores, mineral based companies ₹ 13389.56 crores, service companies ₹ 10311.56 crores and plantation companies ₹ 321.35 crores during the study period. Funds raised from reserves remained the biggest source of internal funds for all the group of companies.

Total Inflow of Funds from Share Capital (Industry-wise Analysis)

Table 8D.3 depicts the inflow of funds from issue of share capital both preference and equity for the industry-wise grouped sample companies (*See on page 201 to 202*).

Table 8D.2 : Inflow of Funds from Internal Sources (Industry-wise Analysis)

(₹ in Crores)

AGRO-BASED COMPANIES (90)

Internal Sources of Funds	2001	2002	2003	2004	2005	2006	2007	2008	Average
Reserves	568.22	–723.12	807.61	923.03	1729.13	5247.13	3374.17	3106.6	1879.09
Revaluation Reserves	83.17	–85.92	6.38	67.5	–337.03	114.27	–34.01	571.07	48.18
Provisions	30.01	17.99	124.25	339.31	258.19	519.86	224.86	302.72	227.15
Accumulated Depreciation	1032.1	1057.66	1266.05	886.35	1171.55	1764.09	2247.12	734.92	1269.98
Total	**1713.5**	**266.61**	**2204.29**	**2216.19**	**2821.84**	**7645.35**	**5812.14**	**4715.3**	**3424.40**

MINERAL–BASED COMPANIES (135)

Internal Sources of Funds	2001	2002	2003	2004	2005	2006	2007	2008	Average
Reserves	1505.2	–963.7	2018.29	4870.46	6914.59	11186.4	20618.6	28894	9380.53
Revaluation Reserves	–69.3	–62.74	137.61	895.96	890.55	–155.83	–109.44	–274.1	156.58
Provisions	362.93	124.7	440.34	791.28	602.97	1634.06	2023.85	2690.8	1083.87
Accumulated Depreciation	1523.01	1902.88	2145.47	2712.48	2428.34	3748.24	3782.29	3905.9	2768.58
Total	**3321.84**	**1001.14**	**4741.71**	**9270.18**	**10836.5**	**16412.8**	**26315.3**	**35217**	**13389.56**

(Contd....)

SERVICE COMPANIES (45)

Internal Sources of Funds	2001	2002	2003	2004	2005	2006	2007	2008	Average
Reserves	4510.87	3615.85	1390.08	4922.57	9875.84	10818.4	15023.7	11413	7696.27
Revaluation Reserves	90.14	630.68	–198.79	–25.28	–135.84	–56.97	776.48	2519.5	449.98
Provisions	151.97	203.05	282.31	2752.25	–590.81	2010.01	–528.32	2957	904.68
Accumulated Depreciation	899.33	905.4	1009.88	1848.19	1308.12	1451.96	731.06	1931.2	1260.63
Total	**5652.31**	**5354.98**	**2483.48**	**9497.73**	**10457.3**	**14223.4**	**16002.9**	**18820**	**10311.56**

PLANTATION COMPANIES (30)

Internal Sources of Funds	2001	2002	2003	2004	2005	2006	2007	2008	Average
Reserves	31.62	3.35	4.6	43.62	203.14	278.42	863.52	371.91	225.02
Revaluation Reserves	–4.05	–66.69	–3.34	–5.48	–10.65	–14.56	–3.67	–32.18	–17.57
Provisions	42.2	–52.74	51.32	–10.74	25.12	36.13	139.92	192.35	52.94
Accumulated Depreciation	85.17	67.99	108.1	81.76	93.75	33.41	86.7	–69.19	60.96
Total	**154.94**	**–48.09**	**160.68**	**109.16**	**311.36**	**333.4**	**1086.47**	**462.89**	**321.35**

Source: Computed from the database collected from www.moneycontrol.com

Table 8D.3 : Inflow of Funds from Share Capital (Industry-wise Analysis)

(₹ in Crores)

AGRO-BASED COMPANIES (90)

Funds Flow from Share Capital	2001	2002	2003	2004	2005	2006	2007	2008	Average
Equity Share Capital	180.03	116.22	96.04	88.14	87.76	259.81	31.19	108.96	121.01
Preference Share Capital	–8.13	201.65	–3.84	–125.85	–78.44	13.76	–32.34	11.09	–2.76
Share Application Money	221.32	–44.19	–214.77	21.96	31.33	199.81	126.7	168.73	63.86
Total	**393.22**	**273.68**	**–122.57**	**–15.75**	**40.65**	**473.38**	**125.55**	**288.78**	**182.11**

MINERAL–BASED COMPANIES (135)

Funds Flow from Share Capital	2001	2002	2003	2004	2005	2006	2007	2008	Average
Equity Share Capital	142.82	253.68	78.97	468.66	297.08	338.09	294.35	468.29	292.74
Preference Share Capital	7.04	132.22	–31.21	–18.11	441.47	160.68	–292.65	–67.39	41.50
Share Application Money	285.18	25.44	129.38	–232.26	–52.41	–36.06	64.52	270.83	56.82
Total	**435.04**	**411.34**	**177.14**	**218.29**	**686.14**	**462.71**	**66.22**	**671.73**	**391.06**

(Contd...)

SERVICE COMPANIES (45)

Funds Flow from Share Capital	2001	2002	2003	2004	2005	2006	2007	2008	Average
Equity Share Capital	303.69	30.55	–113.19	160.12	425.95	533.91	463.64	560.03	295.58
Preference Share Capital	11.01	38.93	237.14	–36.9	–161.57	–48	71.25	105.35	27.15
Share Application Money	–32.81	24.18	–22.07	26.17	–6.57	–27.31	137	–20.51	9.76
Total	**281.89**	**93.66**	**101.88**	**149.39**	**257.81**	**458.6**	**671.89**	**644.87**	**332.49**

PLANTATION COMPANIES (30)

Funds Flow from Share Capital	2001	2002	2003	2004	2005	2006	2007	2008	Average
Equity Share Capital	–1.15	–6.73	20.31	2.2	3.5	1.53	24.67	–31.41	1.61
Preference Share Capital	–15	–0.6	–14.99	–1.46	–2.44	64.97	–63.75	0	–4.15
Share Application Money	9.95	7.26	–19.75	–0.09	1.01	19.17	13.9	–9.78	2.70
Total	**–6.2**	**–0.07**	**–14.43**	**0.65**	**2.07**	**85.67**	**–25.18**	**–41.19**	**0.16**

From the analysis of the table it was observed that in case of agro-based companies, the average amount of funds raised through share capital was ₹ 182.11 crores, in case of mineral based companies it was ₹ 391.06 crores, in case of service companies it was ₹ 332.49 crores and in case of plantation companies, it was ₹ 0.16 crores. The average amount raised from the issue of equity shares by the agro based companies was ₹ 121.01 crores, mineral based companies ₹ 292.74 crores, service companies ₹ 332.49 crores and plantation companies ₹ 1.61 crores. In case of preference shares, the redemption was more as compare to issue in case of agro-based companies. The fresh issue of preference shares registered in the years 2002, 2006 and in 2008 whereas, in 2001, 2003, 2004, 2005 and in the year 2007 the agro-based companies seems to be redeemed their preference shares.

In case of mineral-based companies, the highest amount of preference issue was ₹ 441.47 crores in the year 2005 and the highest amount redeemed was ₹ 292.65 crores in the year 2007. The service companies raised highest amount of ₹ 237.14 crores through issue of preference shares in the year 2003 and the plantation companies raised highest amount of ₹ 64.97 crores in 2006.

Inflow of Funds from Long-term Debts/Loans (Industry-wise Analysis)

Funds raised by sample companies grouped under different industrial groups from long-term loans are shown in table 8D.4. By analyzing the table, we saw that the annual average inflow of funds from long-term loans comprising of both secured as well as unsecured, by the agro-based companies recorded ₹ 3180.97 crores, mineral based companies ₹ 3385.39 crores, service companies ₹ 3525.22 crores and plantation companies ₹ 211.87 crores. No amount has been raised through deferred credits.

The highest amount raised by agro-based companies through secured loans was ₹ 8841.03 crores in the year 2007 and through unsecured loans ₹ 2783.14 crores in the year 2006. In case of mineral based companies, the highest amount raised through secured loans was ₹ 4977.4 crores in 2008 and through unsecured loans ₹ 6792.61 crores in 2006. In case of service companies, the highest amount raised through secured loans was ₹ 3915.7 crores in 2008 and through unsecured loans ₹ 13420 crores in 2006. In case of plantation companies, the highest amount raised through secured loans was ₹ 418.56 crores in 2008 and through unsecured loans ₹ 493.92 crores in 2007.

Table 8D.4 : Inflow of Funds from Long-term Loans (Industry-wise Analysis)

(₹ in Crores)

AGRO-BASED COMPANIES (90)

Funds Flow from Debt/Loan	2001	2002	2003	2004	2005	2006	2007	2008	Total	Average
Secured Loans	861.25	–540.63	85.18	1291.52	1111.67	2856.51	8841.03	5328.3	19834.8	2479.35
Unsecured Loans	63.46	–26.51	–57.52	678.06	14.27	2783.14	1768.25	389.81	5612.96	701.62
Deferred Credit	0.00	0.00	0.00	0.00	0.00	0.00	0.00	0.00	0.00	0
Total	**924.71**	**–567.14**	**27.66**	**1969.58**	**1125.94**	**5639.65**	**10609.3**	**5718.1**	**25447.8**	**3180.97**

MINERAL-BASED COMPANIES (135)

Funds Flow from Debt/Loan	2001	2002	2003	2004	2005	2006	2007	2008	Total	Average
Secured Loans	1619.22	–260.19	1743.7	182.34	–255.35	–1009.5	2387.89	4977.4	9385.54	1173.19
Unsecured Loans	–557.8	58.15	–411.99	1940.7	3660.55	6792.61	3075.71	3139.7	17697.6	2212.20
Deferred Credit	0.00	0.00	0.00	0.00	0.00	0.00	0.00	0.00	0.00	0
Total	**1061.42**	**–202.04**	**1331.71**	**2123.04**	**3405.2**	**5783.16**	**5463.6**	**8117.1**	**27083.2**	**3385.39**

(Contd....)

SERVICE COMPANIES (45)

Funds Flow from Debt/Loan	2001	2002	2003	2004	2005	2006	2007	2008	Total	Average
Secured Loans	725.47	573.52	–193.04	241.83	347.47	737.7	1115.15	3915.7	7463.77	932.97
Unsecured Loans	256.72	1648.17	629.43	–40.26	–507.55	2071.33	3259.76	13420	20738	2592.25
Deferred Credit	0.00	0.00	0.00	0.00	0.00	0.00	0.00	0.00	0.00	0
Total	**982.19**	**2221.69**	**436.39**	**201.57**	**–160.08**	**2809.03**	**4374.91**	**17336**	**28201.8**	**3525.22**

PLANTATION COMPANIES (30)

Funds Flow from Debt/Loan	2001	2002	2003	2004	2005	2006	2007	2008	Total	Average
Secured Loans	85.58	89.88	52.78	127.11	51.86	223.72	336.29	418.56	1385.78	173.22
Unsecured Loans	30.7	–78.68	–48.68	–41.22	30.86	227.86	493.92	–305.6	309.21	38.65
Deferred Credit	0.00	0.00	0.00	0.00	0.00	0.00	0.00	0.00	0.00	0
Total	**116.28**	**11.2**	**4.1**	**85.89**	**82.72**	**451.58**	**830.21**	**113.01**	**1694.99**	**211.87**

Source: Computed from the database collected from www.moneycontrol.com

Inflow of Funds from Current Liabilities (Industry-wise Analysis)

Funds raised by sample companies grouped under industry-wise from current liabilities are shown in the Table 8D.5.

Table 8D.5 : Funds Raised from Current Liabilities (Industry-wise Analysis)

Analysis Funds raised from Current Liabilities *(₹ in Crores)*

Year	Agro Based Companies (90)	Mineral Based Companies (135)	Service Companies (45)	Plantation Companies (30)
2001	460.4	298.5	351.61	–69.75
2002	2005.62	4592.43	1049.37	160.06
2003	736.23	1945.95	220.67	63.71
2004	779.48	1799.79	2322.24	95.09
2005	531.82	2073.5	1351.6	56.64
2006	1436	5304.6	2379.66	238.4
2007	3051.42	4934.1	5649.28	172.52
2008	3307.07	8383.54	8203.81	640.13
Total	**12308.04**	**29332.41**	**21528.24**	**1356.8**
Average	**1538.50**	**3666.55**	**2691.03**	**169.6**
Average per Company per Year	**17.09**	**27.16**	**59.80**	**5.65**

Source: Computed from the database collected from www.moneycontrol.com

From the table 8.5 it was observed that the average amount of funds raised annually by the agro-based companies through current liabilities was ₹ 1538.50 crores with a mean average of ₹ 17.09 crores. The annual average in case of mineral based companies was ₹ 3666.55 crores with a mean average of ₹ 27.16 crores per year per company. The annual average in case of service companies was ₹ 2691.03 crores with a mean average of ₹ 59.80 crores and for plantation companies, the annual average was ₹ 169.6 crores and the mean average was ₹ 5.65 crores. Thus, in terms of total annual average, the mineral-based companies have raised the highest amount through current liabilities whereas, in terms of annual average per company, the service companies has raised highest amount of funds from current liabilities. In the year 2001, plantation companies have made some repayments. The highest borrowings through current liabilities was ₹ 3307.07 crores by the agro-based companies, ₹ 8383.54 crores by the mineral based companies, ₹ 8203.81 crores by the service companies, and ₹ 640.13 crores by the plantation companies, all in the year 2008.

Outflow of Funds for Acquiring Fixed Assets (Industry-wise)

Funds invested in fixed assets by the sample companies grouped under different industrial groups are shown in Table 8D.6 (*See on next page*). From the table it was observed that an average annual investment of ₹ 4602.65 crores were made by agro-based companies in acquiring additional fixed assets during the study period. In case of mineral-based companies, the average was ₹ 7792.23 crores, in case of service companies it was ₹ 6324.68 crores and in case of plantation industries, the average was ₹ 126.17 crores.

The mean average investment i.e. average investment per company per year in fixed assets was ₹ 51.14 crores in case of agro-based companies, ₹ 57.72 crores in case of mineral-based companies, ₹ 140.54 crores in case of service companies and ₹ 5.08 crores in case of plantation companies.

For our study purpose, the term fixed assets consists of gross block and capital work in progress. Gross block is the sum total of all tangible fixed assets of the company valued at their cost of acquisition. Capital work in progress means the stage of assets which is at present not ready for use for which it is intended because of some further processing is required. The year when the asset becomes ready for use, the balance in the capital work in progress account of that particular asset is transferred to gross block account. The negative figure in this account indicates that amount has been transferred from this account to gross block. In case of plantation companies, the gross block shows a negative figure of ₹ 1.24 crores in the year 2008. It indicates that some fixed assets have been sold in that year.

Application of Additional Funds in Current Assets (Industry-wise)

The application of funds by sample companies grouped according to the industry to which they belong, in acquiring additional current assets are shown in Table 8D.7 (*See on page 210*). From the table it was observed that an average of ₹ 1538.68 crores by agro-based companies, ₹ 4545.30 crores by mineral based companies, ₹ 3211.39 crores by service companies and ₹ 111.29 crores by plantation companies were invested in the form of current assets every year. The annual average investment per company was ₹ 71.36 crores by the service companies which was the highest among the group, followed by ₹ 33.66 crores by the mineral based companies, ₹ 17.09 crores by agro-based companies and ₹ 3.70 crores by plantation

Table 8D.6 : Application of Funds in Acquiring Additional Fixed Assets – Industry–wise Analysis

(₹ in Crores)

AGRO–BASED COMPANIES (90)

Fixed Assets	2001	2002	2003	2004	2005	2006	2007	2008	Total	Average
Gross Block	2,223.23	1,669.71	1,725.34	1,987.26	2,910.26	5,981.21	9,391.26	6,619.31	32,507.58	4,063.45
Capital WIP	–101.00	–394.85	399.83	–78.24	1,225.54	3,403.03	2,146.51	–2,287.25	4,313.57	539.20
Total	**2,122.23**	**1,274.86**	**2,125.17**	**1,909.02**	**4,135.80**	**9,384.24**	**11,537.77**	**4,332.06**	**36821.15**	**4,602.65**

Average Investment Per Company = Rs.51.14 Crores

MINERAL-BASED COMPANIES (135)

Fixed Assets	2001	2002	2003	2004	2005	2006	2007	2008	Total	Average
Gross Block	1,606.61	3,865.17	2,875.59	5,481.31	6,329.95	10,806.21	9,941.36	10,359.05	51,265.25	6408.16
Capital WIP	1,303.05	–1,212.56	319.85	1,275.28	2,437.69	–1,799.55	3,333.82	5,415.03	11,072.61	1384.07
Total	**2,909.66**	**2,652.61**	**3,195.44**	**6,756.59**	**8,767.64**	**9,006.66**	**13,275.18**	**15,774.08**	**62337.86**	**7792.23**

Average Investment Per Company = ₹ 57.72 Crores

SERVICE COMPANIES (45)

Fixed Assets	2001	2002	2003	2004	2005	2006	2007	2008	Total	Average
Gross Block	2,176.43	2,380.90	2,659.90	3,686.53	2,083.70	3,600.82	6,306.19	18,189.58	41,584.05	5198.00
Capital WIP	517.11	1,453.59	–1,455.75	–27.89	800.35	4,258.56	3,385.70	81.76	9,013.43	1126.68
Total	**2,693.54**	**4,334.49**	**1,204.15**	**3,658.64**	**2,884.05**	**7,859.38**	**9,691.89**	**18,271.34**	**50597.48**	**6324.68**

Average Investment Per Company = ₹ 140.54 Crores

PLANTATION COMPANIES (30)

Fixed Assets	2001	2002	2003	2004	2005	2006	2007	2008	Total	Average
Gross Block	218.30	102.57	110.05	56.00	106.93	163.65	252.67	–1.24	1,009.43	126.17
Capital WIP	–11.57	5.77	–11.85	6.47	81.62	40.60	172.26	–73.46	209.84	26.23
Total	**207.23**	**108.34**	**98.20**	**62.47**	**188.55**	**204.25**	**424.93**	**–74.70**	**1219.27**	**152.40**

Average Investment Per Company = ₹ 5.08 Crores

Source: Computed from the database collected from www.moneycontrol.com

companies. In case of plantation companies, the year 2001 and 2002 shows a negative application of funds which indicates that some amount of current assets have been sold in those years.

The trend of investment in current assets during the study period has been found to be fluctuating. In case of agro based companies, the highest investment was ₹ 4797.43 crores in the year 2008 and the lowest investment was ₹ 168.44 crores in the year 2005. In case of mineral based companies, the highest was ₹ 9614.97 crores in 2008 and the lowest was ₹ 441.61 crores in the year 2001. In case of service companies, the highest was ₹ 7639.9 crores recorded in the year 2008 and the lowest was ₹ 923.39 crores in 2002. For plantation companies, the highest was ₹ 431.86 crores in 2007 and the lowest was (₹ 102.06 crores), a negative outflow in the year 2001.

Table 8.7 : Application of Funds in Current Assets (Industry-wise Analysis)

(₹ in Crores)

Year	Agro Based Companies (90)	Mineral Based Companies (135)	Service Companies (45)	Plantation Companies (30)
2001	910.57	441.61	1181.28	-102.06
2002	255.43	1132.9	923.39	-35.99
2003	220.79	554.72	962.72	56.54
2004	1426.4	3720.05	2753.12	108.93
2005	168.44	4097.3	3029.58	118.83
2006	2219.21	8530.2	5161.77	281.36
2007	2311.2	8270.68	4039.36	431.86
2008	4797.43	9614.97	7639.9	30.87
Total	**12309.47**	**36362.43**	**25691.12**	**890.34**
Average	**1538.68**	**4545.30**	**3211.39**	**111.29**
Average per Company Per Year	**17.09**	**33.66**	**71.36**	**3.70**

Source: Computed from the database collected from www.moneycontrol.com

Debt-Equity Ratio Analysis of Sample Companies (Industry-wise)

The debt equity ratios of different companies grouped under different industrial groups are shown in the Table 8D.8.

Table 8D.8 : Debt-Equity Ratio of Sample Companies (Industry-wise)

Year	Agro Based Companies (90)	Mineral Based Companies (135)	Service Companies (45)	Plantation Companies (30)
2000	1.47	1.47	0.74	0.67
2001	1.45	1.42	0.58	0.68
2002	1.66	1.63	0.62	0.77
2003	1.63	1.61	0.61	0.8
2004	1.72	1.44	0.59	0.86
2005	1.66	1.27	0.45	0.85
2006	1.53	1.21	0.45	0.97
2007	1.89	1.01	0.49	1.02
2008	1.94	0.88	0.73	1.12
Total	**14.95**	**11.94**	**5.26**	**7.74**
Average	**1.66**	**1.32**	**0.58**	**0.86**

Source: Computed from the database collected from www.moneycontrol.com

From the analysis of the Table 8D.8, it was observed that the agro-based companies had an average D/E ratio of 1.66, the mineral-based companies had an average of 1.32, service companies had 0.58 and plantation companies had 0.86.

In the case of service companies, the ratio was below one throughout the study period. It shows that, the amount of debt in none of the years of our study had ever crossed the equity holding/net worth. The industry had relied less on debt than their own equity funds. The owners of the industry had carried business with a high risk. The nature of business and financial policy of the firm might be primarily responsible for it. A ratio of 1:1 may be usually considered as satisfactory, but there the low ratio (debt being low in comparison to net worth or equity) indicated a larger margin of safety for the long term creditors. The situation of plantation companies was also similar to that of service companies except for the year 2007 and 2008 in which their debt-equity ratio was slightly more than one.

In case of agro-based and mineral-based companies though the average ratio is more than one, yet it is below the standard norm of 2:1. Companies of these two industries have used the debt funds more as compared to equity.

Analysis of Size of Investment of Sample Companies (Industry-wise)

The size of investment in fixed assets and current assets of the industry wise grouped sample companies are shown in Table 8.9 (*See on next page*). On the analysis of the table, it was observed that the annual average growth rate in the size of investment in case of agro based companies was 13.75 per cent, mineral based companies 12.57 per cent, service companies 28.17 per cent and in the case of plantation companies, it was 5.35 per cent.

The annual average growth per company was ₹ 48.13 crores in case of agro based companies, ₹ 60.63 crores in case of mineral-based companies, ₹ 158.86 crores in case of service companies and ₹ 5.88 crores in case of plantation companies. Thus the rate of investment in net fixed and current assets were very fast in case of service companies and it was very slow in case of plantation companies.

Analysis of Asset Structure of Sample Companies (Industry-wise)

The ratio of net fixed assets to total assets by the industries taken in the sample is shown in Table 8D.10 (*See on page 215*).

From the table 8D.10, it was observed that the average ratio of net fixed assets to total assets was 0.44 in case of agro-based companies, 0.36 in case of mineral-based companies, 0.28 in case of service companies, and 0.33 in case of plantation companies. The analysis shows that during the initial years of study i.e. 2000 to 2003, the ratio was more than the average so calculated. But gradually it started decreasing and the year 2008 recorded to be the year in which the ratio of net assets to total assets was the lowest for all categories of companies except for service companies for which, the lowest ratio was recorded in the year 2006 and 2007.

Current Ratio of Sample Companies (Industry-wise Analysis)

The current ratios of sample companies grouped under different industrial groups are shown in table 8D.11 (*See on page 215*).

On analysis of the table 8D.11, it came to the notice that the average liquidity ratio in case of agro passed companies was 1.44, mineral-based companies 1.39, service companies 1.40 and plantation companies 1.44.

In all the group of industries, the average liquidity ratios were more than 100 per cent which was referred as a good ability of the industry group to meet current obligations as and when these become due. So we can say that they had a satisfactory liquidity position. The banker, suppliers and other short-term creditors felt fully secured as the currents assets were enough in comparison to current liabilities.

Table 8D.9 : Size of Investment (Net Fixed Assets + Current Assets) Industry-wise Analysis

(₹ in Crores)

Agro Based Companies	2000	2001	2002	2003	2004	2005	2006	2007	2008
Net Block	12042.97	13234.1	13846.15	14305.44	15406.35	17145.06	21362.18	28506.32	34390.71
Current Assets	7949.03	8859.6	9115.03	9335.82	10762.22	10930.66	13149.87	15461.07	20258.5
Total	13992	22093.7	22[illegible]61.18	23641.26	26168.57	28075.72	34512.05	43967.39	54649.21
Growth		2101.7	367.48	680.08	2527.31	1907.15	6436.33	9455.34	10681.82
Growth Per cent		10.51	3.93	2.96	10.69	7.29	22.93	27.40	24.29

Average Growth Per Company Per Year = 43.13

Average Growth Rate Per Year = 13.75%

Mineral Based Companies	2000	2001	2002	2003	2004	2005	2006	2007	2008
Net Block	25618.48	25702.08	27[illegible]64.37	28394.49	31163.32	35064.93	42122.9	48281.97	54735.15
Current Assets	17145.49	17587.1	18[illegible]20	19274.72	22994.77	27092.07	35622.27	43892.95	53507.92
Total	42763.97	43289.18	46[illegible]34.37	47669.21	54158.09	62157	77745.17	92174.92	108243.07
Growth		525.21	3[illegible]95.19	1284.84	6488.88	7998.91	15588.17	14429.75	16068.15
Growth Per cent		1.23	7.15	2.77	13.61	14.77	25.08	18.56	17.43

Average Growth Per Company Per Year = 60.63

Average Growth Rate Per Year = 12.57%

Service Companies	2000	2001	2002	2003	2004	2005	2006	2007	2008
Net Block	6189.22	7466.32	9441.82	11091.84	12930.18	13705.76	15854.62	21429.75	37688.16
Current Assets	3221.22	4402.5	5325.89	6288.61	9041.73	12071.31	17233.08	21272.44	28912.34
Total	**9410.44**	**11868.82**	**14767.71**	**17380.45**	**21971.91**	**25777.07**	**33087.7**	**42702.19**	**66600.5**
Growth		**2458.38**	**2898.89**	**2612.74**	**4591.46**	**3805.16**	**7310.63**	**9614.49**	**23898.31**
Growth Percent		**26.12**	**24.42**	**17.69**	**26.42**	**17.32**	**28.37**	**29.06**	**55.97**

Average Growth Per Company Per Year = 158.86 Average Growth Rate Per Year = 28.17%

Plantation Companies	2000	2001	2002	2003	2004	2005	2006	2007	2008
Net Block	1674.94	1808.57	1843.15	1845.1	1819.34	1832.52	1962.76	2128.73	2196.68
Current Assets	1144.89	1042.83	1006.84	1063.38	1172.31	1291.14	1572.5	2004.36	2035.23
Total	**2819.83**	**2851.4**	**2849.99**	**2908.48**	**2991.65**	**3123.66**	**3535.26**	**4133.09**	**4231.91**
Growth		**31.57**	**–1.41**	**58.49**	**83.17**	**132.01**	**411.6**	**597.83**	**98.82**
Growth Per cent		**1.12**	**–0.05**	**2.05**	**2.86**	**4.41**	**13.18**	**16.92**	**2.40**

Average Growth Per Company Per Year = 5.88 Average Growth Rate Per Year = 5.35%

Source: Computed from the database collected from www.moneycontrol.com

Table 8D.10 : Asset Structure of Sample Companies (Ratio of Net Fixed Assets to Total Assets) (Industry-wise)

Year	Agro Based Companies (90)	Mineral Based Companies (135)	Service Companies (45)	Plantation Companies (30)
2000	0.46	0.43	0.36	0.37
2001	0.46	0.41	0.32	0.39
2002	0.47	0.41	0.3	0.39
2003	0.46	0.39	0.33	0.38
2004	0.43	0.37	0.29	0.36
2005	0.44	0.35	0.25	0.34
2006	0.41	0.34	0.21	0.3
2007	0.41	0.31	0.21	0.25
2008	0.41	0.26	0.26	0.22
Total	**3.95**	**3.27**	**2.53**	**3**
Average	**0.44**	**0.36**	**0.28**	**0.33**

Source: Computed from the database collected from www.moneycontrol.com

Table 8D.11 : Liquidity Ratio of Current Assets to Current Liabilities (Industry-wise)

Year	Agro Based Companies (90)	Mineral Based Companies (135)	Service Companies (45)	Plantation Companies (30)
2000	1.99	1.74	1.24	1.83
2001	1.98	1.73	1.49	1.87
2002	1.41	1.27	1.33	1.4
2003	1.29	1.15	1.49	1.36
2004	1.34	1.24	1.38	1.34
2005	1.28	1.31	1.53	1.38
2006	1.32	1.37	1.67	1.34
2007	1.18	1.42	1.33	1.49
2008	1.24	1.36	1.19	1.02
Total	**13.03**	**12.59**	**12.65**	**13.03**
Average	**1.44**	**1.39**	**1.40**	**1.44**

Source: Computed from the database collected from www.moneycontrol.com

Correlation between Size of Investment and D/E Ratio (Industry-wise)

The correlation between size of investment and D/E ratio of sample companies grouped according to the nature of industry is shown in Table 8D.12 (*See on next page*).

It was calculated that the correlation between the size of investment and D/E ratio was –0.94636 in case of mineral-based companies, which indicates a fairly high degree of negative correlation. Hence it is clear that a greater proportion of increment of funds year after year were sought from equity sources than from debt sources. The assets base of this industry called more long-term funds from equity source than from debt.

In case of agro-based companies and plantation companies, the correlation was 0.81869 and 0.93384 respectively. In both of the cases there was a high degree of positive correlation between the variables which indicates that, the assets of these two industries required long-term funds more from the debt sources rather than from equity.

With regard to correlation between size of investment and D/E ratio of plantation industries, it was 0.01591, a low degree of positive correlation. It implies that these companies have used debt funds for their asset base, but very lesser extent.

Correlation between Asset Structure and D/E Ratio (Industry-wise)

The correlation between the asset structure and D/E ratio of sample companies grouped according to the nature of industry is shown in Table 8D.13 (*See on page 218*).

The analysis shows that in case of agro-based companies and plantation companies, the correlation between the asset structure and the D/E ratio were –0.61017 and –0.93493 respectively. It indicated a moderate to high degree of negative correlation between the variables in both the cases. It shows that the proportion of fixed assets to total assets is influenced by long-term funds more by equity than debts. So it revealed a higher share of equity funds in the acquisition of total assets.

In the case of mineral based companies and service companies, the correlation between the asset structure and D/E ratio was 0.91533 and 0.69618 respectively. Here the degree of correlation is fairly high and positive in both the cases. This indicates that the asset structures of these two types of industries were influenced by the long term funds raised out of debt capital instead of equity capital.

Table 8D.12 : Correlation between Size of Investment and Debt-Equity Ratio (Industry-wise Analysis)

Year	Agro Based Companies (90)		Mineral Based Companies (135)		Service Companies (45)		Plantation Companies (30)	
	Size of Investment (₹ in Crores) (X)	D/E Ratio (Y)	Size of Investment (₹ in Crores) (X)	D/E Ratio (Y)	Size of Investment (₹ in Crores) (X)	D/E Ratio (Y)	Size of Investment (₹ in Crores) (X)	D/E Ratio (Y)
2000	19992	1.47	42763.97	1.47	9410.44	0.74	2819.83	0.67
2001	22093.7	1.45	43289.18	1.42	11868.82	0.58	2851.4	0.68
2002	22961.18	1.66	46384.37	1.63	14757.71	0.62	2849.99	0.77
2003	23641.26	1.63	47669.21	1.61	17330.45	0.61	2908.48	0.8
2004	26168.57	1.72	54158.09	1.44	21971.91	0.59	2991.65	0.86
2005	28075.72	1.66	62157	1.27	25777.07	0.45	3123.66	0.85
2006	34512.05	1.53	77745.17	1.21	33087.7	0.45	3535.26	0.97
2007	43967.39	1.89	92174.92	1.01	42702.19	0.49	4133.09	1.02
2008	54649.21	1.94	108243.07	0.88	66600.5	0.73	4231.91	1.12
Coefficient of Correlation	0.81869		-0.94636		0.01591		0.93384	

Source: Computed from the database collected from www.moneycontrol.com

Table 8D.13 : Correlation between Asset Structure and Debt-equity Ratio (Industry-wise Analysis)

Year	Agro Based Companies (90)		Mineral Based Companies (135)		Service Companies (45)		Plantation Companies (30)	
	Size of Investment (₹ in Crores) (X)	D/E Ratio (Y)	Size of Investment (₹ in Crores) (X)	D/E Ratio (Y)	Size of Investment (₹ in Crores) (X)	D/E Ratio (Y)	Size of Investment (₹ in Crores) (X)	D/E Ratio (Y)
2000	0.46	1.47	0.43	1.47	0.36	0.74	0.37	0.67
2001	0.46	1.45	0.41	1.42	0.32	0.58	0.39	0.68
2002	0.47	1.66	0.41	1.63	0.3	0.62	0.39	0.77
2003	0.46	1.63	0.39	1.61	0.33	0.61	0.38	0.8
2004	0.43	1.72	0.37	1.44	0.29	0.59	0.36	0.86
2005	0.44	1.66	0.35	1.27	0.25	0.45	0.34	0.85
2006	0.41	1.53	0.34	1.21	0.21	0.45	0.3	0.97
2007	0.41	1.89	0.31	1.01	0.21	0.49	0.25	1.02
2008	0.41	1.94	0.26	0.88	0.26	0.73	0.22	1.12
Coefficient of Correlation	–0.61017		0.91533		0.69618		–0.93493	

Source: Computed from the database collected from www.moneycontrol.com

Correlation between Liquidity Ratio and D/E Ratio (Industry-wise)

The correlation between liquidity and D/E ratio of sample companies grouped according to different industrial groups is shown in Table 8D.14. From the table it is observed that the correlation between the liquidity ratio and D/E ratio of agro-based companies was –0.75268, mineral-based companies –0.06758, service companies –0.78884 and plantation companies –0.7994. So, except mineral-based companies where there was a low degree of negative correlation, in all other cases the correlation between the variables were negative and fairly high. It shows that the current assets to liability position had a negative association with the long-term debt sources. Hence we can say that, these factors were mostly influenced by long-term equity sources. Therefore it can be concluded that, the liquid assets ofthese industries were influenced more by the equity funds than by the debt funds.

Summary and concluding remarks

The ability to raise funds differs according to the nature of business, age size and regions. Therefore, the sample companies were classified on the basis of region, age, size, industry etc. This chapter analyzed the trend and pattern of sources and uses of funds and the capital structure of each group of sample companies.

The region of a company more or less influences its quantum of inflow of funds both debt and equity. They also exert impact on the overall trend of the total sample. Companies were classified into eastern, western, northern and southern regions. The number of companies in eastern region was 34, western region 135, northern region 46 and southern region 85.

From the funds flow analysis of sample companies grouped under four different regions, it was found that the western region which comprises of 135 companies has raised the highest amount of funds among all the four regions during the period of study. The average amount of funds raised by the sample companies of eastern region was ₹ 1832.76 crores, western region ₹ 22205.46 crores, northern region ₹ 5772.78 crores and southern region ₹ 16939.08 crores.

With respect to raising of funds through internal sources, it was found that the eastern region companies raised funds internally ₹ 9229.6 crores in total during the study period with an average of ₹ 1153.7 crores yearly. In case of western region companies, the total amount of funds raised internally was ₹ 105347.84 crores with an average of ₹ 13168 annually, which is the highest among all the four regions. Similarly, the total internal

Table 8D.14 : Correlation between Liquidity Ratio and Debt-Equity Ratio (Industry-wise Analysis)

Year	Agro Based Companies (90)		Mineral Based Companies (135)		Service Companies (45)		Plantation Companies (30)	
	Liquidity Ratio(X)	D/E Ratio (Y)	Liquidity Ratio(X)	D/E Ratio (Y)	Liquidity Ratio(X)	D/E Ratio (Y)	Liquidity IRatio(X)	D/E Ratio (Y)
2000	1.99	1.47	1.74	1.47	1.24	0.74	1.83	0.67
2001	1.98	1.45	1.73	1.42	1.49	0.58	1.87	0.68
2002	1.41	1.66	1.27	1.63	1.33	0.62	1.4	0.77
2003	1.29	1.63	1.15	1.61	1.49	0.61	1.36	0.8
2004	1.34	1.72	1.24	1.44	1.38	0.59	1.34	0.86
2005	1.28	1.66	1.31	1.27	1.53	0.45	1.38	0.85
2006	1.32	1.53	1.37	1.21	1.67	0.45	1.34	0.97
2007	1.18	1.89	1.42	1.01	1.33	0.49	1.49	1.02
2008	1.24	1.94	1.36	0.88	1.19	0.73	1.02	1.12
Coefficient of Correlation	–0.75268		–0.06758		–0.78884		–0.7994	

Source: Computed from the database collected from www.moneycontrol.com

funds raised by northern and southern companies during the period of study were ₹ 21796.17 crores and 83421.13 crores respectively.

Total amount of funds raised by the issue of equity and preference shares were ₹ 3479 crores by western region, ₹ 1250 crores by northern region, and ₹ 2521 crores by southern region. In case of eastern region, the amount of funds raised shows a negative figure of ₹ 4.97 crores indicating that the amount paid towards the redemption of preference shares was more than the amount collected by issue of equity shares.

Companies also raised funds through long-term loans comprising of secured and unsecured loans. The total amount raised through debt or long term loan both secured and unsecured was ₹ 3141 crores by eastern region companies, ₹ 38915 crores by western region companies, ₹ 12941 crores by northern region companies, and ₹ 27435 crores by southern region companies. The common observation for the companies of all the four regions was that they have raised more funds through debt capital as compared to equity, may be due to the reason of easy and availability of cheap debt capital. Not a single company of any region has raised any fund through differed credit.

The annual average inflow of funds from current liabilities was ₹ 287 crores by the eastern region companies, ₹ 3737.59 crores by the western region, ₹ 1274.26 crores by the northern region and ₹ 2766.81 crores by the southern region companies.

The funds so raised by different regions were applied in acquiring fixed assets, current assets, etc. It was found that an annual average of ₹ 938.16 crores were invested in acquiring fixed assets by the eastern region companies. The same in case of western region was ₹ 9327.66 crores, northern region ₹ 2768.21 crores and southern region ₹ 5838.67 crores. Similarly, an annual average of ₹ 241.16 crores were invested additionally every year in current assets by the eastern region companies whereas that in case of western region it was ₹ 4384.07 crores, ₹ 911.64 crores in case of northern region and ₹ 3836.78 crores by the southern region companies.

The debt-equity ratios were calculated from the consolidated balance sheets of the respective regions. For our study purpose, debt includes secured loans, unsecured loans, current liabilities and deferred credits, i.e. all types of debts. Similarly equity or net worth consists of equity share capital, preference share capital, share application money, reserves and revaluation reserves. The debt-equity ratio for the above purpose is calculated by dividing debt by equity. The annual average ratio for the total period was 1.21, 1.24, 1.09 and 0.97 respectively for eastern, western, northern and southern region companies. The average so worked out for all the regions were fairly lower than the generally accepted norm of 2:1.

The annual average of size of investment for the whole period worked out to be ₹ 8925.76 crores for eastern region companies, ₹ 60983.47 crores for western region companies, ₹ 16470.68 crores for northern region companies and ₹ 38470.31 crores for southern region companies. Western region shows the highest with respect to average as well as total size of investments among all the regions.

While analyzing the asset structure of companies of different regions, it was observed that the proportion of net fixed assets to total assets for the eastern region companies varied in between 0.36 to 0.46. In case of western region it was 0.30 to 0.43, northern region 0.32 to 0.34 and in case of southern region it was in between 0.23 to 0.43. The average ratio of eastern, western, northern and southern region companies was 0.41, 0.38, 0.33 and 0.33 respectively.

With respect to the liquidity ratio or current ratio of different regions for the study period, it was observed that it varied from 0.89 to 1.41 with an annual average of 1.07 in case of eastern region companies, 1.23 to 1.77 with an annual average of 1.42 in case of western region companies, 0.96 to 1.87 with an annual average of 1.42 in case of northern region companies and 1.25 to 1.85 with an annual average of 1.48 in case of southern region companies.

The correlation between size of investment and debt-equity ratio for eastern, western and southern region were found to be –0.58349, –0.82911, 0.94371 and –0.74606 respectively.

A high negative ratio in case of eastern, western and southern region indicates that the investments are influenced much by equity funds than by the debt funds. But in case of northern region, the coefficient of correlation shows a positive figure which is 0.94371. This kind of high degree positive correlation indicates that a greater proportion of debt funds are used for acquiring fixed as well as current assets.

The correlation between asset structure and debt equity ratio shows that eastern, western and southern region companies had high degree of positive correlation between the asset structure and D/E ratio. This indicated that the proportions of fixed assets greatly depended on long-term debt funds. In the case of northern region, the coefficient of correlation between the asset structure and debt-equity ratio is -0.01077 which is a very low degree of negative correlation. This indicates that the fixed assets depended negatively on debt funds and positively on equity funds, particularly in case of northern region companies.

The correlation between liquidity and debt equity ratio shows that except for the southern region, all other regions indicated a negative association between the two variables. It implies that the current assets of the companies of those regions were negatively influenced by long-term debts. It might be from short-term sources or from equity sources. The positive correlation shown by southern region indicated that a portion of the long-term debt funds have been invested by the companies of this region in current assets.

The ability of a company to generate internal funds and attract funds from outside is also affected by the age of the company. An attempt has been made to study the capital structure and its components for companies grouped under different ages, viz., very old, old, and new companies. The companies registered before independence i.e. 1947 were grouped under the category 'very old' companies. There were 44 companies in this group. Companies registered after 1947 but before 1980 were grouped under the head 'old' companies. There were 95 companies under this head. Companies came into existence after 1980 were grouped under the head 'new' and there were 161 companies under this category.

While analyzing the total inflow of funds by sample companies, it was observed that in case of very old companies, the average inflow of funds was ₹ 8297.97 crores, in case of old companies the annual average was ₹ 14040.57 crores and in case of new companies the annual average was ₹ 24411.55, which was highest among all the three groups.

After the analysis of the funds raised through internal sources, it was observed that in case of very old companies the flow of funds from internal sources was ₹ 5343.3 crores on an average during the period. The total amount raised from internal sources during the period was ₹ 42746.6 crores. In case of old companies, the total internal funds generated during the period was ₹ 68779.9 crores with an annual average of ₹ 8597.47 crores. Similarly, with respect to new companies, the total funds raised internally amounted to ₹ 108268 crores with an annual average of ₹ 13533.52 crores. In all the three categories, amount generated from reserves which consists of retained earnings, was highest among the internal sources of funds. Funds generated from accumulated depreciation remained the second biggest source of internal funds in all the cases.

It is observed from the analysis of external sources of finances that, an average of ₹ 135.96 crores were raised by the very old companies by issue of equity shares, preference shares as well as through share application money. In case of old companies, the average amount raised was ₹ 253.14 crores and that of for new companies it was ₹ 516.73 crores.

Funds were also generated by all the age grouped companies through long-term loans comprising of secured as well as unsecured loans. On an average every year the very old companies generated ₹ 1350.9 crores of funds through long-term debts and loans. In case of old companies, this yearly average is ₹ 2802.62 crores whereas in case of new companies the average is ₹ 6150.67 crores. Funds raised through current liabilities by the age grouped companies during the study period showed that the average inflow of funds from this source by the very old companies were ₹ 1467.77 crores, old companies were ₹ 2387.32 crores and new companies were ₹ 4210.59 crores.

Funds were invested in acquiring additional fixed assets by the sample companies grouped age-wise. It was observed that an average of ₹ 3030.15 crores were invested in acquiring additional fixed assets by the very old companies. The same in case of old companies were ₹ 5234.29 crores and in case of new companies, it recorded ₹ 10608.26 crores. With respect to investment in current assets, the average investment in additional current assets in case of very old companies were ₹ 1842.45 crores whereas in case of old companies the average was ₹ 2380.25 crores and in case of new companies the average was ₹ 5183.95 crores, being the highest in the group.

After studying the Debt-Equity ratios of age grouped companies of the entire study period it was observed that an average of 1.04 ratio of debt to equity was there in case of very old companies. That in case of old companies was 1.13 and for new companies it was around 1.00. All the averages were below the accepted norm 2:1.

The analysis of size of investment which comprises of the sum of net fixed assets and current assets showed that the average growth rate was 11.88 per cent every year in case of very old companies, 11.74 per cent in case of the old companies and 21.22 per cent in case of new companies. The asset structure which indicates the ratio of net fixed assets to total assets revealed that an average of 36 per cent net fixed assets were there in the total assets in case of both very old and old companies, while that in case of new companies it was 35 per cent. It reflects that companies of all the age groups invested more or less equal proportion of total funds in net fixed assets. The liquidity ratio which reflects the short-term solvency position of the company, i.e. ability to meet short-term obligations showed that an average of ₹ 1.34 worth of current assets were there for covering every rupee of current liability obligations in case of very old companies. In case of old companies, the average ratio was 1.30 and in case of new companies it was 1.60.

The co-efficient of correlation between the size of investment and debt-equity ratio in all the categories are found to be negative. In case of very old companies it was -0.87527, in case of old companies it was -0.86772, and in case of new companies, the correlation was calculated at -0.55028. The correlation between asset structure and D/E ratio of sample companies grouped under age category for all the three groups shows that, the degree of correlation is high as well as positive. This indicates that in case of all the companies, the asset structure was influenced greatly by the long term funds raised through debts and loans rather than the equity capital. Whereas the correlation between liquidity ratio and debt-equity ratio revealed that in case of very old companies, the correlation was +0.24852, in case of old companies the coefficient of correlation is calculated at -0.04209 and in case of new companies the correlation was +0.55918.

The total sample companies were again grouped on the basis of their size, viz., small, medium and large. As on 31st March 2008, the companies having total assets below ₹ 100 crores are grouped under 'small sized companies'. There were 75 of such companies in the total sample which are grouped under this category, which constitute 25 per cent of the total sample. The companies having the total assets value ₹ 100 crores and above but less than ₹ 500 crores are grouped under 'medium sized companies'. There was 98 such type of companies constituting 32.67 per cent of the total sample. Companies having their total assets value worth ₹ 500 crores and above as on 31st March, 2008 are grouped as 'large sized companies', which include 127 companies, about 42.33 per cent of the total sample.

From the analysis of total inflow of funds, it was observed that an average of ₹ 370.69 crores of funds was raised by small sized company with a mean inflow of ₹ 4.94 crores annually by each company under this group. The average inflow of funds in case of 'medium sized companies' was ₹ 3078.18 crores with a mean inflow of ₹ 31.41 crores by each company annually under this group. In case of 'large sized companies', the annual average inflow of funds were ₹ 43300.91 crores and the mean inflow for each company per annum was ₹ 340 .95 crores.

With respect to the funds generated from internal sources, it is found that an annual average of ₹ 133.40 crores was raised by the small sized companies from internal sources. In case of medium sized companies and large sized companies, the inflow of funds from internal sources were ₹ 1468.90 crores ₹ 25872.03 crores respectively. The mean average inflow from such sources was ₹ 1.78 crores in case of a small company, ₹ 14.98 crores in a medium sized company and ₹ 203.71 crores in case of large company.

It was observed that an average of ₹ 43.96 crores were raised by the small sized companies from issue of both preference and equity shares during the period. The same was ₹ 129.15 crores in case of medium sized companies and ₹ 732.72 crores in case of large sized companies. The equity issue as bonus issues causes no inflow of funds.

The average funds generated by small, medium and large sized companies from long-term loans were ₹ 89.66 crores, ₹ 850.31 crores and ₹ 9364.22 crores respectively. Average funds generated from current liabilities were ₹ 103.66 crores by the small sized companies, ₹ 630.09 crores by the medium sized companies and ₹ 7331.93 by the large sized companies.

The funds so raised by the sample companies from internal and external sources were applied in acquiring mainly additional fixed assets and current assets. It was observed that averages of ₹ 114.84 crores were invested in incremental fixed assets by the small sized companies. The average investment in case of medium sized company was ₹ 1552.55 crores and in case of large sized companies, the average application of funds in fixed assets was ₹ 17205.30 crores. The average investments in current assets by small, medium and large sized companies were ₹ 154.31 crores, ₹ 798.56 crores and ₹ 8453.79 crores respectively.

The average D/E ratio in case of small sized companies was 3.04, in case of medium sized companies it was 2.10 and in case of large sized companies it was calculated at 1.00. The average investment position in small sized company was ₹ 3255.46 crores. Such a position in case of medium sized companies revealed ₹ 16456.14 crores and large sized companies ₹ 105138.62 crores. It was observed that an average of 36 per cent of net fixed assets were there in the total assets structure in case of small sized companies. The same was 40 per cent in case of medium sized companies and 35 per cent in case of large sized companies. The average liquidity ratio was 1.61, in case of medium sized companies it recorded a ratio of 1.33 and in case of large sized companies the average ratio was 1.42.

On analysis, it was observed that the correlation between size of investment and D/E ratio in case of small sized company was –0.57129, in case of medium sized companies it was –0.66987 and in case of large sized companies, it was –0.77986. In the case of all the three group of companies there exists a fairly high degree of negative correlation between the size of investments and the debt-equity ratios. It indicated that a greater proportion of investments were influenced more by the long term equity sources than the debt source.

The correlation between asset structure and debt equity ratio of the different sized companies revealed that in case of small sized companies, the correlation was 0.42978, medium sized companies 0.36926 and large companies 0.91474. This implies that, in case of small and medium sized companies, there was a moderate level of influence of the long term debt funds in the acquisition of net fixed assets but the influence of debt funds was much more in case of large sized companies and the influence of equity funds in acquisition of fixed assets was negligible.

The correlation between the current ratio and debt equity ratio of small sized companies was –0.56777, in case of medium sized companies –0.78487 and in case of large sized companies, it was 0.31412. It indicated that the liquidity position of large sized companies was positively influenced by the long term debt sources rather than equity, which was not seen in case of small and medium sized companies.

The Sample companies were again grouped according to the nature of industry, viz., agro based manufacturing industries, mineral based manufacturing industries, service industries and plantation industries. An attempt has been made to study the impact of each industry variable on the overall flow of funds and the capital structure.

The funds flow statement of each group of industry revealed that the amount of funds raised and applied by the companies under different industrial groups is worked out to be ₹ 8325.99 crores, ₹ 20832.58 crores, ₹ 16860.31 crores and ₹ 702.99 crores in average annually by the agro based, mineral based, service and plantation companies respectively.

The agro based companies had generated an average of ₹ 3424.40 crores, mineral based companies ₹ 13389.56 crores, service companies Rs.10311.56 crores and plantation companies ₹ 321.35 crores from the internal sources during the study period.

From the analysis it was observed that in case of agro based companies, the average amount of funds raised through share capital was ₹ 182.11 crores, in case of mineral based companies it was ₹ 391.06 crores, in case of service companies it was ₹ 332.49 crores and in case of plantation companies, it was ₹ 0.16 crores.

The annual average inflow of funds from long term loans comprising of both secured as well as unsecured, by the agro based companies recorded ₹ 3180.97 crores, mineral based companies ₹ 3385.39 crores, service companies ₹ 3525.22 crores and plantation companies ₹ 211.87 crores. No amount has been raised through deferred credits.

It was observed that the average amount of funds raised annually by the agro based companies through current liabilities was ₹ 1538.50 crores with a mean average of ₹ 17.09 crores. The annual average in case of mineral based companies was ₹ 3666.55 crores with a mean average of ₹ 27.16 crores per year per company. The annual average in case of service companies was ₹ 2691.03 crores with a mean average of ₹ 59.80 crores and for plantation companies, the annual average was ₹ 169.6 crores and the mean average was ₹ 5.65 crores.

Funds so raised by the sample companies were mainly invested in acquiring fixed and current assets. Some funds were also applied in the form of fixed deposits, investments, loans and advances and miscellaneous assets. It was observed that an average annual investment of ₹ 4602.65 crores were made by agro based companies in acquiring additional fixed assets during the study period. In case of mineral based companies, the average was ₹ 7792.23 crores, in case of service companies it was ₹ 6324.68 crores and in case of plantation industries, the average was ₹ 126.17 crores. Turning to current assets, it was observed that an average of ₹ 1538.68 crores by agro based companies, ₹ 4545.30 crores by mineral based companies, ₹ 3211.39 crores by service companies and ₹ 111.29 crores by plantation companies were invested in the form of current assets every year.

The results of ratio analysis showed that, the agro based companies had an average D/E ratio of 1.66, the mineral based companies had an average of 1.32, service companies had 0.58 and plantation companies had 0.86. The annual average growth rate in the size of investment in case of agro based companies was 13.75 per cent, mineral based companies 12.57 per cent, service companies 28.17 per cent and in the case of plantation companies, it was 5.35 per cent. The average ratio of net fixed assets to total assets was 0.44 in case of agro based companies, 0.36 in case of mineral based companies, 0.28 in case of service companies, and 0.33 in case of plantation companies. And finally, it came to the notice that the average liquidity ratio in case of agro passed companies was 1.44, mineral-based companies 1.39, service companies 1.40 and plantation companies 1.44.

The results of correlation analysis showed that the correlation between the size of investment and D/E ratio was –0.94636 in case of mineral based companies, which indicates a fairly high degree of negative correlation. Hence it is clear that a greater proportion of increment of funds year after year were sought from equity sources than from debt sources. In case of agro-based companies and plantation companies, the correlation was 0.81869 and 0.93384 respectively. In both of the cases there was a high degree of positive correlation between the variables which indicates that, the assets of these two industries required long-term funds more from the debt sources rather than from equity. With regard to correlation between size of investment and D/E ratio of plantation industries, it was 0.01591, a low degree of positive correlation. It implies that these companies have used debt funds for their asset base, but very lesser extent.

The analysis shows that in case of agro based companies and plantation companies, the correlation between the asset structure and the D/E ratio were –0.61017 and –0.93493 respectively. It indicated a moderate to high degree of negative correlation between the variables in both the cases. In the case of mineral based companies and service companies, the correlation between the asset structure and D/E ratio was 0.91533 and 0.69618 respectively. Here the degree of correlation is fairly high and positive in both the cases.

It was observed that the correlation between the liquidity ratio and D/E ratio of agro based companies was –0.75268, mineral based companies –0.06758, service companies –0.78884 and plantation companies –0.7994. So, except mineral based companies where there was a low degree of negative correlation, in all other cases the correlation between the variables were negative and fairly high. It shows that the current assets to liability position had a negative association with the long-term debt sources.

9 Summary of Findings and Conclusion

The Aim and Utility of the Study

The aim of this concluding chapter is to summarize the key findings of the study and to offer some possible research ideas for future work. The first task is thus to briefly restate the purpose and approach of each chapter, emphasizing the main results and conclusions. This will be followed by the testing of hypothesis and concluding section, which highlights some promising research ideas as were mentioned at chapters' ends.

Key Findings of each Chapter

Key Findings of Chapter — 1

First chapter, 'Introduction' was all about the concept of capital structure, importance of its study, how our study is designed and what is expected from it. We have also stated what would be the structure of our study and the limitations associated with it.

Key Findings of Chapter — 2

Turning to second chapter 'Concept of Capital Structure', we started with the meaning and definition of capital structure. No doubt capital structure decisions are the most complex and controversial area in the field of corporate finance. Financing the firms assets is a very crucial problem and as a general rule there should be a proper mix of debt and equity capital in financing the firm's assets. The exercise of the financial managers in planning for capital structure differs from firm to firm, as no two firms, though similar in nature, operations etc. can have single capital structure. Even a single capital structure cannot suit the same firm through out. In order to know whether capital structure affects the value of the firm, we started analyzing the various capital structure theories.

Among the theories of capital structure, the first one is Net Income Approach on Capital Structure which was propounded by David Durand in 1952. This approach states that firm can increase its value or lower the cost of capital by using the debt capital. Net operating income approach is converse to this approach. This approach contends that the value of a firm and cost of the capital are independent to capital structure. Thus, the firm cannot increase its value by judicial mixture of debt and equity capital. These are two extreme approaches to capital structure.

Solomon developed the intermediate approach to the capital structure in 1963. This traditional theory of capital structure pleads that value of the firm goes increase to a certain level of debt capital and after then it tends to remain constant with a moderate use of debt capital, and finally value of the firm decreases (Solomon 1963). Thus, this theory holds the concept of optimal capital structure.

The modern theory of capital structure began with the celebrated paper of Modigliani and Miller published in 1958. In this paper, they supported the net operating income approach and rejected the traditional theory of capital structure. They contend in their first proposition that the market value of any firm is independent to its capital structure and is given by capitalizing its expected return at the rate appropriate to the risk class. This was theoretically very sound but was based on the assumptions of perfect capital market and no tax world, which were not valid in reality. So, this was corrected in 1963. In correction, they incorporated the effect of tax on value and cost of the capital of the firm; and contend that, in the presence of corporate tax, the value of the firm varies with the variation of the use of the debt due to tax benefit on interest bill.

Jensen and Meckling developed the capital structure theory based on the agency costs in 1976. Firm incurs two types of agency costs—cost associated with the outside equity holders and cost associated with the presence of debt in capital structure. Total agency cost first decreases and after certain level of outside equity capital in capital structure, it increases. The total agency cost becomes minimal at certain level of outside equity capital. Thus, this theory pleads the concept of optimal capital structure. To sum up, through capital structure theories we tried to explain how the mix of debt and equity in the firm's capital structure influences its market value.

The next issue which is taken up in this chapter for discussion is regarding optimality of capital structure. This is one of the most debatable issues in finance. There are two schools of thought in this regard. One school pleads for optimal capital structure and other does against it. Former school argues that judicious mixture of debt and equity capital can minimize the overall cost of capital and maximize the value of the firm. Hence, this school considers capital structure decision as relevant. Latter school of thought led by Modigliani and Miller contends that financing decision does not affect the value of the firm. Since value of the firm depends on the underlying profitability and risk of investment. Despite its theoretical appeal, researchers in financial management have not found the optimal capital structure. But our opinion in this regard is that instead of trying to find out what is an optimal mix of debt and equity that will maximize shareholder wealth, the finance managers should start to find out under what circumstances should leverage be used to maximize shareholder wealth? Why? Because debt and equity have profound long-term implications for corporate governance that far exceed the exigencies of the moment. Before concluding this chapter, we took up the topic of determinants of capital structure for discussion. We have discussed the factors that generally affect the capital structure decisions of a firm like, tax policy of government, inflation rate, capital market condition, etc.

Key Findings of Chapter — 3

The third chapter 'Sources of Corporate Finance' deals with the various sources of company finances. Finance is the life blood of every business. It is a process of converting accumulated funds to productive use. Raising of funds, administration of income and regulation of the flow of funds are the important aspects of finance. Modern corporate world need adequate financing for their long-term existence and profitability.

Acquiring an appropriate amount of finance at the right time is very much important. The financial managers should also be careful in formulation of internal policies concerning the various sources of finance and costs thereof. The sources of finance mainly depend upon the size, age and nature of business. By and large, methods of financing are categorized broadly into equity and non-equity portions of the capital structure. The other divisions of sources of finances are, internal and external, short-term and long-term etc. In this chapter we discussed in detail the various sources of corporate finances.

After that we discussed the factors that should be considered while choosing the sources of finances. We have also tried to find out the preferred source of finance of Indian corporate. The finding says that, Indian companies prioritize their sources of financing (from internal financing to equity) according to the law of least effort, or of least resistance, preferring to raise equity as a financing means 'of last resort'.

Hence internal funds are used first, and when that is depleted debt is issued, and when it is not sensible to issue any more debt, equity is issued.

Key Findings of Chapter — 4

In fourth chapter, 'Liberalization and Capital Structure of Indian Corporate', we presented the scenario of the capital structure of Indian corporate before liberalization. A theoretical study has been undertaken to find out the pattern of corporate financing before liberalization, how liberalization affected the Indian corporate and changes observed in the capital structure decisions of Indian corporate after liberalization.

While trying to find out the preferred source of financing for Indian corporate before 1990's, we came across the study conducted by I.M.Pandey in 1984. In his study, he found that during 1973-81 about 80 per cent of the assets of the companies sampled were financed by external debt and current liabilities. Large-sized companies were more levered though a large number of small firms also courted more debt capital, particularly in pre-liberalization years Before 1990s Indian financial managers courted debt due to its low cost, tax advantages and the complicated procedures to be observed in garnering equity capital. The substitutability of short-term debt for long-term loan was another attraction.

Then we analyzed how liberalization of Indian economy affected the capital structure of Indian corporate. Analysis found that, by the mid-90s, the private capital had surpassed the public capital. The management system had shifted from the traditional family based system to a system of qualified and professional manager One of the most significant effects of the liberalization era has been the emergence of a strong, affluent and buoyant middle class with significant purchasing powers and this has been the engine that has driven the economy since liberalization.

Key Findings of Chapter — 5

During this study we have reviewed some of the noteworthy contributions on capital structure in order to know the views and opinions given by the finance experts on this topic in fifth chapter, titled as 'Review of Literature'. Franco Modigliani and Merton Miller (hereafter called M-M) were the first to present a formal model on valuation of capital structure. In their seminal papers (1958,1963), they showed that under the assumptions of perfect capital markets, equivalent risk class, no taxes, 100 per cent dividend-payout ratio and constant cost of debt, the value of a firm is independent of its capital structure. When corporate taxes are taken into account, the value of a firm increases linearly with debt-equity (D/E) ratio because of interest payments being tax exempted. M-M's work has been at the centre stage of the financial research till date. Their models have been criticized, supported, and extended over the last 35 years.

David Durand (1963) criticized the model on the ground that the assumptions used by M-M are unrealistic. Solomon (1963) argued that the cost of debt does not always remain constant. When the leverage level exceeds the accepted level, the probability of default in interest payments increases thus raising the cost of debt. Stiglitz (1969, 1974) proved the validity of the M-M model under relaxed assumptions whereas Smith (1972), Krause and Litzenberger (1973), Baron (1974, 1975), and Scott (1976, 1977), supported the M-M model, but only under the conditions of risk free debt and costless bankruptcy. When bankruptcy has positive costs, there exists an optimal capital structure which is a trade-off between tax advantage of debt and bankruptcy costs. This trade-off theory was challenged by Miller (1977). He argued that bankruptcy and agency costs are too small to offset the tax advantage of debt. But when personal taxes are taken into account, this advantage is completely offset by the disadvantage of personal tax rate.

Thus, in equilibrium, the value of a firm is independent of its capital structure, even when the market is imperfect. But Miller's model was rejected by DeAngelo and Masulis (1980). They argued that even if bankruptcy, agency and related costs are ignored, introduction of non-debt tax shields is enough for a firm to have an optimal capital structure. And even if these costs are taken into account, an optimal capital structure exists, irrespective of availability of non-debt tax shields.

Masulis (1980, 1983), Brennen and Schwartz (1978), and Jensen and Meckling (1976) also advocated the existence of an optimal capital structure in an imperfect market, while using different mechanisms. Besides, a lot more work has been done on this problem till now, but a formal model, showing the mechanism for determining an optimal capital structure in an imperfect market, is yet to be developed.

In the Indian context, one comes across two works, one by Sharma and Rao (1969) and the other by Pandey (1992). The former tested the M-M model using cross-sectional analysis for engineering companies, wherein the value of a firm was found to be independent of its capital structure after allowing for tax advantage. But the results could not be generalized, as the sample was homogeneous. The other work by Pandey (1992) observed that the M-M theory is not fully valid under Indian conditions. He concluded that, initially, cost of capital and value of a firm are independent of the capital structure changes, but they rise after a certain level.

Key Findings of Chapter — 6

In chapter six, we have explained about the methodology and tools that we have adopted for our study purpose. We have given a brief description about the nature and scope of the study, nature and source of the data, selection and classification of sample, period and objectives of the study, hypothesis constructed and tools and techniques adopted for the study purpose.

For our study purpose, only secondary data is used which is sourced from the website *www.moneycontrol.com*. The information relating to nature of industry, size, age, state and region, company background, value of total assets and annual financial statements of sample companies for the period 1999-2000 to 2007-2008 have been obtained from the same. Keeping in view the scope of the study, it was decided to select companies on the basis of purposive sampling rather than taking the whole thing. Our sample consists of 300 firms from a heterogeneous set of 20 different sectors. For our study purpose we have taken the data of top 15 companies of each sector selected on the basis of their total assets value as on 31st March 2008. The study excludes financial and securities sector companies, as their financial characteristics and use of leverage are substantially different from other companies.

As it is already mentioned that the main objectives of the study was to know:

1. Whether there exist any significant variations in the capital structures of Indian companies and if yes, the reason for it.
2. Whether the age, size, nature and region of a company has a bearing on the capital structure of a company.
3. Whether Indian companies rely more on external sources to meet the financial requirements.
4. Which is the most preferred source of capital of Indian companies i.e. Debt or Equity?

In order to achieve our objectives, first we have classified the total sample companies according to their age, size, region and the industry or sector. For the purpose of analysis, two important techniques, i.e., ratio analysis and funds flow statement analysis have been selected to study the capital structure as these two methods are widely used for the study. The study is related to analysis of various sources of finance and factors influencing the need for generation of different components of finance. It also analyzed the overall trend of internal and external finance and examination of their uses. The pattern of different sources from which the companies raised their capital was also discussed and the impact of such components on the overall trend of capital structure was examined.

Historical funds flow statements are prepared to give source wise detail of the funds raised for assets formation. Such a statement was compiled from the balance sheets of two consecutive years It indicated various means by which funds were obtained and the ways in which these funds were employed.

Ratio analysis is the principal technique used in judging the condition portrayed by the financial statements. The analyst can judge the financial growth and development and the present condition of a business enterprise. Ratio is used as an index or yards stick for evaluating the financial position and performance. It indicates quantitative relationship to make qualitative judgment.

To judge the long-term financial position of a firm, leverage or capital structure ratios are calculated. The current ratio is calculated to indicate the current financial position of a firm. Financial leverage indicates the funds provided by owners and creditors. As a general rule, there should be an appropriate mix of debt and equity in financing the firms' assets. Capital structure ratios are calculated from the balance sheet items to determine the proportion of debt in total financing. They indicate the extent to which the firm has relied on debt funds in financing assets. Net fixed assets to net worth ratio indicate the extent to which equity capital is invested in net fixed assets. Net worth to total assets ratio is a supplementary to determine the security for lenders. Total debt to total net worth ratio indicate the relationship between borrowed funds and owners' capital and is a popular measure to know long-term financial solvency of a firm. Current ratio or liquidity ratio defines relationship between current assets and current liabilities which is widely used to analyze the short-term financial position.

The trend analysis in capital formation/structure is aimed at establishing relationship between sources of funds and uses of funds. The coefficient of correlation is calculated for the total as well as for the classified variables. In the study we have calculated the correlation between size of investment and debt equity ratio, asset structure and debt equity ratio and liquidity and debt equity ratio. The objective is to analyze the impact of capital structure decisions on the operating performance of a company. Debt-equity ratio is taken as a quantitative measure of capital structure. Some operating performance variables, viz. , size of investment, asset structure and liquidity have close interaction with capital structure decisions. The interrelationship was studied with the help of Karl Pearson's coefficient of correlation techniques.

Key Findings of Chapter — 7

Then, we started the seventh chapter to study the sources and application of funds and the capital structure of Indian corporate sector represented by 300 companies taken from 20 different sectors. The different sources from where the corporate sector has raised the funds and the ways and means by which the so raised funds have been utilized have been analyzed in detail. An attempt has also been made to study the relationship existing between long-term sources of funds and fixed assets and between the current assets and current liabilities. Further, the help of ratio analysis is also taken to supplement the findings. The ratio of net worth and net fixed assets i.e. net block, net worth to total assets, total debts to total equities and between current assets to current liabilities have also been computed for the purpose. The analysis on the trend in various sources of inflow of funds and their utilization is confined to nine years covering 2000 to 2008. The different sources of funds used for financing additional fixed investments and current assets formation and their proportion to the total utilization of sources are also analyzed.

An analysis of the total inflow of funds indicated an average inflow of ₹ 46750 crores during the study period. Highest inflow of ₹ 112598 crores were marked in the year 2008. The growth rate was highest in the year 2004 which was 112.84 per cent and the lowest was a negative growth of 13.13 per cent recorded in the year 2003. As a whole the growth trend was fluctuating through out the study period.

By analyzing the internal and external sources, it was revealed that the share of funds created from internal source was 60.54 per cent in average to total source while it was 39.46 per cent in average in case of share of external sources. It indicated that Indian companies prefer more to raise funds from internal sources as compared to external sources.

The internal source comprises of reserves, revaluation reserves, provisions and depreciation. A highest amount of ₹ 43785 crores were generated from reserves in the year 2008 while, ₹ 2784 crores were generated from revaluation reserves in that particular year. The highest amount raised through provisions was ₹ 6142 crores in the year 2008 only. In case of depreciation, the highest amount raised was ₹ 6997 crores in the year 2006. In total, the internal source of inflow of funds indicated a constant growth through out the study period. The only exception to this was in 2001, the total amount of internally generated funds was ₹ 10731.51 crores and the amount generated in 2002 was ₹ 6593.23 crores. This shows that in 2002 the focus towards external funds was more as compared to internal funds. But from 2003 onwards this tendency has been changed and since then it shows a rising trend through out the study.

The external sources of finances are mainly divided into long-term sources and short-term sources. The external long-term sources comprise of funds raised from issue of equity shares, preference shares, share application money, secured loans, unsecured loans and deferred credit. Funds raised from issue of equity shares indicated a highest amount of ₹ 1105 crores in the year 2008 and the lowest was only ₹ 82 crores in the year 2003. The fluctuating trend in the growth of issue of equity shares and the reduction in size in issue of equity share capital indicates that the companies went for repurchasing of shares, or they might have decided to go for debt capital instead of equity or due to reduction in the scale of operation, the fresh issue of equity shares was less.

The highest amount of funds raised through preference shares was ₹ 372 crores in 2003 while the highest amount of redemption or conversion has taken place in the year 2007 to the tune of ₹ 317 crores. Amount raised through preference shares during the study period was not that much attractive which shows a declining interest of companies towards preference shares.

Funds raised through secured loans also indicate a fluctuating trend during this period of study. A negative growth has witnessed in second year i.e. in 2002 indicating the redemption or repayment of the loans or it might be conversion of debentures forming part of the secured loans into equity shares. Funds raised through secured loan were highest in the year 2008 which was ₹ 14639 crores.

Unsecured loans contributed to a great extent. In the year 2001 it has showed a negative contribution indicating either repayment of such loans or conversion of same into shares or secured debentures. But from 2002 onwards it has shown a positive contribution till the end. Except the year 2003 in which the amount raised through unsecured loans was only ₹ 111.24 crores, in all other years a sizable amount has been raised through unsecured loans and particularly from 2006 onwards, the trend has showed a remarkable increase. Highest amount collected through unsecured loan was ₹ 16644 crores in the year 2008. No amount has been raised through deferred credit during the study period. An average of ₹ 11210 crores were flowed in from all the external long-term sources. From the analysis it is concluded that, issue of share capital had never been a major source of long-term finance for the corporate sector. The dependence on debt capital i.e. secured and unsecured loan is more as compared to equity.

Funds also flowed into the corporate sector externally from current liabilities as a short-term source. An average of ₹ 8065 crores were flowed into from this source. Highest inflow from this source was recorded in the year 2008 amounting to ₹ 20534 crores.

The total inflow of funds over the years was utilized in acquiring fixed assets, financial assets, intangible assets and current assets. Out of the total funds available, a major portion was utilized in acquiring the fixed assets. During the period of study, the total funds utilized for the above purpose amounted to ₹ 298747 crores, which constitutes nearly 80 per cent of the total application of funds. Out of the total investment in fixed assets, a heavy chunk has been diverted in acquiring tangible fixed assets like land and building, plant and machinery etc. which is shown under the head gross block. Out of the total investment of ₹ 298747 crores in fixed assets, an amount of ₹ 126372 crores has been invested in gross block i.e. in gross tangible fixed assets and ₹ 24610 crores in capital work-in-progress during the period of study.

It has been found that the average investment in gross tangible fixed assets during the period of study is ₹ 18872 crores but amazingly for the first five years i.e. 2001 to 2005, the total investment is less than the above average figure. But from 2006 onwards, it increased sharply. The amount of investment in other fixed assets i.e. in investments, loans and advances, fixed deposits and in miscellaneous assets constitutes nearly half of the total investment in fixed assets. A heavy chunk of the money has been applied in investments which amount to ₹ 71767 crores. Amount invested in loans and advances and fixed deposits were ₹ 50451 crores and ₹ 26044 crores respectively.

With respect to current assets, the total amount invested during the whole period was ₹ 75253, constituting around 20 per cent of the total application of funds. The average amount of investment in current assets was ₹ 9406 crores.

The highest investment in fixed assets was ₹ 38302 crores in the year 2008 and the highest investment in current assets was also in the year 2008 amounted to ₹ 22083 crores.

After funds flow statement analysis, we started analyzing some of the key financial ratios as ratio analysis can help us to check whether the business is doing better this year than it was last year. At first the debt-equity ratio is analyzed which was calculated from the total inflow of funds of the sample companies. The main objective of analyzing the debt equity ratio was to ensure a proper balance between the owned funds and borrowed funds. The factors, which determine the level of debt-equity ratio, are the nature of industry, size of investment, gestation period, profitability potential, debt servicing capacity, current capital market condition and other economic situation. A high debt-equity ratio shows a relatively larger share of financing by the creditors to the owners and therefore a larger claim against the assets. On the other hand a low debt equity ratio implies high stake of owners and a sufficient safety margins. A ratio of 1:1 is considered to be a satisfactory ratio, although there cannot be any rule of thumb or standard norm. A very low ratio is not considered satisfactory for the shareholders because it indicates that the firm has not been able to use outsider's funds to magnify their earnings.

The debt equity ratio of sample companies indicated a large variance from 0.94 to 1.29. The average ratio of debt to equity for the total period of study was 1.12 which was fairly lower than the generally accepted norm of 2:1 in a developing country like India. This makes it clear that sample companies had followed a conservative policy while deciding the debt-equity mix in the capital structure.

By analyzing the size of investment in fixed and current assets of the sample company, it was observed that the growth in the size of investment was about three-fold in nine years i.e. from 2000 to 2008. Net worth to fixed assets ratio fluctuated in between 0.99 to 1.63 during the period of study, the average being 1.28. It was found that the net worth to fixed assets ratio for all the years under study was more than 1 (i.e. 100%) only except for the first year i.e. in 2000 in which the ratio was 0.99, which is also very nearer to 100 per cent. A ratio of one or above indicates that the money spent on fixed assets was fully financed from the shareholders funds and companies are not dependent on outsiders' funds to finance the fixed assets. It was also observed that the proposition of net fixed assets in the total assets structure remained almost constant with an average of 0.36. The ratio varied in between 0.29 to 0.43.

The proprietary ratio or ratio of net worth to total assets varied in between 42 per cent to 49 per cent, the average being 45 per cent. Thus out of every rupee invested in the total assets of sample companies, the shareholders contribution was ₹ 0.45. The margin was satisfactory.

The principle and convention of finance suggests that a portion of funds should be invested in current assets so as to ease the firm for short-term risks and to ensure liquidity by reducing the burden of current liabilities. Here in case of sample companies, liquidity ratio fluctuated in between 1.24 to 1.76 during the study period. The average ratio for the total period was found to be 1.42. Thus, current assets were more than sufficient to meet current liabilities and the liquidity position was satisfactory. Though the absolute standard was 2:1, in this case the liquidity ratio was in the halfway, indicating a good solvency position, i.e. ability to meet short-term obligations.

The correlation between size of investment and debt-equity ratio was –0.83, indicated a fairly high degree of negative correlation between the two. The relationship between the two implied that though the size of investment had grown, the debt-equity proportion remained insensitive.

The association of fixed assets proportions to total assets with debt equity ratio was found to be +0.94 which implies a high degree of positive correlation between the two. It indicates that there is a direct positive correlation between the debt proportion in the total capital and the investment in fixed assets. The correlation between liquidity ratio and debt equity ratio showed a low degree of positive correlation which is +0.28.

In conclusion, it can only be said that the process of capital structure planning is not a one time job, but needs reviews, revision and monitoring through time, in different situations. Financial executives are to pay adequate attention to the multidimensional implications of the capital structure decision. In order to achieve optimal capital structure, time to time judgments in decision making play a crucial part and influences the capital structure planning process.

Key Findings of Chapter — 8

In attempting to study differences in funds flow and capital mix across firms, a variable wise analysis of funds flow and capital structure of the sample companies had been undertaken. Accordingly, the sample companies had been classified on the basis of region, industry, size group and age group.

The region of a company more or less influences its quantum of inflow of funds both debt and equity. They also exert impact on the overall trend of the total sample. Companies were classified into eastern, western, northern and southern regions. The number of companies in eastern region was 34, western region 135, northern region 46 and southern region 85.

From the funds flow analysis of sample companies grouped under four different regions, it was found that the western region which comprises of 135 companies has raised the highest amount of funds among all the four regions during the period of study. The average amount of funds raised by the sample companies of eastern region was ₹ 1832.76 crores, western region ₹ 22205.46 crores, northern region ₹ 5772.78 crores and southern region ₹ 16939.08 crores.

With respect to raising of funds through internal sources, it was found that the eastern region companies raised funds internally ₹ 9229.6 crores in total during the study period with an average of ₹ 1153.7 crores yearly. In case of western region companies, the total amount of funds raised internally was ₹ 105347.84 crores with an average of ₹ 13168 annually, which is the highest among all the four regions. Similarly, the total internal funds raised by northern and southern companies during the period of study were ₹ 21796.17 crores and 83421.13 crores respectively.

Total amount of funds raised by the issue of equity and preference shares were ₹ 3479 crores by western region, ₹ 1250 crores by northern region, and ₹ 2521 crores by southern region. In case of eastern region, the amount of funds raised shows a negative figure of ₹ 4.97 crores indicating that the amount paid towards the redemption of preference shares was more than the amount collected by issue of equity shares.

Companies also raised funds through long-term loans comprising of secured and unsecured loans. The total amount raised through debt or long term loan both secured and unsecured was ₹ 3141 crores by eastern region companies, ₹ 38915 crores by western region companies, ₹ 12941 crores by northern region companies, and ₹ 27435 crores by southern region companies. The common observation for the companies of all the four regions was that they have raised more funds through debt capital as compared to equity, may be due to the reason of easy and availability of cheap debt capital. Not a single company of any region has raised any fund through differed credit.

The annual average inflow of funds from current liabilities was ₹ 287 crores by the eastern region companies, ₹ 3737.59 crores by the western region, ₹ 1274.26 crores by the northern region and ₹ 2766.81 crores by the southern region companies.

The funds so raised by different regions were applied in acquiring fixed assets, current assets, etc. It was found that an annual average of ₹ 938.16 crores were invested in acquiring fixed assets by the eastern region companies. The same in case of western region was ₹ 9327.66 crores, northern region ₹ 2768.21 crores and southern region ₹ 5838.67 crores. Similarly, an annual average of ₹ 241.16 crores were invested additionally every year in current assets by the eastern region companies whereas that in case of western region it was ₹ 4384.07 crores, ₹ 944.64 crores in case of northern region and ₹ 3836.78 crores by the southern region companies.

The debt-equity ratios were calculated from the consolidated balance sheets of the respective regions. For our study purpose, debt includes secured loans, unsecured loans, current liabilities and deferred credits, i.e. all types of debts. Similarly equity or net worth consists of equity share capital, preference share capital, share application money, reserves and revaluation reserves. The debt-equity ratio for the above purpose is calculated by dividing debt by equity. The annual average ratio for the total period was 1.21, 1.24, 1.09 and 0.97 respectively for eastern, western, northern and southern region companies. The average so worked out for all the regions were fairly lower than the generally accepted norm of 2:1.

The annual average of size of investment for the whole period worked out to be ₹ 8925.76 crores for eastern region companies, ₹ 60983.47 crores for western region companies, ₹ 16470.68 crores for northern region companies and ₹ 38470.31 crores for southern region companies. Western region shows the highest with respect to average as well as total size of investments among all the regions.

While analyzing the asset structure of companies of different regions, it was observed that the proportion of net fixed assets to total assets for the eastern region companies varied in between 0.36 to 0.46. In case of western region it was 0.30 to 0.43, northern region 0.32 to 0.34 and in case of southern region it was in between 0.23 to 0.43. The average ratio of eastern, western, northern and southern region companies was 0.41, 0.38, 0.33 and 0.33 respectively.

With respect to the liquidity ratio or current ratio of different regions for the study period, it was observed that it varied from 0.89 to 1.41 with an annual average of 1.07 in case of eastern region companies, 1.23 to 1.77 with an annual average of 1.42 in case of western region companies, 0.96 to 1.87 with an annual average of 1.42 in case of northern region companies and 1.25 to 1.85 with an annual average of 1.48 in case of southern region companies.

The correlation between size of investment and debt-equity ratio for eastern, western and southern region were found to be –0.58349, –0.82911, 0.94371 and –0.74606 respectively.

A high negative ratio in case of eastern, western and southern region indicates that the investments are influenced much by equity funds than by the debt funds. But in case of northern region, the coefficient of correlation shows a positive figure which is 0.94371. This kind of high degree positive correlation indicates that a greater proportion of debt funds are used for acquiring fixed as well as current assets.

The correlation between asset structure and debt equity ratio shows that eastern, western and southern region companies had high degree of positive correlation between the asset structure and D/E ratio. This indicated that the proportions of fixed assets greatly depended on long-term debt funds. In the case of northern region, the coefficient of correlation between the asset structure and debt-equity ratio is –0.01077 which is a very low degree of negative correlation. This indicates that the fixed assets depended negatively on debt funds and positively on equity funds, particularly in case of northern region companies.

The correlation between liquidity and debt equity ratio shows that except for the southern region, all other regions indicated a negative association between the two variables. It implies that the current assets of the companies of those regions were negatively influenced by long-term debts. It might be from short-term sources or from equity sources. The positive correlation shown by southern region indicated that a portion of the long-term debt funds have been invested by the companies of this region in current assets.

The ability of a company to generate internal funds and attract funds from outside is also affected by the age of the company. An attempt has been made to study the capital structure and its components for companies grouped under different ages, viz., very old, old, and new companies. The companies registered before independence i.e. 1947 were grouped under the category 'very old' companies. There were 44 companies in this group. Companies registered after 1947 but before 1980 were grouped under the head 'old' companies. There were 95 companies under this head. Companies came into existence after 1980 were grouped under the head 'new' and there were 161 companies under this category.

While analyzing the total inflow of funds by sample companies, it was observed that in case of very old companies, the average inflow of funds was ₹ 8297.97 crores, in case of old companies the annual average was ₹ 14040.57 crores and in case of new companies the annual average was ₹ 24411.55, which was highest among all the three groups.

After the analysis of the funds raised through internal sources, it was observed that in case of very old companies the flow of funds from internal sources was ₹ 5343.3 crores on an average during the period. The total amount raised from internal sources during the period was ₹ 42746.6 crores. In case of old companies, the total internal funds generated during the period was ₹ 68779.9 crores with an annual average of ₹ 8597.47 crores. Similarly, with respect to new companies, the total funds raised internally amounted to ₹ 108268 crores with an annual average of ₹ 13533.52 crores. In all the three categories, amount generated from reserves which consists of retained earnings, was highest among the internal sources of funds. Funds generated from accumulated depreciation remained the second biggest source of internal funds in all the cases.

It is observed from the analysis of external sources of finances that, an average of ₹ 135.96 crores were raised by the very old companies by issue of equity shares, preference shares as well as through share application money. In case of old companies, the average amount raised was ₹ 253.14 crores and that of for new companies it was ₹ 516.73 crores.

Funds were also generated by all the age grouped companies through long-term loans comprising of secured as well as unsecured loans. On an average every year the very old companies generated ₹ 1350.9 crores of funds through long-term debts and loans. In case of old companies, this yearly average is ₹ 2802.62 crores whereas in case of new companies the average is ₹ 6150.67 crores. Funds raised through current liabilities by the age grouped companies during the study period showed that the average inflow of funds from this source by the very old companies were ₹ 1467.77 crores, old companies were ₹ 2387.32 crores and new companies were ₹ 4210.59 crores.

Funds were invested in acquiring additional fixed assets by the sample companies grouped age-wise. It was observed that an average of ₹ 3030.15 crores were invested in acquiring additional fixed assets by the very old companies. The same in case of old companies were ₹ 5234.29 crores and in case of new companies, it recorded ₹ 10608.26 crores. With respect to investment in current assets, the average investment in additional current assets in case of very old companies were ₹ 1842.45 crores whereas in case of old companies the average was ₹ 2380.25 crores and in case of new companies the average was ₹ 5183.95 crores, being the highest in the group.

After studying the Debt-Equity ratios of age grouped companies of the entire study period it was observed that an average of 1.04 ratio of debt to equity was there in case of very old companies. That in case of old companies was 1.13 and for new companies it was around 1.00. All the averages were below the accepted norm 2:1.

The analysis of size of investment which comprises of the sum of net fixed assets and current assets showed that the average growth rate was 11.88 per cent every year in case of very old companies, 11.74 per cent in case of the old companies and 21.22 per cent in case of new companies. The asset structure which indicates the ratio of net fixed assets to total assets revealed that an average of 36 per cent net fixed assets were there in the total assets in case of both very old and old companies, while that in case of new companies it was 35 per cent. It reflects that companies of all the age groups invested more or less equal proportion of total funds in net fixed assets. The liquidity ratio which reflects the short-term solvency position of the company, i.e. ability to meet short-term obligations showed that an average of ₹ 1.34 worth of current assets were there for covering every rupee of current liability obligations in case of very old companies. In case of old companies, the average ratio was 1.30 and in case of new companies it was 1.60.

The co-efficient of correlation between the size of investment and debt-equity ratio in all the categories are found to be negative. In case of very old companies it was –0.87527, in case of old companies it was –0.86772, and in case of new companies, the correlation was calculated at –0.55028. The correlation between asset structure and D/E ratio of sample companies grouped under age category for all the three groups shows that, the degree of correlation is high as well as positive. This indicates that in case of all the companies, the asset structure was influenced greatly by the long-term funds raised through debts and loans rather than the equity capital. Whereas the correlation between liquidity ratio and debt-equity ratio revealed that in case of very old companies, the correlation was +0.24852, in case of old companies the coefficient of correlation is calculated at –0.04209 and in case of new companies the correlation was +0.55918.

The total sample companies were again grouped on the basis of their size, viz., small, medium and large. As on 31st March 2008, the companies having total assets below ₹ 100 crores are grouped under 'small sized companies'. There were 75 of such companies in the total sample which are grouped under this category, which constitute 25% of the total sample. The companies having the total assets value ₹ 100 crores and above but less than ₹ 500 crores are grouped under 'medium sized companies'. There was 98 such type of companies constituting 32.67% of the total sample. Companies having their total assets value worth ₹ 500 crores and above as on 31st March, 2008 are grouped as 'large sized companies', which include 127 companies, about 42.33% of the total sample.

From the analysis of total inflow of funds, it was observed that an average of ₹ 370.69 crores of funds was raised by small sized company with a mean inflow of ₹ 4.94 crores annually by each company under this group. The average inflow of funds in case of 'medium sized companies' was ₹ 3078.48 crores with a mean inflow of ₹ 31.41 crores by each company annually under this group. In case of 'large sized companies', the annual average inflow of funds were ₹ 43300.91 crores and the mean inflow for each company per annum was ₹ 340 .95 crores.

With respect to the funds generated from internal sources, it is found that an annual average of ₹ 133.40 crores was raised by the small sized companies from internal sources. In case of medium sized companies and large sized companies, the inflow of funds from internal sources were ₹ 1468.90 crores ₹ 25872.03 crores respectively. The mean average inflow from such sources was ₹ 1.78 crores in case of a small company, ₹ 14.98 crores in a medium sized company and ₹ 203.71 crores in case of large company.

It was observed that an average of ₹ 43.96 crores were raised by the small sized companies from issue of both preference and equity shares during the period. The same was ₹ 129.15 crores in case of medium sized companies and ₹ 732.72 crores in case of large sized companies. The equity issue as bonus issues causes no inflow of funds.

The average funds generated by small, medium and large sized companies from long-term loans were ₹ 89.66 crores, ₹ 850.31 crores and ₹ 9364.22 crores respectively. Average funds generated from current liabilities were ₹ 103.66 crores by the small sized companies, ₹ 630.09 crores by the medium sized companies and ₹ 7331.93 by the large sized companies.

The funds so raised by the sample companies from internal and external sources were applied in acquiring mainly additional fixed assets and current assets. It was observed that averages of ₹ 114.84 crores were invested in incremental fixed assets by the small sized companies. The average investment in case of medium sized company was ₹ 1552.55 crores and in case of large sized companies, the average application of funds in fixed assets was ₹ 17205.30 crores. The average investments in current assets by small, medium and large sized companies were ₹ 154.31 crores, ₹ 798.56 crores and ₹ 8453.79 crores respectively.

The average D/E ratio in case of small sized companies was 3.04, in case of medium sized companies it was 2.10 and in case of large sized companies it was calculated at 1.00. The average investment position in small sized company was ₹ 3255.46 crores. Such a position in case of medium sized companies revealed ₹ 16456.14 crores and large sized companies ₹ 105138.62 crores. It was observed that an average of 36 per cent of net fixed assets were there in the total assets structure in case of small sized companies. The same was 40 per cent in case of medium sized companies and 35 per cent in case of large sized companies. The average liquidity ratio was 1.61, in case of medium sized companies it recorded a ratio of 1.33 and in case of large sized companies the average ratio was 1.42.

On analysis, it was observed that the correlation between size of investment and D/E ratio in case of small sized company was 0.57129, in case of medium sized companies it was –0.66987 and in case of large sized companies, it was –0.77986. In the case of all the three group of companies there exists a fairly high degree of negative correlation between the size of investments and the debt-equity ratios. It indicated that a greater proportion of investments were influenced more by the long-term equity sources than the debt source.

The correlation between asset structure and debt equity ratio of the different sized companies revealed that in case of small sized companies, the correlation was 0.42978, medium sized companies 0.36926 and large companies 0.91474. This implies that, in case of small and medium sized companies, there was a moderate level of influence of the long term debt funds in the acquisition of net fixed assets but the influence of debt funds was much more in case of large sized companies and the influence of equity funds in acquisition of fixed assets was negligible.

The correlation between the current ratio and debt equity ratio of small sized companies was –0.56777, in case of medium sized companies –0.78487 and in case of large sized companies, it was 0.31412. It indicated that the liquidity position of large sized companies was positively influenced by the long-term debt sources rather than equity, which was not seen in case of small and medium sized companies.

The Sample companies were again grouped according to the nature of industry, viz., agro-based manufacturing industries, mineral-based manufacturing industries, service industries and plantation industries. An attempt has been made to study the impact of each industry variable on the overall flow of funds and the capital structure.

The funds flow statement of each group of industry revealed that the amount of funds raised and applied by the companies under different industrial groups is worked out to be ₹ 8325.99 crores, ₹ 20832.58 crores, ₹ 16860.31 crores and ₹ 702.99 crores in average annually by the agro-based, mineral-based, service and plantation companies respectively.

The agro-based companies had generated an average of ₹ 3424.40 crores, mineral based companies ₹ 13389.56 crores, service companies ₹ 10311.56 crores and plantation companies ₹ 321.35 crores from the internal sources during the study period.

From the analysis it was observed that in case of agro based companies, the average amount of funds raised through share capital was ₹ 182.11 crores, in case of mineral based companies it was ₹ 391.06 crores, in case of service companies it was ₹ 332.49 crores and in case of plantation companies, it was ₹ 0.16 crores.

The annual average inflow of funds from long-term loans comprising of both secured as well as unsecured, by the agro based companies recorded ₹ 3180.97 crores, mineral based companies ₹ 3385.39 crores, service companies ₹ 3525.22 crores and plantation companies ₹ 211.87 crores. No amount has been raised through deferred credits.

It was observed that the average amount of funds raised annually by the agro-based companies through current liabilities was ₹ 1538.50 crores with a mean average of ₹ 17.09 crores. The annual average in case of mineral-based companies was ₹ 3666.55 crores with a mean average of ₹ 27.16 crores per year per company. The annual average in case of service companies was ₹ 2691.03 crores with a mean average of ₹ 59.80 crores and for plantation companies, the annual average was ₹ 169.6 crores and the mean average was ₹ 5.65 crores.

Funds so raised by the sample companies were mainly invested in acquiring fixed and current assets. Some funds were also applied in the form of fixed deposits, investments, loans and advances and miscellaneous assets. It was observed that an average annual investment of ₹ 4602.65 crores were made by agro-based companies in acquiring additional fixed assets during the study period. In case of mineral-based companies, the average was ₹ 7792.23 crores, in case of service companies it was ₹ 6324.68 crores and in case of plantation industries, the average was ₹ 126.17 crores. Turning to current assets, it was observed that an average of ₹ 1538.68 crores by agro based companies, ₹ 4545.30 crores by mineral-based companies, ₹ 3211.39 crores by service companies and ₹ 111.29 crores by plantation companies were invested in the form of current assets every year.

The results of ratio analysis showed that, the agro-based companies had an average D/E ratio of 1.66, the mineral-based companies had an average of 1.32, service companies had 0.58 and plantation companies had 0.86. The annual average growth rate in the size of investment in case of agro-based companies was 13.75 per cent, mineral based companies 12.57 per cent, service companies 28.17 per cent and in the case of plantation companies, it was 5.35 per cent. The average ratio of net fixed assets to total assets was 0.44 in case of agro-based companies, 0.36 in case of mineral-based companies, 0.28 in case of service companies, and 0.33 in case of plantation companies. And finally, it came to the notice that the average liquidity ratio in case of agro-based companies was 1.44, mineral-based companies 1.39, service companies 1.40 and plantation companies 1.44.

The results of correlation analysis showed that the correlation between the size of investment and D/E ratio was –0.94636 in case of mineral-based companies, which indicates a fairly high degree of negative correlation. Hence it is clear that a greater proportion of increment of funds year after year were sought from equity sources than from debt sources. In case of agro-based companies and plantation companies, the correlation was 0.81869 and 0.93384 respectively. In both of the cases there was a high degree of positive correlation between the variables which indicates that, the assets of these two industries required long-term funds more from the debt sources rather than from equity. With regard to correlation between size of investment and D/E ratio of plantation industries, it was 0.01591, a low degree of positive correlation. It implies that these companies have used debt funds for their asset base, but very lesser extent.

The analysis shows that in case of agro based companies and plantation companies, the correlation between the asset structure and the D/E ratio were –0.61017 and –0.93493 respectively. It indicated a moderate to high degree of negative correlation between the variables in both the cases. In the case of mineral-based companies and service companies, the correlation between the asset structure and D/E ratio was 0.91533 and 0.69618 respectively. Here the degree of correlation is fairly high and positive in both the cases.

It was observed that the correlation between the liquidity ratio and D/E ratio of agro based companies was –0.75268, mineral based companies –0.06758, service companies –0.78884 and plantation companies –0.7994. So, except mineral-based companies where there was a low degree of negative correlation, in all other cases the correlation between the variables were negative and fairly high. It shows that the current assets to liability position had a negative association with the long-term debt sources.

Summary of Findings

The key findings of all the chapters can be summarized as:

- Indian corporate employ substantial amount of debt in their capital structure in terms of the debt-equity ratio as well as total debt to total assets ratio. Nonetheless, the foreign controlled companies in India use less debt than the domestic companies. The dependence of the Indian corporate sector on debt as a source of finance has over the years declined particularly since the mid-nineties.
- The corporate enterprises in India seem to prefer long-term borrowings over short-term borrowings. Over the years, they seem to have substituted short-term debt for long-term debt. The foreign controlled companies use more long-term loans relatively to the domestic companies.
- As a result of debt-dominated capital structure, the Indian corporate are exposed to a very high degree of total risk as reflected in high degree of operating leverage and financial leverage and, consequently, are subject to a high cost of financial distress which includes a broad spectrum of problems ranging from relatively minor liquidity shortages to extreme cases of bankruptcy. The foreign controlled companies, however, are exposed to lower overall risk as well as financial risk.
- The debt service capacity of a sizeable segment of the corporate borrower as measured by Interest Coverage Ratio and Debt Service Coverage Ratio is inadequate and unsatisfactory.

- Retained earnings are the most favoured source of finance. There is significant difference in the use of internally generated funds by the highly profitable corporate relative to the low profitable firms. The low profitable firms use different forms of debt funds more than the highly profitable firms.
- Loan from financial institutions and private placement of debt are the next most widely used source of finance. The large firms are more likely to issue bonds in the market than small corporate.
- The hybrid securities are the least popular source of finance amongst corporate India. They are more likely to be used by low growth firms. Preference shares are used more by public sector units and low growth corporate.
- Equity capital as a source of fund is not preferred across the board.
- Indian companies prioritize their sources of financing (from internal financing to equity) according to the law of least effort, or of least resistance, preferring to raise equity as a financing means 'of last resort'. Hence internal funds are used first, and when that is depleted debt is issued, and when it is not sensible to issue any more debt, equity is issued.
- Study revealed that an average of 60.54 per cent of the total funds was raised from internal sources whereas external sources contribute only 39.46 per cent of the total funds of Indian companies. It indicated that Indian companies prefer more to raise funds from internal sources as compared to external sources.
- It has been found that, issue of share capital had never been a major source of long-term finance for the corporate sector. The dependence on debt capital i.e. secured and unsecured loan is more as compared to equity.
- Small sized companies relies more on debt capital as compared to large sized companies. The average debt-equity ratio of small sized companies were found to be more than 3:1 whereas in case of large sized companies it is 1:1. This shows that the large sized companies followed a strict conservative policy while deciding the debt equity mix.
- The average debt-equity ratios of manufacturing companies were more than double of the average debt-equity ratio of service sector companies. It indicates that service sector companies relies more on the equity and less on the debt, and vice-versa in case of manufacturing companies.

- The common observation for the companies of all the four regions was that they have raised more funds through debt capital as compared to equity, may be due to the reason of easy availability of cheap debt capital.
- Although the size of the firm, its age, the region to which it belongs and industry-classification contribute to the existing variation in capital structure across industry classes but nature of the industry seems to dominate.
- The study revealed that in terms of total average inflow of funds, western region stood highest as this region is the most industrially advanced region of our country and covers 135 companies out of the total sample size of 300 companies. In terms of mean average southern region has the highest inflow of funds as compared to other regions because most of the large sized companies are situated in this region, which are capable of generating more funds as compared to the companies of other region.
- More specifically, it is the differences in external fund requirement based on technology differences that play a leading role in determining the inter-industry variation in capital structure. This signals that there exists a linkage between product market and capital market. This proves that the capital structure and the determinants of capital structure vary from industries to industries and the nature of the industry acts as a key determinant of the capital structure.
- To sum up, nature of the industry to which the firm belongs to, its size, age and location plays a major role in the determination of the capital structure of the private sector firms of Indian corporate.

Testing of hypotheses

While planning the study, a set of hypotheses have been formulated based on various theories of corporate finance. Those hypotheses have been tested after taking into consideration the total sample analysis and variable analysis. They are discussed below:

***Hypothesis 1**: There exists the variation in the capital structure of firms of a particular industry or among the firms in different industries.*

In order to identify the existence of variation in the capital structure of firms of a particular industry or among the firms in different industries, the total sample is classified into four broad groups of industries namely, agro-based manufacturing industries, mineral-based manufacturing industries, service industries and plantation industries. The group of companies which obtain their raw materials from agriculture like textiles, sugar, edible oil, paper, food processing are grouped under the head agro-based companies. The companies which obtain their raw materials from mining or mineral-based products like chemicals, cement, fertilizer, pharmaceuticals, electric equipment, plastics, construction and housing, mining, fabricated metal etc. are grouped under the head mineral-based companies. The group of companies, which are engaged in plantation of tea, coffee and rubber, are categorized as plantation companies. The companies which do not manufacture, but are involved in rendering services like transport, computers software, hotel etc. are called service companies.

When we analyzed the proportion of debt and equity in the total capital structure of different industrial groups through debt-equity ratio, we found that the agro-based companies had an average D/E ratio of 1.66, the mineral-based companies had an average of 1.32, service companies had 0.58 and plantation companies had 0.86.

In the case of service companies, the ratio was below one throughout the study period. It shows that, the amount of debt in none of the years of our study had ever crossed the equity holding/net worth. The industry had relied less on debt than their own equity funds. The owners of the industry had carried business with a high risk. The nature of business and financial policy of the firm might be primarily responsible for it. A ratio of 1:1 may be usually considered as satisfactory, but there the low ratio (debt being low in comparison to net worth or equity) indicated a larger margin of safety for the long term creditors. The situation of plantation companies was also similar to that of service companies except for the year 2007 and 2008 in which their debt-equity ratio was slightly more than one. In case of agro-based and mineral-based companies though the average ratio is more than one, yet it is below the standard norm of 2:1. Companies of these two industries have used the debt funds more as compared to equity.

The variation in the debt-equity ratio was also observed, when we analyzed the debt-equity proportion of the sample companies after grouping them into different regions, different sizes and different ages. Thus, it is evident that the capital structure of firms are systematically different across industry classes so far as the debt financing as a proportion of total capital is concerned. Although the size of the firm, its age, the region to which it belongs and industry-classification contribute to the existing variation in capital structure across industry classes but nature of the industry seems to dominate. More specifically, it is the differences in external fund requirement based on technology differences that play a leading role in determining the inter-industry variation in capital structure. This signals that there exists a linkage between product market and capital market. Hence the hypothesis that there exists the variation in the capital structure of firms of a particular industry or among the firms in different industries holds good.

Hypothesis 2: *Indian companies prefer internal sources of finance rather than external to meet their financial requirement.*

Analyzing the funds flow statement of the total sample companies, it was observed that the per centage of funds raised from internal sources during the study period was 58.77 per cent of the total funds raised whereas from external sources it was 41.23 per cent. In case of sample companies grouped according to the region to which they belong, it was also observed that the internal sources contributed more than the external sources. The respective share of internal source was 62.95 per cent, 59.30 per cent, 47.19 per cent 61.56 per cent in case of eastern, western, northern and southern region companies. With regard to companies grouped according to their age, it was also observed that the internal sources contributed 64.39 per cent, 61.23 per cent and 55.43 per cent of the total funds for the very old group, old group and new group of companies respectively. When the companies were grouped according to their size, it was observed that the contributions to the total funds from the internal sources were 35.98 per cent, 47.71 per cent and 59.74 per cent for the small sized, medium sized and large sized companies respectively. With regard to sample companies divided industry-wise, it was seen that the internal contribution to the total source was 41.12 per cent, 64.27 per cent, 61.15 per cent, and 45.71 per cent for the agro-based companies, mineral-based companies, service companies and plantation companies respectively. Thus, barring to few exceptions like small and medium sized companies in size group and agro-based companies and plantation companies in industrial group, this hypothesis holds good for all other categories and groups of companies.

Hypothesis 3: *The region to which the company belongs to influences the quantum of inflow of funds (both debt and equity).*

The validity of this hypothesis has been examined for the sample companies classified under different regions. The techniques used for analyzing the data are the historical funds flow analysis and ratio analysis. By analyzing the inflow of funds for individual regions, it is observed that the quantum of inflow was more in case of western region companies in comparison to other region. The average amount of funds raised by the sample companies of eastern region was ₹ 1832.76 crores, western region ₹ 22205.46 crores, northern region ₹ 5772.78 crores and southern region ₹ 16939.08 crores. The annual average inflow of funds per company was ₹ 53.90 crores, ₹ 164.48 crores, ₹ 125.49 crores and ₹ 199.28 crores respectively for eastern, western, northern and southern region companies. This reveals that in terms of total average inflow of funds, western region stood highest as this region is the most industrially advanced region of our country and covers 135 companies out of the total sample size of 300 companies. In terms of mean average southern region has the highest inflow of funds as compared to other regions because most of the large sized companies are situated in this region, which are capable of generating more funds as compared to the companies of other region. Hence, the hypothesis that the region of a company influences the quantum of inflow of funds holds good.

Hypothesis 4: *Age of the company has a bearing on its ability to generate internal funds and to attract funds from outside.*

During the process of classification, the sample companies are grouped according to their age, viz., very old, old and new companies. The companies have generated funds internally mainly by way of reserves, revaluation reserves, provisions and depreciation. The average annual inflow of funds from internal sources in case of very old companies found to be ₹ 5343.3 crores, whereas the total amount raised from internal sources during the period was ₹ 42746.6 crores. In case of old companies, the total internal funds generated during the period was ₹ 68779.9 crores with an annual average of ₹ 8597.47 crores. Similarly, with respect to new companies, the total funds raised internally amounted to ₹ 108268 crores with an annual average of ₹ 13533.52 crores. For each individual company of these three groups, the average annual generation of internal funds comes to ₹ 121.43 crores, ₹ 90.5 crores and ₹ 100.25 crores for very old, old and new companies respectively. It shows that the age of the company has a bearing in generating internal funds. With respect to attracting funds from outside, the average annual inflow of funds for each individual company of different age group is calculated at ₹ 2954 crores, ₹ 5443 crores and ₹ 10878 crores respectively for the very old, old and new companies. All these analysis clearly indicates that the age of the company has an influence on its ability to generate funds, internally as well as externally. Hence, the present hypothesis holds good.

Hypothesis 5. *Size of the company has a bearing on its capital structure.*

For the purpose of analyzing the capital structure of the sample companies according to their size group, they are divided as small, medium and large sized companies. From the debt-equity ratio calculated for these groups, it revealed that the average D/E ratio in case of small sized companies was 3.04, in case of medium sized companies it was 2.10 and in case of large sized companies it was calculated at 1.00.

In case of small sized companies, the D/E ratio varied in between 2.07 to 5.24 and the average was much higher than the standard norm of 2:1. It indicates that in case of small sized companies, the component of debt was more in the capital structure as compared to the equity. In case of medium sized companies, the D/E ratio varied in between 1.76 to 2.46 leading to an average of 2.10, which is slightly above the standard norm of 2:1. But in case of large sized companies, the ratio varied in between 0.86 to 1.17 with an average of 1.00. This shows that the large sized companies followed a strict conservative policy while deciding the debt equity mix.

Thus, in case of small sized companies a higher debt-equity ratio of more than three on average indicates that they are more dependent on debt capital whereas in case of large sized companies, a debt-equity ratio of one on average indicated that their dependence on debt is less than the standard norm. This shows that the large sized companies followed a strict conservative policy while deciding the debt equity mix. A low ratio of 1.00 means that the company is exposing itself to a large amount of equity. The difference is found only because of the difference in size of the company. Hence, the hypothesis that says the size of the company has a bearing on its capital structure is perfectly valid.

Hypothesis 6: *Nature of the company i.e. the industry to which it belongs to plays an important role in deciding the capital structure of the company.*

We have also grouped the sample companies according to their nature of industries. After conducting the ratio analysis, we found that the agro-based companies had an average D/E ratio of 1.66, the mineral-based companies had an average of 1.32, service companies had 0.58 and plantation companies had 0.86.

In the case of service companies, the ratio was below one throughout the study period. It shows that, the amount of debt in none of the years of our study had ever crossed the equity holding/net worth. The industry had relied less on debt than their own equity funds. The owners of the industry had carried business with a high risk. The nature of business and financial policy of the firm might be primarily responsible for it. A ratio of 1:1 may be usually considered as satisfactory, but there the low ratio (debt being low in comparison to net worth or equity) indicated a larger margin of safety for the long term creditors. The situation of plantation companies was also similar to that of service companies except for the year 2007 and 2008 in which their debt-equity ratio was slightly more than one. In case of agro-based and mineral-based companies though the average ratio is more than one, yet it is below the standard norm of 2:1. Companies of these two industries have used the debt funds more as compared to equity.

From the analysis of the size of investment of the industry-wise grouped companies, it was observed that the annual average growth rate in the size of investment in case of agro-based companies was 13.75 per cent, mineral based companies 12.57 per cent, service companies 28.17 per cent and in the case of plantation companies, it was 5.35 per cent. The annual average growth per company was ₹ 48.13 crores in case of agro-based companies, ₹ 60.63 crores in case of mineral-based companies, ₹ 158.86 crores in case of service companies and ₹ 5.88 crores in case of plantation companies. Thus the rate of investment in net fixed and current assets were very fast in case of service companies and it was very slow in case of plantation companies.

The analysis of asset structure shows that, the average ratio of net fixed assets to total assets was 0.44 in case of agro-based companies, 0.36 in case of mineral-based companies, 0.28 in case of service companies, and 0.33 in case of plantation companies.

Thus it can be concluded that the results are different in all the cases for different types of industries. This confirms the fact that the nature of the company or the industry to which it belongs has a bearing on the capital structure of the company. Hence, the hypothesis holds valid.

Further Extension of the Study and Research Ideas

Any research study can explore only a limited field of knowledge. There are many aspects which need to be researched further. In the present case also there is a considerable scope for further research. Data for the purpose of analysis have been collected chiefly from secondary sources which have their own limitations. A more useful study can be done by collecting data from primary sources. This will enhance the scope of the study and will have a better insight into the capital structure. The period of study is confined to nine years which can be further extended. Lastly work-based on a finer classification of the industries may provide stronger and more stable results. However, it is hoped that the analysis presented in this study will act as a base for further extension of this important investigation.

Bibliography

BOOKS

1. Anthony Robert, *'Financial Statement Analysis'*, (Homewood, III, Richard D Irwin, inc.) 3rd Edition, 1971, p. 297.
2. Anthony Robert, *'Analysis of the Financial Statements'* (New York, DUN & Bradstreet), 4th Ed. 1969, p. 207.
3. Beraneck W., *'Working Capital Management'*, (Belment, Wordsworth), 1968, 4th Ed. p. 301.
4. Bhalla V.K., *'Financial Management and Policy'*, Anmol Publications, New Delhi, 3rd Edition, 2002.
5. Chandra Prasanna, *'Financial Management — Theory and Practice'*, Tata McGraw-Hills, 5th Edition, 2002.
6. Donaldson, M. Charles, *'Basic Business Finance'*, (Homewood, Illinois), 3rd Ed. 1966, p. 1541.
7. Gordon. M. J.; *'The Investment, Financing and Valuation of Corporation'*; Homewood III; Irwin; 1962.
8. Guthmann, G. Harry, *'Analysis of Financial Statements'*, (Prentice Hall of India Pvt. Ltd., New Delhi), 1976, p. 157.
9. Kishore R.M., *'Financial Management'*, Taxmann, 6th Edition, 2005.
10. Khan M.Y., Jain P.K., *'Financial Management'*, Tata McGraw- Hills, 4th Edition, 2004
11. Kotrappa G; *'Contemporary in Business Finance'* by Omprakash Kajipet; Discovery Publishing House; New Delhi; 1st Edn; 2000; pp. 70-75.
12. Kohler E.L., *'A Dictionary for Accountants'*, p. 393
13. Mayer R.R., *'Capital Expenditure Analysis'* (Prospects Hights, iii, Wave Land) Ed.3, 1978, Chapter—2, p. 109.
14. Pandey I.M., *'Capital Structure and Cost of Capital'*, Financial Management (Vikas Publishing House Pvt. Ltd., New Delhi), 8th Ed., 2005.

15. Peterson, Pamela (1999) '*Analysis of Financial Statements*' New York: Wiley. p. 92.
16. Rustagi R.P., 'Financial Management — Theory, Concepts and Problems', 2nd Edition, 2005.
17. Sharma R. K., Gupta S.K. , '*Management Accounting, Principles and Practice*', Kalyani Publishers, New Delhi, 1996, pp. 5.1.
18. Solomon E., 'The Management of Corporate Capital', (New York, The Free Press) 1959, 2nd Ed., p. 107.
19. Vishwanath S.R., '*Corporate Finance — Theory and Practice*', Response Books, 2nd Edition, 2007.
20. Wixon R, Kell W.G. , Bedford N.M., — '*Accountants Hand Book*', 1970, p. 39.

JOURNALS, PERIODICALS AND MAGAZINES

1. Baron, D P (1974). 'Default Risk, Home-made Leverage and M-M Theorem,' *American Economic Review*, 64, pp. 176-82.
2. Baron, D P (1975). 'Firm Valuation, Corporate Taxes and Default Risk,' *Journal of Finance*, 30, pp. 1251-64.
3. Baxter, N.D.; 'Leverage, Risk of Ruin and the Cost of Capital'; *Journal of Finance*; Vol. 22; Sep.1967; pp. 395-403.
4. Bhat. K. and Ramesh. K. 'Determinants of Financial Leverage: Some Further Evidence'; *The Chartered Accountant*; Vol. 9; No. 9; 1980; pp. 451-456.
5. Bhole L M '*Financing of Private Corporate Sector in India: Trends and Determinants During 1966-67 to 2000-01*'.
6. Bradley, Jarell and Kim; 'A Review of Research on the Practices of Corporate Finance'; *South Asian Journal of Management*; Vol. 9; No. 4; July-Sep 2002; pp. 29.
7. Brennen, M J and Schwartz, E S (1978). 'Corporate Income Taxes, Valuation and the Problem of Capital Structure,' *Journal of Business*, pp. 103-15.
8. Brenan M.J., 'A New Look at the Weighted Average Cost of Capital', *Journal of Business Finance, Spring* 1973, Vol. 21, No. 1, March 1966, p. 73.
9. Carelton. W.T. and Siberman.I.H.; 'Joint Determination of Rate of Return and Capital Structure; An Econometric Analysis'; *Journal of Finance*; Vol.32; June 1977; pp. 811-821.
10. DeAngelo, Harry and Masulis, M S (1980). 'Optimal Capital Structure under Corporate and Personal Taxation,' *Journal of Financial Economics, 8*, pp. 3-29.
11. Durand, David (1963). 'The Cost of Capital in an Imperfect Market: A Reply to M-M,' *American Economic Review*, 53.
12. Ferri. M.G. and Jones.W.H. 'Determinants of Financial Structure; A New Methodological Approach'; *Journal of Finance*; Vol. 34; No. 3; June 1979; pp. 631-644.
13. Gangadhar V., Yadagiri M., 'Sourses and Application of Funds', *Finance India*, Vol. IX, March 1995, p. 53.
14. Gupta, M.C,; ' The Effect of Size, Growth and Industry on Financial Structure of Manufacturing Companies'; *Journal of Finance*; Vol. 24; No. 3; June 1969; pp. 517-529.

15. Jensen, M and Meckling, W (1976). 'Theory of the Firm: Managerial Behaviour, Agency Costs and Ownership Structure,' *Journal of Financial Economics*, 3, pp. 305-60.

16. Kraus, A and Litzenberger, R H (1973). 'A State Preference Model of Optimal Financial Leverage,' *Journal of Finance*, 28, pp. 911-22.

17. Masulis, M S (1980). 'The Effect of Capital Structure Changes on Security Prices: A Study of Exchange Offers,' *Journal of Financial Economics, 8*, pp. 139-78.

18. Masulis, M S (1983). 'The Impact of Capital Structure on Firm Value,' *Journal of Finance, 38*, pp. 107-25.

19. Mathew T. '*Optional Financial Leverage the Ownership Factor Finance India*', Vol. 5; No. 2; June 1991; pp. 195-201.

20. Miller, M H (1977). 'Debt and Taxes,' *Journal of Finance*, 32, pp. 261-73

21. Modigliani, F and Miller, M H (1958). 'The Cost of Capital, Corporation Finance and the Theory of Investment,' *American Economic Review*, 48, pp. 261-97.

22. Modigliani, F and Miller, M H (1963). 'Corporate Income Taxes and the Cost of Capital: A Correction,' *American Economic Review*, 53, pp. 433-43.

23. Modigliani, F and Miller, M H (1966). 'Estimates of Cost of Capital to Electric Utility Industry 1954-1957,' *American Economic Review*, 56, pp. 333-91.

24. Mohanty; 'A Review of Research on the Practices of Corporate Finance'; *South Asian Journal of Management*; Vol. 9; No. 4; July-Sep 2002; p. 29

25. Ram Kumar Kakani. 'The Determinants of Capital Structure - An Econometric Analysis'; *Finance India*; Vol. XII; No. 1; March 1999; pp. 51-69

26. Rajan G. Raghuram and L. Zingales, (1998), 'Financial Dependence and Growth', *American Economic Review*, Vol. 88, pp. 559-586.

27. Rajeswar Rao K., Sadanandan R., 'Impact of Capital Structure Decisions on Operating Preference of State Enterprises of A.P. — A Correlation Analysis', *Finance India*, Vol. IX, No. 1, March, 1995, p. 76.

28. Sarkar, J. and S. Sarkar, (2000), 'Liberalization, Financing Pattern and Corporate Performance in India', IGIDR.

29. Scott Jr., J H (1976). 'A Theory of Optimal Capital Structure,' *Bell Journal of Economics*, Spring, pp. 33-54.

30. Scott Jr., J H (1977). 'Bankruptcy, Secured Debt and Optimal Capital Structure,' *Journal of Finance*, 32, pp. 261-73.

31. Sharma, R and Rao, H (1969). 'Leverage and the Value of the Firm,' *Finance Journal*, 24.

32. Smith, V L (1972). 'Default Risk, Scale and Home-made Leverage Theorem,' *American Economic Review*, 62.

33. Solomon, Ezra (1963). 'Leverage and the Cost of Capital,' *Journal of Finance*, 18, pp. 273-79.

34. StiglitzJE (1969). 'A Re-examination of M-MTheorem,' *American Economic Revieiv*, 59, pp. 784-93.

35. Stiglitz, J E (1974). 'On the Irrelevance of Corporate Financial Policy,' *American Economic Review*, 62, pp. 851-66.

36. Toy.N., Stonehill A., Rammers.L. and Beekhuisen.T; 'A Comparative International Study of Growth, Profitability and Risk as Determinants of Corporate Debt Ratio in the Manufacturing Sector'; *Journal of Financial and Quantitative Analysis*'; Vol. 9; No. 1974. pp. 875-886.

37. Venketesan. S; 'Determinants of Financial Leverage: An empirical Extension'; *The Chartered Accountant*; 1983; pp. 519-527.

WEBSITES

1. http://findarticles.com/p/articles/mi_m3257/is_8_59/ai_n14920105
2. http://peregrin.jmu.edu/~drakepp/principles/module7/coc.pdf
3. http://www.enotes.com/small-business-encyclopedia/capital-structure
4. http://www.investopedia.com/articles/basics/06/capitalstructure.asp
5. http://www.westga.edu/~bquest/2002/rethinking.htm
6. http://www.dynamic-equity.com/vcmag03.htm
7. http://quickfinancecheck.org/capital-gearing
8. http://www.scribd.com/doc/22615511/Financial-Management-Notes
9. http://www.elearning.strathmore.edu/file.php/582/Financing.docx
10. http://www.bized.co.uk/learn/accounting/financial/sources/capital.htm
11. http://wiki.answers.com/Q/Types+of+long+term+sources
12. http://www.coolavenues.com/forums/showthread.php?t=11359
13. http://mostlyeconomics.wordpress.com/2007/06/06/capital-structure-of-indian-companies
14. http://www.chillibreeze.com/articles/India-liberalization.asp

Index